Autumn
watch

Spring
watch

Winter
watch

THE
ALMANAC
2019

THE
ALMANAC
2019

A Nature Companion
for the British Year

MICHAEL BRIGHT &
KAREN FARRINGTON

1 3 5 7 9 10 8 6 4 2

BBC Books, an imprint of Ebury Publishing
20 Vauxhall Bridge Road,
London SW1V 2SA

BBC Books is part of the Penguin Random House group of companies
whose addresses can be found at global.penguinrandomhouse.com

Penguin
Random House
UK

This book is published to accompany the television series entitled *Springwatch*
first broadcast on BBC Two in 2018. *Springwatch* is a BBC Studios production.

Series producer: Chris Howard
Executive producer: Rosemary Edwards

First published by BBC Books in 2018

www.penguin.co.uk

A CIP catalogue record for this book is available from the British Library

ISBN 978 1 785 94367 6

Commissioning editor: Albert DePetrillo
Project editor: Bethany Wright
Design: seagulls.net
Production: Phil Spencer

Printed and bound in Great Britain by Clays Ltd, Elcograf S.p.A.

Penguin Random House is committed to a sustainable future
for our business, our readers and our planet. This book is made
from Forest Stewardship Council® certified paper.

MIX
Paper from
responsible sources
FSC® C018072

CONTENTS

FOREWORD

It's unlikely to start with a pair of golden eagles displaying in a thunderstorm or a close-up view of a bittern booming, or a purple emperor pitching up on your nose. More likely an interest in natural history will be seeded by something far more humble, homely even, some little moment of simple magic that ignites a spark which burns for a lifetime and fuels a constant curiosity and hunger to see, hear, smell and touch an unravelling cascade of life.

A ladybird is all it took for me, I think, or maybe it was a tadpole… By the time I met a slow worm and found a blackbird's nest it was already the reason to get up and get out in the garden. A glimpse of a fox got me over the fence and a lust for kestrels got me on a bike and cycling the lanes. A car took me past Go, without the £200, and directly to Scotland, where aged 23 I finally caught up with those eagles displaying. All the while my knowledge of and passion for the UK's wildlife had been growing and exploding, and, at the age of 57, it is still progressing in that direction. I wouldn't say that 'home is where the heart is' but the fields and woods and streams, rivers and lakes, the heaths and the moors, the bogs, the beaches and the bits of wasteland behind the bike sheds that lie beyond the door… that is where my home has been and it's where my heart beats fastest.

It's true that, like many, I've carried my interest overseas. I've been tickled by the exotic, but when I walk among the oaks, when the bluebells squeak beneath my soles, when the tawnies screech and the fox barks and the first brimstone bursts brilliantly from the hedge to announce spring, it's more relevant. I feel part of it. I'm not a tourist picking postcards. I'm a caring custodian of a community which nurtures me and which I love immeasurably in return.

And of course I'm not alone. The viewers of *Springwatch* share that affinity en masse. It's at the core of why the series endures: it's about our companions in our backyard, the creatures we know and know about. They are 'ours': although many are shared as they move around the globe, we have a connection with them, and that, combined with the care it engenders, means we always want to know more.

The most exciting thing for a naturalist is not what they know; it's what they don't know. Because learning new things about old friends is so good! And this Almanac is packed full of novel and exciting facts, practical advice to facilitate you going out to discover things yourself and suggestions of how to make the most of the tremendous differences between the seasons. I love the monthly fox update. For me this forms a calendar through their lifecycle and behaviour: spring is fox cubs, winter is the braying adults in the cold, black woods. And I love data too, so the sunrises, sunsets, sunshine hours and temperatures are all invaluable when it comes to planning encounters with our wildlife. It's also got history, with the wonderful quotes from Gilbert White's *Natural History of Selborne* and loads of fascinating cultural references to the relationships we have or had with our natural neighbours. It's a great repository of interesting things, ordered around an annual cycle and thus a true almanac... and don't we love an almanac!

But most of all, this book is a toolkit. It's loaded with ideas and filled with teases to tempt you off the sofa and out into the real world. And when you get there you will see that a lot of that world is in trouble. We live in a strange age for naturalists. I often wonder what people like Gilbert White would make of the world now. His was a time of plenty, when plants and animals were in massive abundance, but his was also an era of very basic exploration and science. Now we live in a ravaged landscape where many species struggle to survive, but thanks to remarkable technologies we learn more about them more quickly than ever before. It's a paradox and a problem… but we have solutions. We can restore habitats, re-introduce species and recover their populations, but in truth we are not doing it quickly or widely enough. And that's where you and this almanac come in. If you meet wildlife, you will connect with it, and when you connect you will generate an affinity, in time a love for it. With that will come a concern, a care, a desire to protect and nurture it. But in these desperate times caring is no longer enough to ensure a healthy future for our wildlife. You must take action, must make a difference. Our wildlife needs us, and it needs us more than ever.

Chris Packham
New Forest, 2018

INTRODUCTION

It seems to me that the natural world is the greatest source of excitement; the greatest source of visual beauty; the greatest source of intellectual interest. It is the greatest source of so much in life that makes life worth living

David Attenborough

When it comes to wildlife, Britain boasts a compelling breadth and depth which ensures that we are a nation with plenty of natural riches.

The advantages of getting up close and personal with nature are well documented. Visiting an open space enhances mood and improves fitness. That's perhaps why such a vast number of people regularly choose to spend time outside, going al fresco for a few hours to entire days each week.

Natural England monitors how the English use the countryside and in the year ending February 2016 we made 879 million visits to parks in towns and cities, 446 million trips to woodlands and forests and 519 million trips along paths, cycle tracks and bridleways.

In total there were 3.1 billion excursions to the great outdoors recorded in that year alone.

And why not? There are so many compelling sights and enchanting sounds to enjoy in England, Wales, Scotland and Northern Ireland. Depending on the season, there are spectacular displays of wild flowers and foliage bathing parks and verges – and that's just the start.

There are 101 species of those to be found in the British Isles, including 28 native terrestrial mammals, 18 native bats, 25 cetaceans and 13 introduced or naturalised species.

Thanks to mysterious migration, birds come and go – and sometimes a stiff wind blows some unexpected feathered visitors to our shores – but at present the list of those you might expect to find here, compiled by the British Ornithologists' Union, stands at 574.

These figures are dwarfed by those of terrestrial or airborne insects, as there are 24,000 species in the UK, according to the Royal Entomological Society.

Typically, these are the undervalued members of the British wildlife scene although most of us have the opportunity to witness first hand their lifestyles, just by stepping outside into our backyards.

Still, observing nature risks becoming a lost art, given the sheer variety of ways people today might choose to spend their free time.

As a pastime it was pioneered by those who arguably had much more time for reflection, notably Gilbert White (1720–93) from Selborne, Hampshire, acknowledged as the father of English ecology. He was a gardener, ornithologist and naturalist and made short notes that recorded the passing of the seasons as he saw it from his parsonage.

'The air is soft. Violets blow. Snow lies under hedges. Men plow.'
he wrote on 8th March 1783.

'Green woodpecker laughs at all the world. Storm-cock [mistle thrush] sings.'
he recorded on 16th April 1770.

'Rabbits make incomparably the finest turf, for they not only bite closer than larger quadrupeds but they allow no bents to rise; hence warrens produce much the most delicate turf for gardens.'

he noted on 17th August 1775.

At a time when little was accurately recorded about the order of the natural world he was full of questions, only trusting what he saw with his own eyes and deduced with his mental acuity.

Unconvinced by local accounts that swallows spent the winter underwater, he devoted much time looking for 'secret dormitories' where he suspected they resided during harsh weather. On one occasion he shouted through an ear trumpet at a hive to see if bees responded to loud noises.

Despite a few red herrings, he was encouragingly systematic in his approach, at one stage outlining his study of bird song like this:

'For many months I carried a list in my pocket of the birds that were to be remarked; and as I rode or walked about my business, I noted each day the continuance or omission of each bird's song; so that I am as sure of the certainty of my facts as any man can be of any transaction whatsoever.'

If his previously made, well-ordered notes carefully penned in Italian style didn't answer all his questions they certainly lightened the load for the generations of naturalists who came later.

His book, *The Natural History of Selborne*, first published in 1789, has appeared in 300 editions and has never been out of print. It is reputedly the fourth most published work in the English language, after the Bible, the works of Shakespeare and John Bunyan's *The Pilgrim's Progress*.

Springwatch presenter Chris Packham has acknowledged Gilbert White as an early influence, saying: 'His descriptions were so vivid that I was able to rebuild this landscape so far away in time.'

Science has since solved many opaque issues that left White and others scratching their heads, although sometimes evidence-based revelations bring forth more questions.

Today, *Springwatch* and its sister programmes, *Autumnwatch* and *Winterwatch*, are the happy meeting point for cutting-edge science and old-style observation.

Modern technology used to film birds on their nests or water voles by their burrows captures nature with a clarity and intimacy never witnessed before.

Cameras trained on the nests of small birds in *Springwatch 2017* monitored 81 eggs, 44 of which fledged; a success rate of 55 per cent.

In total the web cameras trained on those nests were watched by viewers for 15,000 hours or 617 days.

In the face of triumph or tragedy, filmmakers and viewers alike watched the story unfold with the same sense of wonder that enveloped Gilbert White centuries ago. Presenters may be scientifically savvy but they remain merely intrigued onlookers, just like viewers, as the ecosystem takes control.

As *Springwatch* producer Rosemary Edwards puts it: 'We are respectful observers of the natural world.'

Thus the connection between wildlife and mankind, often now devoted to mitigating the damage he has wreaked in it, remains as potent and resilient now as it has for centuries.

This *Springwatch Almanac* aims to strengthen that bond, providing a monthly guide to what's occurring in the great outdoors. Nothing if not wide-ranging, it will direct you to national sites of interest as well as to unexpected treasures a stone's throw from your windows and doors. There's inspiration to join some of the nation's most exciting monitoring projects, watching nature in action then collecting data, as well as tips on where to immerse yourself in stunning spectacles, backing up one of the programme's key underlining themes – that nature remains accessible to all.

JANUARY

With fleeting days and lingering nights, January doesn't seem like the obvious time to hit a nature trail. But, with appropriate clothing and footwear, there're plenty of reasons to step outside to make the most of the British winter. While some of the country's wildlife sleeps deeply through the worst of the weather, you might see amorous squirrels and hear lovelorn foxes. Even the dreariest day is lightened by the sound of robins and blackbirds, the birds most likely to sing loud and long in January. Birds of prey like sparrowhawks, hen harriers and numerous owls are still hard at work scouring green patches for food. Indeed, Britain's birdlife is particularly rich, with the ranks of domestic birds having been reinforced by migrants from Iceland, Greenland, Scandinavia and Siberian Russia – and more visible than ever with the lack of leaves on trees. When a flock of birds rises as one and flies overhead, the sound of scores of beating wings is inevitably breathtaking.

Sunrise and sunset times for Britain's capital cities

1st January	☀ Sunrise	☀ Sunset
Belfast	08.48	16.09
London	08.05	16.02
Cardiff	08.17	16.15
Edinburgh	08.43	15.49

Burning the bush

At 5 o'clock in the morning on New Year's Day, the country folk of Herefordshire would take down a globe, made from a tangle of the two 'magical trees' hawthorn and mistletoe, which hung in the kitchen all year. It was carried to the first field that had been sowed with wheat and thrown onto a large fire of burning straw and dry bushes. The menfolk would encircle the fire and sing, the song ending in 'Auld-Ci-der' delivered as a deep growl; Herefordshire being a key cider-growing area. The ceremony, known as the Burning of the Bush, ensured that the evil spirits of the old year were burned, and crops would be plentiful in the coming year. During the ceremony, the womenfolk would weave a new globe and it was hung in the kitchen until the following New Year. No house was safe, unless it had its protective globe hanging in the kitchen. The tradition is kept alive in Much Marcle, but on the Saturday closest to 6th January each year.

Several slow-worms found under the bottom of an old hay-rick in a torpid state, but not without some motion.

Gilbert White, 28th January 1788

 ## Tweet and greet

Squealing and snorting heard from the wilds of a riverbank indicate the presence of one of Britain's shyest birds. The water rail is heard more often than it is seen, with its peculiar grunts known as 'sharming'. It is most likely to be spotted when vegetation is stripped back in winter or if the water freezes, forcing it to forage in the open. Although it enjoys similar habitats to the familiar moorhen, observers are unlikely to know they are nesting there. So secretive is the water rail that it's proved impossible to accurately establish how many live in the UK.

Water rails have long red bills, small tails and are substantially grey, with barred black and white flanks. The resident population is joined in winter by a population from Scandinavia. However, it remains difficult to track the migration of water rails because they travel under cover of darkness. It is known, however, that one bird ringed in Lancashire in the winter of 1990 was killed the following year by a cat in Belarus, 2,000 miles away.

 Track facts

Wild animals are experts in subterfuge as they don't want to be seen as they go about their business. But they can't help but leave clues relating to their movements, especially in January when there is mud or perhaps even snow on the ground. Even with crisp outlines it can be tricky to distinguish a domesticated dog from a patrolling fox. But these fundamental ground rules will help you discern one surreptitious night-time garden visitor from the next.

- A **fox** has four toes, with two forward-facing digits flanked by two others, ahead of an oval pad. Sometimes claw marks can be detected too. Similar to a dog print, a fox print is typically smaller, measuring about five centimetres long and four centimetres wide.

- A **badger** has five toes with claw marks almost certainly visible. The claws on the hind foot are likely to be shorter and nearer to the squat pad.

- A **rabbit** leaves close-set tracks, with hind feet that are larger than forepaws. As rabbits are sociable creatures, there tend to be numerous similar tracks in the same area.

- **Deer** have splayed, cloven hooves, frustratingly similar in appearance to those of sheep, goats and cattle – although presumably you will be able to rule out all the latter trekking across your property. Each deer track looks similar to an upside-down broken heart. The biggest domestic variety is

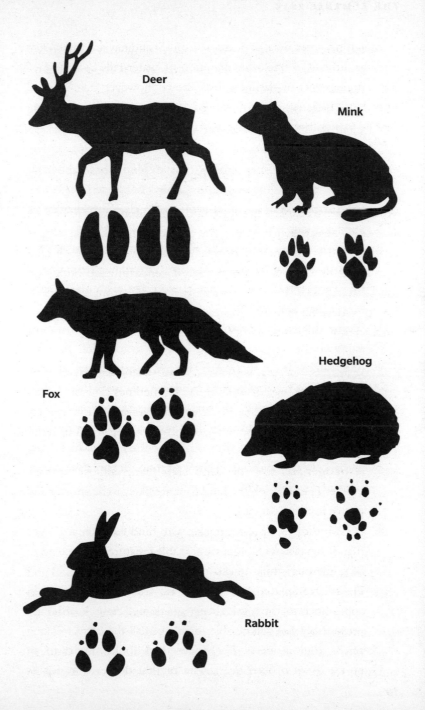

Deer

Mink

Fox

Hedgehog

Rabbit

red deer, descending in size through fallow to roe and finally muntjac deer. The hoof of a muntjac deer is about a third of the size of its red cousin.

 Wild boar are also cloven-hoofed animals, but their tracks are wider than those of deer and often register the imprint of a dew claw at the rear.

 Otters have five toes although the webbing that links them is not always visible in mud or snow. Alongside its substantial rear pad there might be evidence of drag marks from its low-lying tail.

 Weasels, stoats, polecat, mink and **pine marten** tracks are difficult to tell apart, other than by size, ranging from one to four centimetres. All have five clawed toes, with males being bigger than females.

 Water voles and **brown rats** also leave similar footprints, although the toes of a rat are forward-facing while the toes of a water vole are splayed. It also has a shorter heel.

 Hedgehogs have narrow feet and five toes, with three facing forward and two each side, surrounding a central pad.

 Squirrels have five toes on their rear legs and four on their small front feet, as the fifth is often poorly developed. Claw marks generally show up in snow or mud. Behind the toes are signs of multiple pads.

 Little breeders

Little owls will be pairing up this month, with courtship loud and vocal thanks to frequent calls between the couple. The male also brings gifts of food to his new partner before the business of breeding gets underway.

Scottish wildcats come into season. Despite the caterwauling and stinky scent marking associated with this, few people will be aware of those clues as Scottish wildcats live in remote locations and avoid human contact. After a gestation period lasting a little over two months, an average of three or four wildcat kittens will be born.

Squirrels are starting to feel frisky. Keep an eye on tree canopies to see squirrels playing a cavorting kiss chase after the female has emitted a powerful scent, enough to attract numerous interested males. In addition to dashing from one branch to the next there is tail flicking, barking calls and the beating of feet, which will help distinguish the courtship ritual. An energetic pursuit of the female squirrel ends when she mates with the most athletic of the males.

 ## Statistically speaking...

Thanks to the UK Met Office, there are arrays of statistics stretching back decades sufficient to thrill the most ardent weather watchers. Today there's a network of weather stations around the country that feed back information on temperatures, hours of sunshine and depth of rainfall. It's easy to understand how accurate information has been gathered in the recent past. Of course, that wasn't always the case with present coverage evolving from small beginnings. Nothing daunted, the Met Office has applied detailed analysis to derive monthly averages which give an overall picture of UK weather down the years. The country's best meteorological brains have looked at defined areas and the ways they are affected by climate to come up with the most relevant figures available. It was, the Met Office admits, a complex and challenging task but their figures are the best estimate for weather-obsessed British people, more than half of whom talk about it at least once every six hours while almost 70 per cent check a forecast at least once a day.

Highest and lowest average temperatures (°C) recorded for January since 1910

	Highest		Lowest	
England	9.7	1916	-4.9	1963
Wales	9.2	1916	-5.2	1963
Scotland	8.3	1989	-4.1	1945
Northern Ireland	9.4	1916	-3.0	1963

 Britain's favourite fish

1. Brown trout
2. Stickleback
3. Tench
4. Perch
5. Pike
6. = Roach/Basking shark
7. Bass
8. Cod
9. Mackerel

When it came to voting in the quest to find Britain's favourite fish in 2016 there was one clear winner. The brown trout, with its spotted back and cream-coloured belly, garnered more than one-fifth of all votes cast in the poll organised by fish photographer Jack Perks, with the backing of groups including the Shark Trust and the Institute of Fisheries Management.

In winter the extraordinary behaviour of the female brown trout puts many expectant mums to shame as she takes on the daunting task of cleaning a riverbed. The female attacks the gravel where she intends to lay eggs by turning on her side and beating the ground briskly with the flat side of her tail, shifting mucky sludge as she does so. With luck, evidence of her work can be seen from above the water as the cleaned gravel is lighter in colour than the rest.

Only when the silt is dispersed will a female begin to spawn. But her elaborate preparations will have attracted the attentions of a passing male fish who, eager to fertilise the eggs, will then shadow her, nudging her abdomen with his nose as he does so. Often, more than one male fish will crowd around. Usually, the biggest male will drive off smaller hopefuls.

She will lay between 100 and 300 orange eggs that cascade into the gravel where they will be protected from predators but also oxygenated by flowing water, thanks to the cleaning process.

After the fry feasts on the inside of the egg it begins eating insect larvae like its parents, before graduating to small fish and flying insects.

On average, brown trout are between 50 and 80 cm long and weigh in at two kilos but the British record stands at nearly 14 and a half kilos.

In Britain it is a barometer fish: when the waterways are clean and clear it flourishes but when there's pollution the population falters. Thankfully, improved waterway management means that today it can be found in virtually all rivers and canals.

Runner-up in the competition was another river fish, the smooth-bodied stickleback – usually a child's first catch using net and bucket – which may have rampant nostalgia to thank for fuelling 16 per cent of the vote, with the olive-green tench in third place, just three points behind.

Year of the Fox

Winter nights can be long, dark – and sometimes extremely noisy, thanks to the antics of resident red foxes.

The chill night air is often split by the shrill screams of a vixen. In response the dog fox fills the silence between shrieks with sets of monosyllabic barks at regular intervals. With more than 40,000 urban foxes and 200,000 living in the countryside, the January wails are familiar to many householders.

It's a busy month for the fox population. Aware that vixens are receptive for as few as three days, dog foxes will be shadowing a prospective partner. She may well see off a few suitors before settling on one deemed acceptable. Like dogs and wolves, the pair will remain conjoined for an hour after mating in what's known as 'the copulatory tie'. At least the night-time noises end once the deed is done.

 ## This little chiggywig went to market ...

There's special affection in Britain for the humble woodlouse, with no creature gathering a greater collection of names. A 150-strong list drawn up in 2002 was deemed far from exhaustive.

Lovers of the dark and damp, there are something like 45 different woodlouse species in the UK. Admittedly, one is hard to distinguish from the next, although some roll up into a ball while others don't.

They are crustaceans rather than insects but even when they shed their exo-skeleton there's little to warrant this slew of cute-sounding terms of endearment. Indeed, they have some particularly nasty habits like eating their own faeces as well as rotting plants and fungi. They also exude ammonia through their shells, to get rid of bodily waste.

As woodlice travelled with the colonists, these old-style names can now be found worldwide. Here's our top 20 favourites and where they came from.

1. Chiggypigs – Devon
2. Choogeypigs – West Country
3. Chiggywigs – Devon
4. Chisel bobs – Devon

5. Granfer greeks – Devon
6. Horace – Devon
7. Cudworms – Shropshire
8. Slunkerpigs – Bristol
9. Grammasows – Cornwall
10. Cheeserockers – Kent
11. Billy Buttons – Yorkshire
12. Cheeselogs – Surrey
13. Cheeseybobs – Surrey
14. Slaters – Scotland
15. Leatherjackets – East Midlands
16. Dampers – Tyneside
17. Ticktocks – Bedfordshire
18. Crunchy bats – North Wales
19. Ogopogos – Sussex
20. Parson pigs – Isle of Man

Spot the difference?

Most of us are familiar with resident song thrushes, the gardener's friend that uses stones to smash snail shells and can hold a tune.

But in winter you might easily mistake the song thrush for a visiting redwing or fieldfare, together known as the winter thrushes.

The redwing is Britain's smallest thrush, just a tad behind the song thrush in dimensions. They share the spotted breast with their melodious cousins but are distinguishable by a rusty-red underside of the wings.

Although there's a tiny breeding population that chooses to stay in the UK all year round, if you spot one in your garden it is surely one of the 8.6 million that migrate here in the winter from breeding grounds in Scandinavia or Continental Europe, appearing from September onwards.

When the weather is clement they hang out in hedgerows, happy with a diet of berries and worms. Only when the snow descends will they appear in gardens.

Fieldfares are bigger, weighing in at a similar size to the domestic mistle thrush. They share the speckled undercarriage but have a grey head, long black tail and predominantly rich-brown body plumage. Like mistle thrushes they stand upright and hop with attitude. Every year some 680,000 fieldfares appear in Britain.

Both redwings and fieldfares are sociable birds and usually appear in numbers to feed but fieldfares are the more intimidating of the two.

Observers claim to have seen them ram other birds in flight and take aim before defecating on intruders into their territory. When they begin a phased departure in March, there must be palpable relief among some in the bird population.

Snow and starvation

In 1963 Britain suffered 'The Big Freeze'. Snow began to fall on Boxing Day 1962 and the thaw didn't arrive for weeks. By New Year's Eve some 95,000 miles of roads were snowbound. It took 80 men over a week to dig out three trains buried by snow on Dartmoor. Thankfully, protracted Arctic blasts like this are rare – and the ensuing effect on people's lives are well reported. But what happened to wildlife in that terrible winter?

Some species slept their way through it, snug in their nests. A slow heart rate and low body temperature during this extended bout of inactivity helps conserve energy when food is scarce. Hedgehogs, dormice and bats would have been more at risk from unseasonably warm weather, enticing them out of hibernation prematurely and leaving them vulnerable to a cold snap.

Others skipped the country, including swallows, cuckoos and painted lady butterflies, who always head for warmer climates before the winter months. Some birds, including lapwings, redwings and fieldfares, fly south at the first blizzard.

Foxes and birds of prey tend to carry on as normal, capitalising on the difficulties caused to their quarry in the snow. But remaining small birds – who must eat at least one-third of their body weight every day to survive – were badly hit. Today more householders put out bird food as a matter of course, easing their plight. However, extreme conditions have since revealed that birds, including starlings and sparrows, will turn cannibal to survive.

Worse off still were the wintering wildfowl and waders, left ice-bound and unable to feed in estuaries and marshes. With the bounty of the mud flats being ice-bound, starvation and cold weather would become a killer combination.

The effect on hedgehogs, moles and badgers, who rely on slugs and worms for food, wasn't recorded but it is known that hundreds of thousands of birds perished during the Big Freeze. Yet by a quirk of nature populations recovered in as little as five years, as two or three broods were successfully hatched annually making up for the shortfall in numbers.

 # Highest and lowest hours of sunshine recorded for January since 1929

☀	Highest		Lowest	
England	77.3	1959	20.2	1996
Wales	82.3	1933	22.6	1996
Scotland	57.2	1959	20.3	1996
Northern Ireland	77.1	1959	21.5	1996

Pleased to meet you ... again

Majestic and soaring, the red kite is now a familiar feature in British skies again. But in Victorian times it was nearly wiped out as it was viewed as vermin. Those that weren't poisoned by game keepers were subject to the malevolent attentions of egg collectors and taxidermists. Red kites became extinct in England in 1871 and in Scotland, eight years later, leaving a diminishing population in Wales. Yet centuries before that this scavenger bird was welcomed as it cleared up rubbish left on the streets, including the bodies of dead animals.

By the middle of the 20th century the entire UK population was reduced to just a couple of Welsh breeding pairs. There were so few that before long this small red kite population was being impacted by a 'genetic bottleneck', that is, there were no new genes being introduced to make the population more robust. Conservationists braced themselves for the long haul, beginning a re-introduction scheme in the Chilterns in 1989, with red kites being brought from Spain to fill the gap. No one knew if the bold experiment would work. But a decade later chicks from the Chilterns were used to repopulate other parts of Britain.

In fact the scheme proved so successful that a red kite was spotted in London in 2006 for the first time in decades – the same year a pair bred for the first time in Derwent Water, Cumbria. It's now possible to see red kites, with their rich reddish-brown feathers and dark forked tail, across large swathes of Britain, with the exception of the West Country, with breeding pairs numbering about 1,800.

Red kite strongholds include the Chilterns, the Brecon Beacons, Dingwall in Scotland, the Derwent Valley, Gateshead, Harewood House, Yorkshire, Top Lodge, Northamptonshire and along the M40 between Buckinghamshire and Oxfordshire.

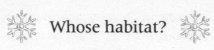

Whose habitat?

ESTUARY

Wrap up warm and head for the coast this month where the mouths of Britain's rivers are swarming with birds. A quarter of all European estuaries are within the United Kingdom which, coupled with its comparatively mild weather, makes the exposed riverbeds an ideal destination for congregations of waders. Why do they fly here? There are 200,000 kcals buried beneath every square metre of estuary mud in the form of lugworms, shellfish and plants. As long as exceptionally cold weather doesn't make it ice bound there will be plenty of food to see them through to the breeding season.

By the time slow-moving rivers make it to the sea their waters are rich in nutrients which helps the invertebrates at the bottom of the food chain to thrive. Estuaries are generally more sheltered, warmer and less salty than open waters. In cold weather, estuaries in the west are more favoured by birds from east-coast or northern European colonies. In severe snaps you might even see kingfishers and grey herons drawn away from frozen waterways to more accessible feeding grounds on the coast.

For the inexperienced bird observer waders are usually large in size and substantial in numbers. If they remain obligingly still under your gaze, it may be because they are recovering from long migratory flights. Typically, they have long legs and penetrating beaks. With no hind toe, the sanderling has an unusual gait, especially noticeable when it runs.

Beyond that, it can be more challenging to discern knot from plover. Look out for differences in beak shape, leg colour, plumage and call.

If it's any consolation to newcomers, even the most experienced eye struggles to tell where an observed bird hails from or where it will head to a few months down the line.

There are, for example, oystercatchers spotted trawling British estuaries that were born and bred in this country. However, other populations of oystercatchers have flown in from Norway to graze alongside their UK cousins. The complexities of bird populations and migratory patterns are still unfolding.

The largest of the waders are curlews, whimbrels and godwits. Smaller waders include sandpipers and phalaropes. Winter visitors from the Arctic include knot, sanderlings and purple sandpipers.

They are joined by migrants from across northern Europe, including grey plovers, whooper swans, bewick swans and avocets.

Resident birds include oystercatchers, lapwings, redshanks, dunlins and grey plover. The rarest sights are greenshanks, ruffs and dotterel.

One of the biggest threats to wader populations has been urban regeneration. As lesser-used industrial sites give way to prestige development, birds are squeezed out of their territories. Research showed that when some 200 hectares of estuary were lost with the installation of the Cardiff Bay barrage the survival rate of redshank fell by 44 per cent.

To witness the wading bird spectacles, go to the estuaries of the Dee in Cheshire, the Mersey, Morecambe Bay in Lancashire, the Exe in Devon, the Severn in Avon, the RSPB reserve at Snettisham, WWT Caerlaverock in Scotland, Oare Marshes in Kent, Pagham Harbour in West Sussex and Blakeney Point in Norfolk.

 ## A rose by any other name

Expect primroses to be among the first flowers to fragment the grey winter suit that the landscape has been wearing for months. Primroses, the Queen's favourite bloom or so BBC's *Gardeners' Question Time* was told, are the county flower of Devon where clusters of them light up the bases of hedges and woodlands in electric fashion.

Their name comes from the Latin 'prima rosa' and it is also known as butter rose, early rose and golden rose. Although it patently isn't a rose it is among the first flowers to bloom. The pale, almost luminous petals with a burnt orange heart measure about three centimetres across and are borne on single stalks. Sometimes they appear as early as December while cold winters delaying their life cycle will mean the last flowers don't die off until May.

Look out for two different types of primrose flowers presenting the flower's reproductive parts differently so as to ensure successful cross-pollination. Some have what's called a pin-eyed stigma, a greenish disc, coming from the tube at the base of the flower which is essentially the female element of the process. Lying out of sight a little way beneath the stigma are the male anthers. Other types are called thrum-eyed flowers, a bud of anthers on top enclosing the stigma.

An insect collecting nectar at the base of the neck from the pin-eyed stigma inevitably picks up pollen from the lower-lying anthers in the middle of its proboscis. It is then ideally placed to transfer this to the stigma of a thrum-eyed flower when it probes for nectar there. Conversely, gathering nectar at a thrum-eyed flower the top of an insect's proboscis is coated with pollen which can be most easily passed on before it goes down the throat of the pin-eyed stigma primrose.

Former prime minister Lord Benjamin Disraeli had a particular fondness for the flower and Queen Victoria sent a wreath of them to his funeral on 26th April 1881. Afterwards, it was used as a symbol for the politically motivated Primrose League, formed in his memory to support the Conservative party.

Highest and lowest rainfall in millimetres recorded for January since 1910

	Highest		Lowest	
England	159.9	2014	14.2	1997
Wales	301.4	1948	11.7	1997
Scotland	293.8	1993	38.6	1963
Northern Ireland	192.3	1928	31.6	1997

 ## Great bird table expectations

An annual bird table survey has revealed the visitors you are most likely to see in your garden during January.

Every year the RSPB asks supporters to sit comfortably for an hour during a designated time slot in January and count the birds that fly into their garden. Those who don't have a garden or yard can go to a local park to find out what's going on there. Then the numbers are collated, with the information provided by citizen scientists being examined by experts who draw conclusions about how well each bird species is faring.

In 2018 a total of 6,764,475 bird sightings were put into the mix, the result of some 420,500 submissions.

The Big Garden Birdwatch has taken place every year since 1979. It's helped to raise the alarm about drastically declining bird populations as well as highlight success stories.

Statistics provided by bird watchers across the UK helped prove that starling numbers had declined by 81 per cent since 1979. Even though they remain a common sight, far fewer have been appearing in gardens. Meanwhile, the wood pigeon population has soared by more than 50 per cent. This year, the Big Garden Birdwatch showed the sightings of goldfinches rose by 11 per cent against the previous year, with a rise of five per cent in the number of greenfinches, halting what has been a catastrophic decline in the species.

It also points to regional variations, with coal tits edging into the top ten in Scotland and magpies proliferating in Northern Ireland. Chaffinches appeared in the top ten of Scotland, Wales and Northern Ireland but not in England.

Using the 2018 results, here is a list that will tell you what you are most likely to see at your bird table in January in the UK as a whole.

1. **House sparrow** – Squabbling sparrows still make themselves heard at the bird table but they are nonetheless a conservation concern, with their population declining by 71 per cent in just 30 years, according to RSPB figures.
2. **Starling** – Initially they seem a drab-looking bird but up close their feathers are oily black with shimmering greens and purples outlined in brown and dotted with speckles. Perhaps it's this finery that gives them sufficient chutzpah to cheekily impersonate other bird cries.
3. **Blue tit** – White-cheeked, blue-crowned and yellow-chested blue tits are a bird table favourite. At Pensthorpe in North Norfolk *Springwatch* cameras filmed blue tits bringing mint into a nest, which one French study says is to lessen bacteria living on the chicks, subsequently enhancing their survival.
4. **Blackbird** – Originally at home in woodlands, the blackbird has adapted to suburban gardens where its superb song rings out sometimes in darkness, if it is fooled into the belief that dawn is breaking by the presence of street lamps. It's one of the first birds to strike up in the year, and can be heard as early as January.
5. **Wood pigeon** – Although its grey plumage is easy on the eye wood pigeons are not necessarily welcomed by gardeners for their habit of attacking crops like cabbages, sprouts and

peas. They waddle when they walk because the total weight of feathers on their bodies is greater than the weight of their skeleton.

6. **Great tit** – The biggest of the UK's tit family, it has a distinctive two-tone song. British great tits now have longer beaks than their Dutch counterparts, thought to be a tweak of evolution in response to the comparative abundance of bird feeders in Britain.

7. **Robin** – Cute it may be but the red breast of the fiercely territorial robin is used to challenge all-comers. About one in ten robin deaths occur in vicious scraps among themselves. Defending their territories all year round means it is often possible to hear robins singing on Christmas Day.

8. **Long-tailed tit** – With tails longer than their bodies and weighing less than a pound coin, these birds are team players, operating in flocks of 20 and huddling in a line on branches in cold weather, taking turns at taking the warm centre spot.

9. **Chaffinch** – It's the pink-chested male that overshadows the duller-coloured female, although both flash white wing bars. *Springwatch* cameras focussed on one bird table revealed that dominant males compress their head feathers, lower their heads and gape when a competitor for food perches nearby.

And here are ten more birds you may get as visitors this month:

1. **Siskin** – These fork-tailed finches – bird table visitors until they head off to forests in March to breed – registered an increase in number in 2018.

2. **Brambling** – A winter visitor from Scandinavia and Siberia that flocks with chaffinches and flashes a white rump in flight.

3. **Greenfinch** – In its winter plumage of olive brown, the yellow tail flashes are muted but still apparent. Parent birds feed the young regurgitated seeds.

4. **Waxwing** – With its crest and black mask it is a glamorous visitor that feasts on rowan berries and sounds like a sleigh bell ringing. Expect flocks to turn up when berry harvests in Scandinavia are poor.

5. **Blackcap** – Previously it fled British winters for southern Spain but now it's thought abundant garden feeders have encouraged it to stay put in the south.

6. **Snow bunting** – Another Scandinavian guest that is more likely to be seen on north and east coasts although a small domestic population has made its home in Scotland.

7. **Goldcrest** – Britain's smallest breeding bird generally prefers conifers but can be tempted to a bird table with crushed mealworm. Although they nest inaccessibly in the highest pine trees, *Springwatch* cameras filmed one crammed with nine fledglings.

8. **Chiffchaff** – Another bird that's now choosing to spend winters in Britain, often found in the unlikely environs of a sewage farm, feasting on insects. Tantalisingly similar to a willow warbler, the chiffchaff has black rather than pale legs and will only burst into song atop a tree that measures more than five metres in height.

9. **Wren** – A well-rounded bird with long legs, a loud voice and an upright tail, its population suffers in cold winters. They may be small but the males have plenty of energy, looking after up to three nests in the spring, having timed their parental roles so perfectly that they move on to a second brood only after the first have fledged.

10. **Bullfinch** – More at home in rural areas than towns, males were kept as caged birds in Victorian times for their striking pink plumage and ability to mimic songs.

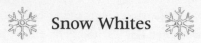 Snow Whites

As the skies darken with the season, the mountain hare turns from brown to white in conjunction with the first Highland snowfalls.

Slightly smaller than the more familiar brown hare, which was introduced to Britain by the Romans, it feasts on grass in the summer and heather and bark in the winter. Indigenous to Scotland, they can nonetheless be seen down south after being given a helping hand.

Mountain hares – also known as blue, white or Irish hares – were re-introduced to the Peak District two centuries ago, after disappearing from England during the last Ice Age.

To us it seems a filthy habit but the hare eats its own droppings. Thus food is twice digested to get the best nutritional value it can yield. This is called refrection and happens among rabbits and hares – but is pivotal for mountain hares after their daily diet disappears under a blanket of snow.

Mating starts in January and it's now that a female will deflect the unwanted attentions of a male suitor with a swift right hook. No, it's not two males resorting to blows over a favoured female when hares start to box. One of the feisty fighters will be female. Boxing like this is her final flourish before a 50-day gestation period.

Spotting a mountain hare in its dense winter coat on a snowy vista can be a challenge, although those prominent ears remain dark-hued. Despite three different layers of insulating fur, the mountain hare needs plenty of rest to conserve energy. It is sometimes easier to spot a golden eagle hunting for its favourite prey and work out from that where the hare – a Jack if it's male or a Jill if it's female – might be hiding.

With snow not necessarily a certainty, the mountain hare coat sometimes retains shades of brown to keep it camouflaged in all weathers. A quick thaw leaves the hare more readily identifiable, being white against the greys and greens of a bare mountainside until March when it gets its spring ensemble.

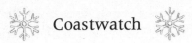

Coastwatch

Intrepid winter walkers will head to British beaches this month to search the strand-line for treasures washed up by seasonal storms. Here are the top five finds:

1. **Sea bean** – a polished seed from tropical forests washed down distant rivers and carried to British shores on the currents.
2. **Ambergris** – from the intestines of sperm whales, this waxy substance found in all shapes and sizes is still highly valued in the perfume industry. As it comes from the rear end of the whale, its scent is often unsurprisingly musky. With colours ranging from gold to grey, it has a soft, clay-like consistency. Don't confuse it with palm oil, often found on beaches and toxic to dogs.
3. **Dead sea creatures,** like crabs, jellyfish and seabirds that have succumbed to cold weather or challenging tides. In particularly violent weather the beach might be carpeted with corpses. If you find a dolphin or a whale contact the Cetacean Strandings Investigation Programme. It collects the dead bodies and carries out post mortems to help find out why the animal has died.
4. **Plastic.** It's a sad fact that most of the items washed up on British beaches will be made of plastic. According to the British Science Association, 37 per cent of beach pollution comes in the form of rope or net fragments. In descending order, it is then plastic or foam fragments, food wrappers, bags, bottles, fishing lines, container caps, fabric pieces, plastic containers and straws. Happily, beach clean-ups are bang on trend, attracting more volunteers than ever before. Waste plastic is choking oceans around the world. It presents a threat to sea life that gets tangled up with large pieces of plastic and may ingest small nurdles, or plastic pellets. Most

washed-up items were initially discarded on land. But some items fell off the back of a ship. On a few Cornish beaches it is still possible to locate some of the 4.8 million pieces of Lego washed overboard when a container ship was struck by a freak wave off Land's End in 1997. Giant pipes measuring 2.4 m in diameter and 480 m in length were washed up at Winterton and Sea Palling in 2017 after being swept off a ship.

5. **Driftwood** has been turned from beach nuisance to bijoux furniture by enterprising finders. Anything made from wood smoothed and bleached by the sea commands high prices.

 ## Blinded by the lights

On a few dark winter evenings people in Scotland and northern England are treated to dazzling light shows, courtesy of the aurora borealis.

Green, pink, yellow, blue and violet flourishes scrolling across the night sky are a natural phenomenon that happen as electrically charged particles from the sun enter the earth's atmosphere. Focussed on the magnetic North Pole, the spectacle is more intense the further north you go and only the most ideal climatic conditions render them visible in Britain at all.

However, latest research points to these bright lights being a factor in a catastrophic whale stranding incident in 2016.

Most of us are oblivious as young male sperm whales make their way up the British and Irish west coasts in the autumn, heading for the Arctic in search of squid. Although they measure between 10 and 20 metres in length and weigh in between 35 and 45 tons, they nonetheless slip past largely unnoticed. The only way to know you've spotted one of these deep-diving leviathans is to see water coming from the blow hole on the left side of its boxy head, at a jaunty forward angle.

32

Twenty-nine of the giants were washed up on beaches that bordered the North Sea in February 2016, including four at Skegness and two at Hunstanton. Now research at the University of Kiel has blamed the carnage on the displays yielded by the aurora borealis in the previous month which, it is claimed, disrupted the whales' natural navigation system.

Usually, the pull of the earth's geo-magnetic field would have taken the whales back south on the same Atlantic Ocean route.

However, this time the whales were drawn down into the funnel of the North Sea, with devastating consequences. Scientists in Germany believe two major solar events in January and December prior to the strandings would have caused short-term shifts in the magnetic field, extending more than 450 km.

The proof remains far from conclusive, but NASA described the theory as 'well founded'.

 ## Fungus foray

One flash of colour in an otherwise dreary winter woodland palette comes in the form of the birch polypore. It's easily identified as it

grows on only silver or common birch trees, spreading out from the trunk like a bulging disc that can measure up to 20 cm across. This distinctive growing habit has won it the name of birch bracket although it is also known as razor strop and birch conk. Young growths are pale or coffee-coloured on the smooth upper surface and white or grey on the underside, which houses the spores. It's a feature seen in woods all year round

and the fungus can reputedly be used to sharpen knives and hold a spark to light camp fires.

Despite a bitter taste it has traditionally been used in medicine down the centuries. A 5,300-year-old mummy found in the Italian Alps had pieces of polypore in his possession, presumably to fight infection.

 ## Sunrise and sunset times for Britain's capital cities

31st January	☀ Sunrise	☀ Sunset
Belfast	08.13	17.01
London	07.39	16.48
Cardiff	07.51	17.01
Edinburgh	08.07	16.44

FEBRUARY

Although February is the shortest month of the year, it sometimes feels like it will never end. Spring is by now so keenly anticipated that days without a glimmer of sunshine accompanying a small but appreciable rise in temperature are endured rather than enjoyed. But the first signs of the forthcoming season are there to be observed: early nesting birds, the foliage of the first flowers poking through the soil crust and veils of tree pollen in flight. And Britain's birds and animals aren't resentfully idle, waiting for better weather. They are getting on with the serious business of procreation, occasionally sharing with us the rituals that they've indulged in for generations. With tree branches bare and vegetation withered, it is a fine time to witness how the countryside starts to stir.

Sunrise and sunset times for Britain's capital cities

1st February	☀ Sunrise	☀ Sunset
Belfast	08.11	17.03
London	07.37	16.50
Cardiff	07.49	17.02
Edinburgh	8.05	16.46

 ## Candlemas Day

Candlemas is on the 2nd February. People take candles to church on this day, where they are blessed and then used during the rest of the year. Before electricity candles were important, and not simply for decorative purposes.

It is also the day of snowdrops. The windows of monasteries, abbeys and churches were once decorated with the pure white flowers to celebrate the feast of the Purification of the Blessed Virgin Mary, exactly 40 days after the birth of Jesus. In pre-Christian times, this day was the 'Feast of Lights', celebrating the increasing strength of the sun as winter was giving way to spring. It was also important in predicting the weather, but not in the way that you'd think. A bright, sunny Candlemas Day means there is more winter to come, but a stormy day shows that the worst of the winter is over.

Skylarks mount & essay to sing House sparrows get in clusters & chirp & fight. Thrushes whistle.

Gilbert White, 16th February 1774

 ## Why don't woodpeckers get headaches?

It's a tantalising question that's perplexed everyone who has had their winter peace disturbed by the rhythmic rat-a-tat of a wood-pecker's beak.

Hitting a tree trunk 20 times every second with some consid-erable force would be enough to give most animals a dangerously sore head. But the woodpecker has a tough skull that's not given to fractures. Its brain snugly fills the cavity inside the skull leaving little room for fluid, so it isn't badly shaken by the drumming. Also, a web of bone and muscle hold the skull and brain securely in place.

From late January to April the aim of the woodpecker pecking is to define territory and attract a partner so the more resonant, the better. Consequently, they are more likely to choose hollow trees which ring out more loudly than the dense bark of a solid trunk.

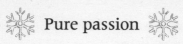 Pure passion

Some people collect stamps, others hoard spoons or street signs. Then there are galanthophiles, people who indulge themselves with snowdrops. Everyone is lifted by the sight of snowdrop drifts in February, among the first flowers to break cover after winter and certainly one of the most arresting. The scientific name for snowdrops is galanthus, which translates to milk flower and the early bloom is traditionally linked to hope and purity.

Originally 19 species grew wild in Europe and Asia, notably in Turkey. Many of the UK's significant snowdrop sites today are linked to former religious institutions; Norman monks who were convinced by their medicinal properties planted them in vast numbers, misguidedly hoping to treat anything from headaches, frostbite and confusion with both flower and bulb. Soldiers who fought in the Crimean War were so beguiled by snowdrops they brought them home to plant in gardens.

Snowdrops need careful handling as the bulbs are poisonous. That's perhaps why a single snowdrop bloom in a house was considered a symbol of death.

Since the 19th century horticulturalists here have cultivated and crossed different varieties, so now there are stripy, scented and single varieties as well as those with yellow splashes, multiple petals and bell shapes. Among the most sought after are those that are green tinged, or virescent. Bulbs for the rarest varieties go on sale for hundreds of pounds.

The lure of the nodding flower can lead people into dangerous obsession. Galanthomania has led to crime, with trowel-brandishing thieves moving silently along grasslands and stripping private gardens, public parks and grass verges of prized specimens. Collectors now rarely label the most valuable to stem flower bed thefts and sometimes employ security guards to patrol during peak snowdrop flowering season.

If you can't grow your own there's still no need to resort to bulb burglary. Scores of gardens open their gates to visitors this month to share their dazzling snowdrop displays. There's a National Collection at the Cambo Estate in Fife, Scotland, where there are 350 varieties on display while at Colesbourne Park in Gloucestershire there are 250 different types. Contact the National Trust, the National Garden Scheme or Great British Gardens for more suggestions in your neighbourhood.

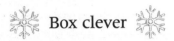

Box clever

With February comes National Nest Box Week, an initiative begun by the British Trust of Ornithology in 1997 to give British birds new accommodation. It's the time of year birds' thoughts turn to homes and families and just the right moment to place a nest box at their disposal.

More than 20 different British bird species are likely to take up residence in bird boxes, which can be homemade or shop-bought. Consider the project from a bird's eye view before you start.

All birds have unexplained preferences when it comes to nesting. Sparrows head high, to house eaves, while robins, wrens and blackbirds go low, probably to take advantage of the protection that dense vegetation offers. Great tits prefer to nest lower than blue tits. But there are plenty of options that will embrace any likely inhabitants.

Look for a sheltered spot that's protected from rain, sun and the prevailing wind – which is likely to be facing the north east – and tilt the house forward slightly so rain bounces off the roof. It should also be concealed from domestic cats. Most bird boxes are safe at a height of between one and three metres off the ground, on a tree, shed or house wall. Open-fronted boxes should be hidden behind vegetation to give occupants the best chance of survival. If you have a problem with squirrels, consider reinforcing the entrance hole with a commercially made metal plate.

There's no need for an outside perch as that might be used by a predator for easy access to vulnerable chicks. Site the box away from any existing bird feeders as hungry visitors could disturb the nesting pair. Don't put it near other nest boxes either, for fear of inciting competition. Only house and tree sparrows and house martins are happy nesting in a colony.

Do pick a box made of wood that's at least 15 mm thick and be generous with the amount of floor space inside so as many eggs as possible can be accommodated. Birds will lay enough eggs to fill the space available so a restricted size means fewer chicks.

If you are making the nest box yourself, be sure the bottom of the entrance hole is at least 125 mm from the floor of the nest box, to keep the hatchlings from tumbling out. Do not use CCA pressure-treated timber in case its arsenic content has an adverse effect on birds.

Remember to clean it out at the end of the nesting season. Use galvanised metal fixings that won't rust in the elements.

Size is important when it comes to bird boxes. Think about which birds you hope to attract as new neighbours and choose accordingly.

- ❄ Biggest nest box – Barn owl, jackdaw, kestrel, stock dove, tawny owl.
- ❄ Big nest box – Great spotted woodpecker, little owl, starling.
- ❄ Open-fronted nest box – Pied wagtail, robin, spotted flycatcher.
- ❄ Medium nest box with oval hole – Swift.
- ❄ Medium nest box with 45-mm hole – Starling.
- ❄ Small nest box with round, 25-mm hole – Blue, coal and marsh tit.

❄ Small nest box with round, 28-mm hole – Great tit, tree sparrow and pied flycatcher.

❄ Small nest box with round, 32-mm hole – House sparrow, nuthatch.

Sometimes even the most appropriately sited nest box is studiously ignored by the local bird population. It could be because there are ample natural sites in the vicinity or that it's on the boundary of pre-existing bird territories. If it stays empty for several years it might be fruitful to re-site it.

Highest and lowest average temperatures (°C) recorded for February since 1910

🌡	Highest		Lowest	
England	10.4	1998	-4.0	1947
Wales	9.8	1998	-4.4	1947
Scotland	8.7	1998	-4.9	1947
Northern Ireland	10.3	1998	-2.5	1947

 # Year of the Fox

It's a more peaceful month for foxes and their neighbours now night-time screaming has come to an end, with the pregnant vixen presently devoted to finding a suitable den. Her chosen sites will be under sheds, on waste ground or in previously used holes in hedge banks. She becomes more secretive and usually only leaves her chosen earth under cover of darkness.

While young males will have been driven off by their parents, it's a different story for juvenile vixens. They are often permitted to stay in the vicinity of their parents, in exchange for some cub care once the litter of young arrive. Dominant vixens won't allow youngsters like these to breed but there are advantages to living at home. They enjoy regular meals in a secure territory that they know well.

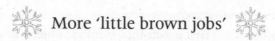 More 'little brown jobs'

Bird watchers often lament the way one small dun-coloured bird looks much the same as the next as it flits across a binocular lens at speed, so much so that they are now universally known as 'little brown jobs'.

The same description could apply to Britain's small furry mammals; all petite, brown and, it seems initially at least, with few outstanding traits. All British rodents will be at large during the winter months with the exception of the dormouse, which hibernates.

A checklist of four items will quickly determine what kind of little rodent you are looking at.

- ❄ Mice have large eyes, long tails, big ears and a pointed snout.
- ❄ Voles have small eyes, short tails, petite ears and a rounded snout. (Brown rats, black rats, grey squirrels and red squirrels are larger members of the same family.)

After that, identification gets a bit tougher. House mouse is the one found inside our homes where they thrive on our detritus. Shredded

paper and fabric, alongside a strong rodent smell, might indicate their presence. But sometimes the mouse you find in your house is a stray one from outside that is altogether better-smelling and certainly less persistent.

Meanwhile, the term field mice is often wrongly applied as this is a generic term that applies to everything that isn't house mouse, that lives outside. Having said that, outdoor mice are extremely similar. Wood mice and yellow-necked mice were only identified as distinct species in 1894. Furthermore, the wood mouse is also called a long-tailed field mouse. No one said mouse nous would be easy!

The abundant wood mouse – the one you are most likely to see – is nocturnal which is why it has those large ears and eyes common to animals that forage in the dark. But that also makes it prime prey for owls, foxes, stoats and others. It has big feet that help it to jump and climb. From nervousness rather than personal pride, it spends unusual amounts of time grooming.

With a life expectancy of less than a year it's no surprise to learn its reproduction cycle is swift, spanning just seven weeks from conception to adulthood.

If a wood mouse is caught by the tail it can shed the end of it in a bid to escape. The missing piece will, however, never grow back.

Closely related yellow-necked mice are bigger and lighter in colour, with a distinctive collar of amber fur. They are also tree climbers in pursuit of food. There are far fewer in existence than the 38 million wood mice estimated to live in our countryside.

Rarely seen harvest mice are the smallest rodents in Europe and can weigh as little as a two-pence coin. While both wood mice and yellow-necked mice dwell mostly underground, the blunt-nosed harvest mouse devotes some time to making a tightly woven ball nest about the size of an orange for breeding, elevated in tall grasses. It manages the necessary aerial acrobatics to do this by having a prehensile tail that it uses like a fifth limb. Mostly vegetarian, it will also tuck into small insects.

The smallest of the voles is the bank vole, active day and night. It differs from wood and harvest mice by having a shorter tail and moving more sedately around its habitat of woodland, grassland and hedgerow. Darker-hued field voles have stubby tails by comparison and are less likely to be seen, being mostly nocturnal and spending much of their time burrowing in soil. Typically, field vole populations peak every four years, then fall back again.

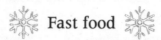

Fast food

In *Winterwatch 2018* a deer carcass was left on a Scottish crag with cameras trained on it, to monitor the meal times of majestic golden eagles in the vicinity. Carrion is an important resource for eagles during the winter months but still, programme makers thought the meat would last some time. In fact, during just 14 visits over 11 days all meat was stripped from the bones, even before there were eaglets to be fed. It shed some light on the amount of time a golden eagle must feed each day to stay alive.

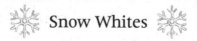

Snow Whites

At any time of year the ptarmigan is hard to glimpse as it is a high-living grouse that, stone-grey, blends with boulders in the summer and has entirely white plumage in the winter months, melting into a landscape that's covered with winter snow. Only a pair of dark eyes and a beak make it distinguishable in a white-out.

One of its secrets of survival is feathers, and not just those warming its plump body. It has feathery feet which act like snow-shoes and help the ptarmigan to walk on even the softest covering. In translation its Latin name means silent hare foot.

Those same feet will dig a hole in the snow so the ptarmigan can shelter from icy winds.

There are also feathers in its nostrils, helping to filter the ice from the air it breathes. Although you'd never know it to look at them, there're feathers on the outside of the eyelids too, insulating another body part vulnerable to the cold.

Unusually, ptarmigans moult three times in a year, turning from white to brown and then grey, to best blend with the bleak Highland backdrop it calls home.

 ## Little breeders

While we mark romance on Valentine's Day, nature has its own extraordinary array of courtship unfolding in February. Swing by your local lake this month and you might be among those fortunate enough to witness great crested grebes indulging in a balletic annual ritual that precedes mating.

The first indicator that their delightful dance is imminent is the fanning of the chestnut ruff around their heads. Then comes a shallow dive by one bird, attracting the attention of its prospective partner. There follows a spell of neck flexing and bending, inter-rupted by vigorous head-shaking, with one bird mimicking the other so they appear in almost perfect time. There may also be some preening and parallel swimming before the next and most impres-sive stage of the wooing gets underway, with both birds diving deeply and surfacing with beaks full of water weeds. They rise up out of the water and rush towards each other clutching these gifts until their bellies meet, with webbed feet paddling the surface of the water like frantic tap dancers before the more mundane business of nest-building begins.

Great crested grebes are a conservation success story. Their plumage became a fashion must-have after it was featured in the

Great Exhibition of 1851 and the resulting trade reduced their population to an estimated 32 breeding pairs in Victorian England. However, protection measures saved the birds, which can now be found all over the United Kingdom.

It's certainly a lot easier to spot this sublime routine than to observe the courtship of waxwings, which begins as early as February but is restricted to passing a berry or fruit between beaks until it is swallowed. Only after this subtle ritual will they copulate.

It's also the month that frog spawn starts appearing. Frogs have been hibernating in the mud at the bottom of ponds, taking oxygen on board through their skins. As the days lengthen and when the temperature reaches 5 degrees Celsius, they emerge with males croaking to attract a female. During mating he grips her tightly using a soft pad on the inner finger of each front foot, a hold that's called amplexus, using his back legs to see off rivals.

You'll probably notice newly laid spawn in the morning as mating happens overnight, comprising as much as 3,000 eggs that will take about 10 days to hatch, after which they will feast firstly on algae, later moving on to meat. Although the sight of frog spawn is often deemed the first sign of spring, the eggs remain vulnerable to cold snaps and won't be replaced as there is no second spawning.

Beneath the ground baby badgers are being born to mums who mated months previously. Badger sows enjoy delayed implantation, meaning they can mate at any time but keep the fertilised eggs in their womb. This means cubs are born in spring, when there's bountiful food and better weather. The sett will already be lined with fresh bedding, sometimes dragged a considerable distance. You might not see the young in the vicinity of a sett for a while but watch out for black and white hair caught in wire fencing, scratch marks on trees caused as badgers clean their claws, piles of used bedding and smelly badger latrines on the outskirts of the area.

Highest and lowest hours of sunshine recorded for February since 1929

☼	Highest		Lowest	
England	119.6	2008	28.1	1940
Wales	109.1	2008	35.7	1966
Scotland	91.7	2003	34.8	1993
Northern Ireland	101.1	2004	24.4	1993

 ## Spot the difference?

If they sat side by side, it would be easy to see that a stoat was much bigger than a weasel. Stoats are rat-sized animals while the more diminutive weasel is about twice the size of a house mouse.

The bad news is, these secretive creatures are never together because although both are from the same family, called mustelids, they generally don't inhabit the same neighbourhoods. Seen apart and usually departing at speed, it suddenly becomes a major challenge to tell one from the other.

Their sinuous bodies share a similar colour scheme with a reddish-brown back and a white throat, chest and belly. However, the colour demarcation line in weasels, the country's smallest carnivore, is uneven whereas in stoats it is straight.

At just 17–24 cm, the weasel – perpetually hungry – hunts day and night for small prey like mice and voles, running with a flat gait. They are perfectly designed for hunting in tiny burrows. On camera *Springwatch* proved the truth of an old saying, that a streamlined weasel could pass through a wedding ring; but using a skull rather than a live animal.

Stoats, measuring some 20–30 cms, bound along with a distinctively arched back. Thankfully there is one sure-fire way of picking out the stoat as it always has a black tip on the end of its tail which you might glimpse as it dashes back to cover.

Weasels begin looking for mates this month, although the pairing is short-lived as it will be the mums alone who bring up the April-born kits. Stoats are also single mums but reproduce differently, carrying a fertilised egg from the previous summer.

Both stoats and weasels were once said to 'dance' in front of prey, possibly to hypnotise before pouncing. However, another theory is that if they start to gyrate it is because a parasitic worm *Skrjabingylus nasicolais* is putting unbearable pressure on their brains and they move this way and that to shake off its effects.

The stoat is itself much smaller than other mustelids, like the polecat, pine marten and mink. Next biggest in size to the stoat is the polecat, which has pale cheeks and dark guard hairs. Then comes the dark-furred mink, often mistaken for an otter although it is smaller with a thinner tail. The pine marten is the biggest of this bunch and the most agile climber. The size of a cat and with a huge bushy tail, its stronghold is Scotland where research shows it has assisted a revival in the fortunes of the red squirrel by preying on its more prolific grey cousin.

Tweet and greet

Bird song is still sparse in February but the tune of one of the thrush family sitting on its high perch is so pronounced it can be heard above the monotonous drumming of bad weather. The ability of the mistle thrush to sing even during winter squalls has earned it the name of 'storm cock' but it also has a variety of other monikers in different corners of the country.

- Big felt – Northern Ireland
- Big Mavis – East Lothian

- ❄ Bull thrush – Hampshire
- ❄ Bunting thrush – Cumbria
- ❄ Corney keevor – Antrim
- ❄ Crackle – East Suffolk
- ❄ Fen thrush – Northamptonshire
- ❄ Holm screech – Devon, Dorset, Cornwall
- ❄ Jay pie – Wiltshire
- ❄ Mizzly Dick – Northumbria
- ❄ Norman gizer – Yorkshire
- ❄ Skirlock – Derbyshire

Mistle thrushes are bigger than song thrushes, have larger breast spots and tend to silver rather than brown on their wings. In bouncing flight they can be distinguished by the white corners on their wings.

Their song is less pleasing to the ear than the more honey-hued song thrush. Mistle thrushes sing in short phrases, in a minor key, making their tunes sound melancholy.

When they are unhappy the song is replaced by the ratchet of a football rattle. They eat worms and other invertebrates but it is mistletoe berries that are a great favourite. And it is the rattling sound that fills the air when they defend a tree from all-comers in a bid to preserve a winter food supply.

 ## Whose habitat?

CITYSCAPE

When inner city became urban sprawl there was not only a mass of new housing but many more gardens as well. In turn they became havens for elements of wildlife whose natural habitat had been swallowed up, with some species of birds like robins and wrens thriving on ornamental plant berries and foxes ultimately adapting well to the changing environment. Victorians also introduced parks into the heart of the new industrial cities, another place for wildlife to re-invent themselves and an ideal habitat for grey squirrels; introduced to Britain from North America in the 1870s as a fashionable new attraction on country estates. Park ponds became home to all kinds of water fowl, with Canada geese becoming familiar visitors. Pigeons were probably the biggest winners from expanding cities, in terms of population.

But through the suburbs and into the cities came railways, bearing steam trains that puffed out toxic smoke. In London plane trees seemed the answer as both leaves and bark – and all the pollution absorbed by them – were shed annually so there was a fresh start the following year. Spotted laurel shrubs and privet were also robust choices in the face of the smoke-inspired smog. Only when steam engines gave way to a new age of technology did the narrow corridors surrounding railway lines become fully utilised by wildlife.

During and after the Second World War, bomb sites became a refuge for wildlife as plants colonised scenes of devastation. Rosebay willowherb quickly colonises areas that have been torched; hence its nickname, fireweed. London bomb sites became a favourite venue for nesting black redstarts. As new buildings reached for the sky there were fresh opportunities for birds like peregrine falcons who swapped steep natural cliffs for high-rise buildings and the lofty ledges they provided. And the debris created by an expanding human population provided a further food bonus for some other birds with seagulls capitalising on rubbish dumps and sparrows and starlings cleaning up at outdoor cafes. Gravel pits created by construction booms down the decades have also doubled as wildlife sanctuaries, along with reservoirs made to provide water for expanding populations. Four disused Victorian reservoirs at Barnes, in south-west London, have been turned into a 105-acre nature reserve – the WWT Wetland centre – that attracts common and unusual birds including Jack snipe, heron, bittern, hen harriers and short-eared owls.

 ## Pleased to meet you … again

Five centuries ago native beavers were hunted to extinction in Britain, killed for their thick pelt and the glands that produced water-proofing oil called castoreum, which was supposed to be medicinal.

It turns out that those 16th-century hunters probably caused ecological damage on a grand scale. Beavers are natural engineers and the work they do in coppicing wood and building dams helps reduce flood threats and improves biodiversity. The monitored re-introduction of Eurasian beavers in Scotland and Devon has helped clarify some of the advantages a beaver population may bring.

By slowing the flow of water, the construction work of a beaver colony prevents a deluge further downstream, which might ruin people's homes and livelihoods. The dams trap the silt before it can block natural drainage gullies, as well as containing agricultural pollution. However, unlike man-made dams, those built by beavers

are leaky and temporary so water continues to trickle through slowly, saving land below from drought in summer months.

In the vicinity of the beaver lodge the landscape changes into a wetland, encouraging other species to thrive. Trees are gnawed away at the base but the felled trees quickly sprout again and increased light invites more plants to bloom. A burgeoning population of water-based invertebrates in the newly created pond brings forth more insect and bird life. The number of frog spawn clumps in the vicinity of one trial site has increased by a factor of 100.

Still, not everyone wants to welcome back this busy plant-eating rodent and the new ecosystem it brings. The farming fraternity fears that productive land might be inundated as the pond created by the beaver backs up in wet weather. Innovations like the 'beaver deceiver' – a pipe that lowers water deemed too high at a particular location – might help soothe commercial concerns. There are suspicions that the presence of beavers alters the flow of rivers and impedes fish travelling up streams to spawn. At the moment, though, the benefits of having beaver families back in Britain seem to outweigh the negatives cited so far.

 Pollen power

It's the time of year when the greys and browns of the British countryside are disrupted by small yellow clouds as the hazel tree sets its seed. The wind-borne drifts are pollen released from a male seed spike or catkin, aiming randomly for the intimate heart of a small,

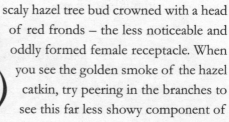

scaly hazel tree bud crowned with a head of red fronds – the less noticeable and oddly formed female receptacle. When you see the golden smoke of the hazel catkin, try peering in the branches to see this far less showy component of the procreation process. Ideally, the bud that's fertilised will belong to a different hazel tree. Male catkins develop before female buds to enable the widest possible distribution of pollen. When trees and plants rely on wind for pollination like this rather than passing insects it's a game of chance and that's why so many tiny particles set off on a journey that for most will be fruitless. The few that hit the target will produce a hazelnut in the autumn. In turn, there's only a very limited chance for that hazelnut to plant itself and grow into a tree.

Although it is one of the acknowledged early joys of spring, few people have sufficient land for these trees; there's a garden alternative in the bewitching shape of the corkscrew hazel, suitable for the back of borders, which will ensure you always glimpse this fascinating phenomenon as it happens.

The hazel tree boasts one of the brightest coloured catkins although it's by no means the only British tree to produce them. Other familiar examples are the fluffy catkin that emerges from the luxuriantly furry bud of goat and grey willows. Sever branches of these and place in a vase to watch the transformation at close quarters. Silver birch trees have firmer two-tone catkins, those on walnut trees are short, fat and green while the white poplar has attractive long red catkins but, grown at the top of the tree, they are hard to see without binoculars.

 'Ducks are a-dabbling, up tails all'

Inevitably February with its chill rain brings good weather for ducks. It was Ratty in Kenneth Grahame's *Wind in the Willows* who rhapsodised about ducks and their feeding habits, with yellow bills 'all out of sight, busy in the river!'

Although the book appeared more than a century ago, the delight of watching ducks hasn't diminished over the decades. And there are plenty of them overwintering in Britain this month alongside domestic dwellers, with scores of waterways playing host to decorative dabblers. Whether it's a village pond, river, canal, gravel pit, reservoir, estuary or wetlands trust, they will be nesting at a place near you.

Even in the heart of the city ducks are at home, as the population in St James's Park in London illustrates. A restricted number of pelicans, which have the second largest wing span of any living birds, have been living on the water there for 350 years, after being presented to King Charles II by the Russian Ambassador. They have never successfully bred because, as the House of Lords was told in a debate on the subject in 1995, pelicans tend not to produce fertile eggs unless they are part of a larger flock, numbering more than 10 birds. However, an increase in the number of pelicans in the park would be matched by a decrease in the populations of other waterfowl there as they would predate on the young.

You might not spot pelicans on your local waterway but other ducks of the 17 species that live alongside them in this royal neighbourhood, bordered by The Mall and a stone's throw from Buckingham Palace, are common everywhere, with males almost always in eye-catching glossy attire while females are frequently a dowdy brown.

Adaptable mallards are among the most familiar of British ducks but the glistening bottle-green head of the male never fails to impress. The loud, flat quack that's strongly associated with mallards is, in fact, the contact call of the female. From the male you hear more of a quiet whistle. An estimated 710,000 spend the winter in Britain.

Pintail Duck

Shoveler Duck

Tufted Duck

Pintails are elegant specimens with a brown head, long neck, pointed wings and a tapering tail. While only between nine and 33 pairs breed in the UK, the overwintering population amounts to 29,000.

With a winter population of 210,000, the UK is home to a significant percentage of north-west European teal, with visitors from Scandinavia, Iceland and Siberia making the most of the milder climate. It is a small duck with a chestnut head and a green path drawing back from its eye. For centuries it has been a source of food, with its bones being identified at a Roman settlement in Hampshire. Several thousand pairs remain here for the breeding season.

Whistling wigeon ducks, with their round heads and small bills, come from the same cold outposts as teal, appearing in numbers some 440,000 strong in the winter.

Shelducks, easily distinguished by their bright red bills and chestnut breast, are large enough to be mistaken for geese. These piebald paddlers are mostly to be found at the coast or in estuaries.

There's no mistaking the shoveler duck moving low on the surface with its black spoon-shaped bill that's fitted with a comb-like structure used to sift food from the water. Most of the 18,000 shoveler ducks that spend their winters here are found in the south and east of England.

It's easy to distinguish the male goldeneye too, for its black and white body plumage, an iridescent head, yellow eye and white cheek. Adult male tufted ducks have a purplish sheen to their heads and a quiff. While Britain was colonising across the globe in Victorian times the tufted duck settled here in 1849, probably in the wake of the zebra mussel, a food source which had made its way here a few decades previously on the hulls of ships. Grey-brown pochards are easily missed as they are quiet types who are frequently diving underwater while the surface-feeding gadwall, also with unassuming plumage and rarely found in the west, can be distinguished by a black and white wing edge.

Where to see overwintering ducks:

- Rutland Water Nature Reserve
- Dee Estuary
- Mersey Estuary
- The Wash, East Anglia
- Belfast Lough, Northern Ireland
- Solway Firth, Scotland
- RSPB Ribble Discovery Centre, Lytham St Annes, Lancashire
- RSPB Pagham Harbour, Sussex
- RSPB Rainham Marshes, East London
- RSPB Exminster and Powderham marshes, Devon
- London Wetland Centre, West London

Highest and lowest rainfall in millimetres recorded for February since 1910

	Highest		Lowest	
England	134.8	1923	8.5	1921
Wales	271.4	1923	3.5	1932
Scotland	278.1	1990	10.3	1932
Northern Ireland	193.6	1990	4.8	1932

 ## Sensational seasonal spectacles: Heronries

Heronries are ungainly nest clusters perched in the tree tops, pricked out high along a cold winter skyline. Sizes vary, usually in accordance with food supply, but the biggest heronries can host scores of pairs. Yet these days heronries are getting bigger than ever, with new residents moving into the neighbourhood.

Once they were exotic visitors, rarely seen on British shores, but in the past 25 years England and Wales have been colonised by little egrets, probably as a result of increased temperatures, and they are now familiar sights in estuaries of the south, east and south west. Little egrets have snowy-white feathers with elegant plumes on their heads. It's easy to spot their black legs too, although their yellow feet are sometimes more difficult to distinguish as they are mostly seen pacing around in shallow water. They were initially seen in significant numbers in southern Britain in 1989 and bred for the first time at Brownsea Island, Dorset, in 1996. Now there are more than 1,000 nesting pairs. Although their spread north has so far been restricted to north Wales it seems likely they will push boundaries further still.

They nest alongside the more numerous grey herons. (Almost 11,000 occupied grey heron nests were recorded by the British Trust for Ornithology in 2016.)

Heronries are best seen in February as the birds return to their ramshackle nests among the branches when there are no leaves to shield them from view. After some running repairs are carried out, they're deemed ready for eggs which may start to appear by the middle of this month.

Luckily, the taller grey heron – Britain's most widespread predatory bird – with its black, white and silver plumage and pterodactyl flight has tolerated the new kids on the block, although *Springwatch* cameras once caught one little egret in the act of stealing stray sticks from a grey heron's nest to line its own.

This ready acceptance is possibly because they feed in different ways, with herons occupying one spot like a statue waiting for passing prey while little egrets stay on the move, kicking up the mud with their golden toes to uncover items of food.

Both lunge forward in a straight line to retrieve their respective dinners, thanks to a hinged sixth vertebra in their kinked necks that permits the arrow-straight punch. Thanks to a sharp 15 per cent angle in the heron's bill and a 14 per cent angle in the beak of the little egret there is little displacement of water as they do so, giving them maximum opportunity to hit their targets.

Witness for yourself the sight of precarious-looking heron and little egret nests with their tall occupants at Cleeve Heronry in Somerset, Besthorpe Nature Reserve in Nottinghamshire, Ellesmere in Shropshire, Trentabank Reservoir in the Peak District, Hilgay Heronry in Norfolk and Waltham Abbey SSSI in Essex.

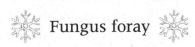

Fungus foray

YELLOW BRAIN FUNGUS

The eye-catching yellow brain fungus has a gelatinous quality that renders it almost slimy when it rains and hard when the weather is dry. An autumn or winter fungus, it can be revived from a shrivelled state by a rain shower to release spores once more. Although it has one to six centimetre lobes which make it look like a brain, the Greeks felt it better resembled a human's middle intestine. A common fungus, it favours fallen branches of birch and hazel trees.

However, it will grow on most wood and years ago any family unfortunate enough to have it appear on a gate were at one time thought to have been cursed by witches. This supernatural association has given it an alternative name: witches' butter.

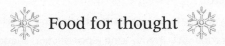

Food for thought

In winter, keeping the bird feeding station brim-full of nuts and seeds seems the obvious option. According to latest Royal Society figures, 48 per cent of households in Britain feed the birds, not just in winter but all year round.

This is undoubtedly a boost to the bird population, at a time when natural habitats are shrinking, and there's been a corresponding hike in numbers as far as some species are concerned.

As birds flock to feed it gives householders the chance to observe wildlife at its most entrancing and diligent backyard bird watchers have taken part in surveys that have significantly extended scientific data.

But those with the best of intentions may be killing with kindness. Sometimes the food used to tempt birds to the table is poor quality so it doesn't enhance avian health and may quickly become disease-ridden. Birds regularly drawn to the same table will themselves become a ready supply of food for predators. Also, says the Royal Society, crowding and competition at feeding stations causes stress.

Recognising that bird tables are a much-loved part of British gardens today, the Society has proposed a few commonsense solutions.

Damp food is quickly contaminated. Bird diseases like salmonella are spread by droppings. (Even human health can be compromised with a build-up of bird poo.) There are also other, less-known bird diseases that are spread through food and feeders. So for the sake of good health and hygiene it's important to dispense with mouldy food, to thoroughly clean feeders and rotate feeding sites.

One way of helping hungry birds is to freeze autumn windfalls and thaw them before scattering around the garden when the weather gets cold.

There's another option open to gardeners, which will help all birds bridge the hungry gap, not just the nut and seed eaters. There are plants and trees that will provide birds with berries in the depths of January when other garden vegetation has been thoroughly pilfered already. Holly, mistletoe and ivy plants all bear berries that are never a first choice for birds but will provide a calorie-rich meal in the absence of other alternatives. Spindle and dog roses may already be stripped of their fruits but climbing pyracantha plants, cotoneaster bushes and Mountain Ash trees are usually still yielding a meal for birds in winter. At the coast the acidic sea buckthorn is still prolific for birds that are running out of options.

 ## Sunrise and sunset times for Britain's capital cities

28th February	☼ Sunrise	☼ Sunset
Belfast	07.13	17.58
London	06.46	17.39
Cardiff	06.58	17.51
Edinburgh	7.04	17.45

MARCH

Straddling winter and spring, unpredictable March has much to recommend it in terms of the natural world. Author Charles Dickens wrote about March days that were summer in the light and winter in the shade. That's weather we all recognise and it's enough to keep many people inside. Yet, incredibly, butterflies may well be on the wing, with small white, green-veined white, painted lady, small copper and holly blue all spotted in the southern half of Britain in March 2018. It's clement enough for numerous migrant birds to make their way back to Britain in preparation for the nesting season ahead and skittish hares are racing around the countryside in bunches when they normally travel alone. The calendar highlights some key reasons to be outside. During March it is World Frog Day, entirely apt as spawn will be in ponds. There are also days devoted to sparrows (to raise awareness about their catastrophic decline in numbers), forests and World Meteorological Day is celebrated on the 23rd which, in 2018, had as a slogan 'weather ready, climate smart'.

Sunrise and sunset times for Britain's capital cities

1st March	⛅ Sunrise	⛅ Sunset
Belfast	07.11	18.00
London	06.44	17.41
Cardiff	06.56	17.53
Edinburgh	07.02	17.47

 ## David, Patrick and the lady

On St David's Day (1st), it is said that whoever finds the first daffodil will be rewarded with gold rather than silver, and on St Patrick's

Day (17th) before the saint adopted the flower, the shamrock was used traditionally to ward off witches and fairies, who plagued everyone at the end of winter. Lady Day (25th) is the first of the English 'quarter days' – the others being Midsummer Day (24th June), Michaelmas Day (29th September) and Christmas Day (25th December), all of which are close to an equinox or solstice. Until 1752, Lady Day was New Year's Day in the Julian calendar. It was the start of the legal and financial year, when land leases ended and others began, so farmers and their families would be moving to new farms. A hangover from this is the start of the UK tax year on 6th April, the equivalent of the 25th, but in the Gregorian calendar.

> Rooks are continually fighting & pulling each other's nests to pieces: these proceedings are inconsistent with living in such close community. And yet if a pair offers to build on a single tree, the nest is plundered & demolished at once.
>
> Gilbert White, 10th March 1775

 ## Winter marched on

Spring weather isn't a certainty in March, as Britain found out to its cost in 1891 when the country was gripped by an icy blast that lasted four days and cost 200 lives.

February had been dry and relatively sunny that year so no one was anticipating the blizzard that began on the evening of 9th March.

The South West was particularly hard hit, with hundreds of people being trapped on ten trains that ground to a halt to become enveloped in snow.

Things were even worse at sea, as one *Times* correspondent reported:

> One of the most awful nights ever known here is being experienced in the Channel tonight. The gale of this afternoon has increased into a hurricane, accompanied by a blizzard. The sea in the harbour is so rough that the waves are washing over the quays, and great excitement prevails, the greatest difficulty being experienced in holding the vessels to their moorings.

Thirteen people died when the ship *Bay of Panama*, bound for Dundee with a cargo of jute, was wrecked on the Cornish coast.

It wasn't until June that year that the last vestiges of snow disappeared from Dartmoor.

 ## Pleased to meet you ... again

With World Osprey Week falling this month, there's particular reason for Britons to celebrate.

Once numerous, ospreys virtually disappeared from the United Kingdom in the middle of the 19th century. For too long they were the target of greedy egg collectors and taxidermists, then the population was poleaxed by a loss of habitat. The final breeding record of the era in England was in Somerset in 1847 while a pair clung on in Scotland until 1916.

Today they are back in numbers in Scotland and are also to be found in Wales, Cumbria, Northumberland and Rutland Water.

The repopulation is mostly thanks to birds from Scandinavia who came back by choice to colonise northerly nesting sites. In 2001 chicks from Scotland were moved to Rutland where they made themselves at home. Since then, 117 young ospreys have successfully fledged there.

Now there's the possibility that Rutland is a staging post for the repopulation of other English sites where they once proliferated, including Norfolk, Derbyshire and Somerset. Once dubbed 'fish hawks', ospreys have white bellies, dark wings and brown eye patches, with a loose crest on their heads. They stand out from other raptors but sometimes it's difficult to distinguish at a glance the difference between ospreys and big gulls.

Ospreys are brilliantly designed to hunt fish, with reversible outer toes so they can grip prey with two toes in front and two behind. Their feet also have backwards-facing scales and protruding needle points to secure their fish feasts. When they dive in the water their nostrils close over to keep the water out and oily plumage prevents them from becoming waterlogged.

It's this month that ospreys start arriving back in Britain from West Africa, having spent the winter in Senegal and The Gambia – and lucky bird watchers in the south of England might spot them passing through.

Adult ospreys prefer to return to places they know and wildlife experts have built platform nests which they readily accept, although fledglings stay away for several years until they are old enough to rear families of their own.

As they have returned from the brink of extinction in Britain, ospreys have become judiciously monitored. In a happy spin-off there are a dozen observatories in operation with web cams focussed on nests between March and September, when migration begins again.

Spot an osprey here

 Bassenthwaite Lake, Cumbria
Cors Dyfi, Powys
Loch of the Lowes, Perth and Kinross
Rutland Water, Rutland
Wigtown, Dumfries and Galloway
Loch Garten, Highlands
Rothiemurchus Trout Fishery near Aviemore

Highest and lowest rainfall in millimetres recorded for March since 1910

	Highest		Lowest	
England	149.3	1947	7.8	1929
Wales	278.7	1981	21.0	1944
Scotland	238.5	1994	28.7	1929
Northern Ireland	146.8	1992	16.4	1953

Year of the Fox

It's the month that fox families celebrate new arrivals. After a pregnancy lasting about 52 days, the cubs are born weighing about 100 g; blind, deaf and unable to maintain a steady body temperature. Their attentive mother even has to prod them into urinating and defecating. It means the vixen must stay close at hand to keep them alive. It's now the role of the dog fox and any subordinate females to find food for themselves and her as she cares for a litter that's usually about five strong – although the record is 13. An increased number of cubs is usually a response to a high mortality rate. If the dog fox is late with dinner the vixen will bark from the mouth of the earth, presumably in a bid to hasten his return. The male soon adopts the hang-dog expression of a put-upon spouse. If he can, he'll take the easy option and raid any domestic hen coops or rabbit houses in the vicinity.

 ## Spot the difference

When it comes to corvids, the term 'bird-brained' simply will not do. Time and again, members of this mighty bird family that includes crows, jackdaws and rooks have proved they have ample intelligence, particularly when it comes to finding food. American research has found they are capable of sophisticated skills like recognition and communication – and will hold a grudge for generations. Royal Society experiments showed that rooks could solve a problem cooperatively, without training, while other studies have reported crows using tools to access food. The assumption now is that they have brains that are, in ratio, the size of a chimp's.

For humans, it's sometimes a challenge for our brains to tell these dark, chattering birds apart. Here's a guide to assist with identification.

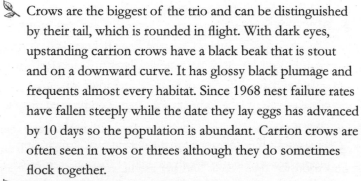

- Crows are the biggest of the trio and can be distinguished by their tail, which is rounded in flight. With dark eyes, upstanding carrion crows have a black beak that is stout and on a downward curve. It has glossy black plumage and frequents almost every habitat. Since 1968 nest failure rates have fallen steeply while the date they lay eggs has advanced by 10 days so the population is abundant. Carrion crows are often seen in twos or threes although they do sometimes flock together.
- Their close cousins, hooded crows, are two-tone with grey neck and black head feathers, and proliferate more in

Scotland, Northern Ireland and parts of Wales. Sometimes hooded crows from Scandinavia take winter refuge here. For decades both carrion and hooded crows were considered as one, looking and sounding alike and behaving in a similar way. Indeed, interbreeding between the two makes it even more difficult to tell them one from another.

Rooks are slightly smaller, more numerous than crows and more likely to make their homes near farmland and pastures. Sociable birds like these are often found in groups. They can be picked out by their peaked crowns and are barefaced with a grey, thinnish beak. Watch out for their 'baggy trousers' – a loose bloom of feathers beneath their bodies. They thrive on a diet of worms.

A 40 per cent increase in the rook population was recorded between 1975 and 1996, possibly reflecting how well the bird had adapted to changes made in farming methods.

Jackdaws are the smallest of this group, with a wing span at least 20 cm shorter than those of rooks and crows. But the key difference is not size and shape but colouring. With silvery heads, black foreheads and a bright eye that glints, jackdaws are easier to pick out even when they do flock together with crows and rooks.

Although *Springwatch* cameras captured a jackdaw emptying a swallow nest of hatchlings, the British Trust for Ornithology study of nesting jackdaws in Leicestershire revealed that while 81 per cent of their diet was meat, none was derived from nest robbing. It comprised mostly invertebrates.

There are other members of the corvid family, including monogamous ravens, which are bigger than the rest as well as being heavy-headed with a wedge-shaped tail and deeper call. As they have long-lasting partnerships and dwell year round on their territories they tend to lay eggs early, having on average three chicks per nest. It is one of the smartest of the family. A raven's brain has 153 million neurons per gram while a chimp has 16.6 million neurons per gram, giving the raven nine times greater capacity.

 Choughs are also corvids – these are much rarer and can be found at cliff sites in Scotland, Ireland, Wales and only lately in Cornwall, but are better distinguished by their coral-red beaks and legs.

Highest and lowest average temperatures (°C) recorded for March since 1910

🌡️	Highest		Lowest	
England	13.3	1998	1.6	1962
Wales	12.3	1948	-1.7	1962
Scotland	10.9	2012	-3.1	1947
Northern Ireland	12.0	2012	-1.2	1919

Sensational seasonal spectacles: the wonders of Wordsworth

March sunshine brings forth a flush of yellow flowers acid enough to sting the eyeballs as daffodils and celandines come to the fore. Both have been sufficiently dazzling to evoke verse from one of our greatest poets.

Most gardens boast a daffodil or two in spring. But these cultivars are bolder and brasher than elegantly nodding wild daffodils with their slender leaves that are found in diminishing numbers these days.

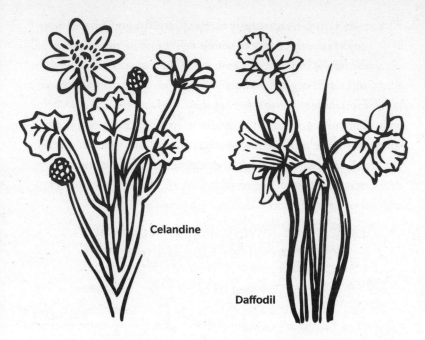

Celandine

Daffodil

Relics from the last ice age, they are also known as the Lenten Lily as they are normally at their best during Easter. They were the inspiration for Romantic poet William Wordsworth who famously wrote about 'a host of golden daffodils'. More than just a lyrical tribute, it's now a measure by which visitors to the Lake District can mark the way the seasons are changing.

Wordsworth wrote the poem sometime after seeing the array of flowers on the shores at Ullswater as he walked with his sister Dorothy, who recorded the moment in her diary in an entry dated 15th April 1802. Now the flowers are just as likely to be going full pelt by the middle of March; the blooming is linked to weather conditions.

Once prolific, wild daffodils have become marginalised with agricultural expansion. In addition to Ullswater they can be seen in hosts at Farndale in Yorkshire, Dunsford nature reserve on east Dartmoor, Devon, Wentwood Forest, Gwent, George's Hays in Staffordshire, Oysters Coppice nature reserve in Wiltshire, Stocking

Spring Wood in Wheathampstead, Hertfordshire and what's known as the golden triangle, centred on Newent in Gloucestershire.

Although Wordsworth wrote one poem devoted to daffodils, albeit an immensely famous one, he penned three in praise of the humble celandine. It's the species that blankets gardens and fields with shiny green leaves and golden stars that reach out in early spring sunshine, then vanish entirely before the summer flowers bloom. Technically speaking it's the lesser celandine, a member of the buttercup clan, that we are talking about. (In fact, it is not a close relation of greater celandine, part of the poppy family.)

In one his affection for it is plain:

> 'There is a flower that shall be mine,
> 'T is the little Celandine.'

In another he remarks on how the abundance of celandine, an often-ignored spring flower, is one of nature's riches:

> 'Pleasures newly found are sweet,
> When they lie about our feet.'

Finally he remarks on how the flower is so responsive to sunshine, folding away when it rains:

> 'There is a Flower, the lesser Celandine,
> That shrinks, like many more, from cold and rain;
> And the first moment that the sun may shine,
> Bright as the sun himself, 'tis out again!'

This star-shaped flower is known by a variety of names appropriate to its cheerful appearance; brighteye, butter and cheese, frog's foot, spring messenger and golden guineas.

It is also called pilewort thanks to a long-standing belief in its curative powers regarding haemorrhoids. As this was rooted in the observation that the twisted tubers of the plant look a bit like piles its efficacy doesn't seem like a nailed-on certainty.

And it is the swiftly spreading tubers that make it an enemy to gardeners who view this as a weed rather than, as Wordsworth did, a natural wonder.

March madness explained

For at least 600 years hares have been saddled with an unwarranted reputation for insanity thanks to the familiar idiom 'mad as a March hare'.

It's their skittish behaviour in spring that has led to the charge of madness, with leaping, chasing and boxing part of a courtship ritual that isn't necessarily restricted to March. Like their close cousins, the mountain hares, it is the females who are ready to land a punch if a male misjudges his advances. It's also a test of the male's strength. And if he is unable to withstand the blow, well, he wasn't ideal mating material anyway.

They are also unfairly associated with foolishness with widespread use of the term 'hare-brained'.

It's a saying that's again rooted in the spring antics associated with hares, which are relatively short-lived affairs. There's nothing reckless or imprudent about their behaviour in the remaining months of the year. Like every other species, it's devoted to survival.

Hares are often mistaken for rabbits, a relation that was likewise introduced in the distant past. Both have white tails but there are key differences between the two, with hares being larger, longer-limbed and having taller ears with black markings at the tips. Their faces are more chiselled than those of a rabbit, and their bulging eyes further to the side. Apart from the springtime cavorting, hares are solitary creatures, while rabbits are community-minded.

Hares don't have the comparative luxury of a burrow but live in the open, in forms, merely shallow depressions in the ground. That's where their young, leverets, will be born with open eyes and fully furred.

During the day the leverets are left alone in the undergrowth by the doe or jill who goes away to graze. They stay perfectly still, so they don't attract the attention of passing predators. But for the first month she returns every evening to feed them, until they can care for themselves.

Hence it's a common misconception that leverets found in a field have been deserted, when in fact they are waiting patiently for their evening meal. The Hare Preservation Trust asks well-intentioned passers-by not to pick up the babies unless there is a clear and present danger that threatens their well-being.

Although at 42 days a hare's pregnancy lasts for a dozen days longer than a rabbit's, a jill will still breed several times a year.

Dwindling hare populations, particularly in the south west of England, have been put down to changes in agricultural practices which have reduced their food and shelter. While autumn-planted crops assist them during the winter months, it means the food available in the spring for leverets is too mature and indigestible. Farm machinery and pesticides take their toll and hares are regularly on the menu for stoats, badgers, foxes, crows and birds of prey.

Hares rely on their extraordinary rapidity to evade predators. With powerful hind legs, they can reach speeds of between 35 mph and 45 mph and are Britain's fastest land mammals.

If hares took part in the Olympic 100 metres final, they would finish in just five seconds.

If there's anything hare-brained about these creatures it's a habit of freezing in the face of danger, including combine harvesters and the like, when they are capable of outrunning them.

Being the subject of field sports and folklore, the hare is known by numerous other names, including Aunt Sarah, Old Sally, bandy, Katie, maudkin, puss, scavernick, poor wat and wintail.

The Hare Preservation Trust is compiling information to help discover where hares are still to be found in Britain. Send your sightings to the organisation to improve their data.

See boxing hares at Lyme Park, Cheshire, RSPB Havergate Island, Suffolk and Anglesey, North Wales.

 # Golden moments

When golden eagles become a couple, the relationship is likely to last for life.

There is a curious flight pattern observed between February and May which, for years, was seen as part of their courtship. 'Skydancing', as it was termed, involved swooping and wheeling at speeds of 100 mph in a series of steep dives and climbs. At a high point in the cycle they beat their wings three or four times before plunging downwards once more.

Odder still was their habit to fly high with twigs, stones or mud in their beaks which they would drop – then plummet to retrieve.

But latest research in America points to the undulating flight displays being more about the defence of territories than the nurturing of a relationship.

Soaring golden eagles patrol a home range containing night-time roosts and at least one nest site, or eyrie, often perched on cliff ledges.

When researchers saw 15 displays performed by several

pairs of golden eagles in north Colorado, they spotted that it was normally initiated by the appearance of an intruder on the home range. Copulation between the birds occurred all year round but didn't necessarily happen after the inspirational displays.

Perhaps the birds are protecting their nests; wisely so as they represent a good deal of hard labour. Golden eagle nests are substantial structures of branches, twigs and heather, made more comfortable with a lining of greenery. The biggest found in Scotland in 1954 was 4.6 metres deep and had been used for 45 years.

 ## Angry birds

For some householders spring is marked by irate window tapping from garden birds. It's a somewhat eerie phenomenon but there's no cause for undue alarm.

In fact, it is birds reacting to their own reflection. Seeing a potential rival nearby is perceived as a threat by those defending their newly defined territories and they try to see off the encroaching bird with some belligerent beak action. According to the RSPB, the birds most likely to indulge in this kind of threatening behaviour are pied wagtails, goldcrests, long-tailed tits and chaffinches.

 ## Little breeders

Toads and roads are a toxic combination, at least as far as the toad is concerned. But the overwhelming nocturnal instinct to find a partner draws unfortunate amphibians to the same dangerous hotspots every year.

Setting off from the hideaways where they spent winter, they head for their ancestral breeding grounds – and they are oblivious as to whether a busy road dissects the route.

It takes considerable time for a toad recently awoken from its winter sleep to get from one kerb to the next. It will be slower still after a mild winter when it will have spent valuable sleep time being mobile and using up precious energy reserves.

Now toad supporters are taking action to reduce numbers killed in the annual toad carnage.

During the past 30 years an increasing number of special patrols have been established to help during toad migrations, with brightly dressed volunteers armed with torches and buckets picking up the at-risk amphibians during the evening and night-time and taking them across the road to safety.

Common toads begin to spawn when the mercury hits seven degrees Celsius. They are on the move for anywhere between a week or two, depending on the weather; choosing rainy spells over a dry period for this activity. Sometimes the crossing point is marked by a Department of Transport warning sign.

Volunteers not only save the lives of toads but, by monitoring their activities, also contribute valuable data to Froglife, the national charity that organises these patrols. Although the science is far from exact, these figures do offer a view on toad triumphs and catastrophes.

Figures collated by Froglife show that when the scheme started in 1987 there were 40 patrols that helped 14,259 toads, with more than 2,000 being helped at one site alone – Wentwood Reservoir in Newport, Gwent.

In 2017 patrollers went to work on 155 sites, plucking 84,784 toads to safety with more than 7,000 being assisted at Selbrigg in Norfolk.

Still, with an estimated 20 tonnes of toads meeting their end between Tarmac and tyre each year, it seems the common toad population has declined by as much as 68 per cent despite the best efforts of volunteers.

Even when the treacherous road crossing has been successfully negotiated, female toads may still be in peril.

Males wrestle one another to win the right to fertilise a female's eggs, which don't appear in clumps like frog spawn but in ropes that are found draped around plants.

And sometimes the battle continues on her back and she is inadvertently drowned in the process.

Although toad tadpoles are themselves toxic to fish only an estimated five per cent will reach sexual maturity.

If you have spotted an unmanned toad crossing point or want to help on toad patrol, contact Froglife.

Arrivals and departures

For some people it's a mystery that great numbers of birds should choose to spend their summers in the UK.

Many bird species turn their backs on the surefire certainty of summer sun in the Mediterranean and North Africa to head for Britain where the weather is, to put it mildly, more changeable. At the same time, we Brits are boarding planes and heading in the opposite direction.

But warm, wet weather helps insects to thrive – and that's the main attraction. Food supplies down south shrivel up with the lack of rainfall, leaving a potentially harmful competition for limited resources. Visitors want to breed here where food is relatively abundant, giving their young the best chance of survival.

Perhaps the real mystery about migration isn't the choice of destination but how the birds that embark on this treacherous journey succeed at all.

Birds will only stay alive if they have fattened up enough beforehand, if the weather is benign, if there aren't obstacles like aircraft or tower blocks in their path and if they don't get lost.

Although science is still only just getting to grips with the miracle of migration, it is thought that a sense of smell, sharp eyesight, the earth's magnetic field and even the pattern of stars helps birds find the same location, year after year.

There's no certainty about precisely when the visitors who have ticked all the boxes above will pitch up but, using figures compiled by Birdtrack, a bird watcher-led group, these are the birds you are mostly likely to see in March in the south of England.

- Wheatear
- Chiffchaff
- Sand martin
- Ring ouzel
- Swallow
- Willow warbler
- Blackcap
- Stone-curlew
- Little ringed plover
- Sandwich tern
- House martin
- Tree pipit

As for departures, Bewick's swan and white-fronted geese are heading off this month.

 ## Tweet and greet

Among the March arrivals is the ring ouzel, or mountain blackbird. Having wintered in the Atlas Mountains of North Africa, it's a bird that relishes the British uplands where it will nest either on a crag or the ground. In the Cairngorms, the North Yorkshire moors, the Peak District and Dartmoor, its arrival is greeted as an indisputable sign of spring. The ring ouzel looks much like a blackbird but for a bright-white gorget or crescent emblazoned across its breast, which appears duller among females. It sings in similar tones too. In the spring it feasts on beetles and earthworms while later in the year it is juniper berries on the menu. In the United Kingdom there are estimated to be no more than 7,500 breeding pairs, a decline

Sandwich Tern

Sand Martin

Wheatear

Chiffchaff

of more than two-thirds, which has put it firmly on the red list. However, in Europe its population seems stable and worldwide numbers are not a cause for concern. At the moment, it's thought that drier summers in Britain are affecting its preference for worms, along with the disappearance of juniper bushes which is taking its toll the rest of the year.

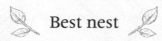

Best nest

By now the business of nest-building is underway for most birds, and completed for some. It's considerable effort for something that's not a permanent home. The majority favour a tightly woven cup made from grasses, moss, leaves and stalks – indeed any material they can manipulate with their beaks – but there are some distinguishing features. Robins, blackbirds and wrens are likely to choose sites close to the ground where there is dense cover while others head for the high branches.

- **Blackbirds** – The substantial cup nest built by the hen is held together by mud, then lined with fine grass. She turns as she builds, so moulding the nest to the shape of her body. The building process may well take two weeks and sometimes the same nest is used for second broods.
- **Rooks** – Nests are visible soon after the process starts, with rooks selecting twigs and dropping them among chosen bare branches. Although at the start it seems fruitless as many fall through, some will get trapped in position and then the speed of building work will accelerate. Finally, the nest will be shrouded in leaves as they begin to grow back.
- **Wrens** – Males build the domed nest while females line it with feathers.

🌿 **Reed warbler** – They construct a deep woven basket in which to bring up their young. But no one has yet fathomed how they begin the nest-building process, winding grass around three, four or five reed stems that are drawn together to support the nest.

🌿 **Song thrush** – Similar to a blackbird nest in dimensions, the song thrush chooses to line its nest with a mix of mud, clay, rotten wood or even cow dung that's mixed with saliva to form a hard cork-like base.

🌿 **Swallows** – Swallows and house martins use mud pellets mixed with saliva to bind their cup-shaped nests together. These effortless fliers have been monitored making as many as 1,200 trips a day to collect nesting material, primarily between 6 am and 8 am to allow the mud maximum time to harden.

🌿 **Long-tailed tits** – A bird experiencing some success in population numbers, notably in urban areas, it builds an oval-shaped nest with a single entrance that's then smothered with lichen for camouflage. One Victorian ornithologist, William McGillivray, counted 2,379 feathers in the construction of one long-tailed tit nest. The birds then withdraw for a couple of weeks before egg laying starts.

🌿 **Chaffinches** – Nesting in tree forks, the chaffinch gathers spiders' webs to make sticking patches that will anchor the nest like mortar. Goldfinches also build with spiders' webs

In March you can lend birds a hand by collecting the kind of natural fibres that add a touch of luxury to their nests. That might include pet fur, hair from brushes, strands of pure wool, feathers, twigs, bits of string and small strips of cloth. Bundle them together with string and hang them in a tree so they can be accessed by birds easily and safely.

Cast of thousands

When it comes to holding up the ecosystem it's the humble earthworm that is doing the hard yards.

With every living thing dependent to some degree on top-quality soil in which good bacteria, fungi, flowers and foodstuffs can flourish, the unseen labours of the earthworm keep the ground beneath our feet in tip-top condition.

Both ends of these extraordinary environmental engineers work in concert to our advantage. One end munches through debris scattered on top, pulling dead leaves into their burrows, while the other deposits faeces that enriches the soil and improves its structure. It's recycling in its purest form and precisely the reason why so many people have domestic wormeries, in which a community of worms goes to work to transform vegetable peelings into glorious compost. Back in the ground, they let oxygen in and carbon dioxide out by burrowing.

The idea that earthworms are one of the vital building bricks of ecology isn't a new one. Gilbert White was convinced of it and eminent naturalist Charles Darwin, whose observations and experiments were initially considered radical and inflammatory, published a book about earthworms in 1881, six months before he died, which was the result of a lifelong passion for the often overlooked underground tunnellers.

In it he wrote:

> When we behold a wide, turf-covered expanse, we should remember that its smoothness, on which so much of its beauty depends, is mainly due to all the inequalities having been slowly levelled by worms ...

The plough is one of the most ancient and most valuable of man's inventions; but long before he existed the land was in fact regularly ploughed, and still continues to be thus ploughed by earth worms. It may be doubted whether there are many other animals which have played so important a part in the history of the world, as have these lowly organised creatures.

According to the Earthworm Society of Great Britain, there are 27 species of earthworm in the UK, which come in all sizes and colours.

No matter how familiar they are, there remains something of the science fiction around them. They have no eyes and no head but are sensitive to light, preferring the security of soil than the scrutiny of passers by. Only at night or during rain do they willingly come to the surface. In extreme cold and hot weather, they will burrow deep into the soil in search of warmth and moisture.

Worms are hermaphrodites, which means each has male and female attributes. Nonetheless, they must mate to procreate, winding themselves around one another in a layer of mucus for up to three hours as sperm is swapped. The thickened part of the body or saddle then produces a mucous tube that moves up the body to combine sperm and egg.

Happily, there's no shortage of earthworms. Best guesses claim there might be 1,000 in every cubic metre of soil, 2,000,000 per football field and 8,000,000 in a hectare.

And that's fortunate because they are on the menu for all kinds of animals. An estimated 60 per cent of a badger's intake consists of earthworms while moles need to eat 50 g of worms a day for survival. Frogs and toads like to feast on them, as do birds.

It's this month, after birds arrive exhausted from migration then when chicks begin to hatch, that a diet of worms is the key to survival. Watch carefully as hungry birds do a spot of 'worm charming', drumming their feet on the ground to imitate the vibration of rain, in the hope of luring worms to the surface.

More troublingly, earthworms are also prey for the purple, slimy New Zealand and Australian flat worms, unwelcome Antipodean visitors who first squeeze then dissolve their victims in a bodily mucus that contains digestive enzymes.

Despite their profound importance in our lives, comparatively little is known about the earthworm and its lifestyle. The Earthworm Society is looking for citizen scientists to help establish more data.

 ## Spring equinox

20th March	☀ Sunrise	☀ Sunset
Belfast	06.24	18.37
London	06.01	18.13
Cardiff	06.13	18.26
Edinburgh	06.13	18.26

 ## Whose habitat?

WOODLANDS

It's about the most important habitat in the country, supporting all kinds of mammals, amphibians, birds, butterflies and insects.

In Britain there are 3.16 million hectares of woodland, a figure that's doubled since the Second World War.

The charitable Woodland Trust is a major contributor, having planted 38 million trees since its formation in 1972.

In addition, it works to restore ancient woodlands and save areas under threat.

But there are plenty of concerns about trees in Britain, given the effects of pollution, disease and encroaching human activity.

Only 13 per cent of the country is now covered in trees. This compares with 38 per cent for the EU as a whole. Of that 13 per cent only one-third is planted with native trees. Six thousand years ago three-quarters of Britain was forested.

With the International Day of Forests falling on 21st March, it's a timely moment to list some of the vast array of creatures who rely on it – from tiny insects to alpha mammals – as a reminder never to be complacent about this vital habitat.

Mammals

Look out for signs of badgers, foxes, fallow deer, roe deer, red deer, muntjac, pine martens, stoats, weasels, grey squirrels, red squirrels, bank voles, dormice, yellow-necked mice, hedgehogs and assorted bats.

Birds

A by-no-means-exhaustive list of birds you might spot in woodlands starts with songbirds like nightingales, song thrushes, fieldfares, redwings, mistle thrushes and blackbirds.

Among the owl family tawny, long-eared, little and barn owls are usually represented while there are birds of prey including sparrowhawks and goshawks.

Using eyes and ears, you might be able to identify robin, redstart, dunnock, cuckoo, wood pigeon, jay, tree creeper, capercaillie and woodcock as well as coal, crested marsh and blue tits and three varieties of woodpecker.

Amphibians

Frogs, toads and all varieties of newt are to be found in woodlands, specifically in those shallow ponds, while adders, grass snakes, smooth snakes, slow worms, common and sand lizards favour wooded areas with glades in which they can soak up the sun.

Outnumbering all the above by some considerable margin are the invertebrates in the butterfly, beetle, spider and moth families, plus other assorted insects. They languish at the bottom of the food chain but if they didn't thrive under the forest canopy then few of the other animals would too. It's also home to a vast array of plants, fungi and, obviously, trees.

Not everything listed above will be dwelling in your local woodland. Red squirrels are only found in specific pockets of the country and pine martens are most likely to be living in Scotland.

Indeed, no one knows exactly about the distribution of wildlife in the country's woods and forests. And here's where you come in. The Woodland Trust would like to know more about where our animals live and how weather and climate change might be affecting them.

Go to the website and enter a record of exciting sightings and contribute to Nature's Calendar, a database containing millions of records that's used by researchers across the UK.

Highest and lowest hours of sunshine recorded for March since 1929

☼	Highest		Lowest	
England	172.8	1929	57.2	1984
Wales	209.4	1929	60.5	1936
Scotland	153.0	1929	58.2	1936
Northern Ireland	172.8	1929	50.2	1996

Who's who of poo

One way of identifying which animals are living in the habitats near you is identifying the calling card they can't help but leave behind.

Any creature that eats must defecate too, which becomes vital evidence for nature detectives. The clues are in its shape, size, colour and consistency. Look closely and you might see what they had for their last meal. Remember, never touch it with your hands, for reasons of hygiene. If you want to investigate what they've been eating, use a stick to probe the poo.

 Fox – Dark brown or black, and often deposited on a garden lawn, it looks suspiciously like the work of a local dog. But fox poo is distinctive for being tapered to a hairy point, as well as being pungent. In the countryside the remains of fur, feathers and bones may well be apparent. But this won't be the case among urban foxes who will probably have got their last meal from a domestic bin.

 Badgers – Badger poo is softer and sausage-shaped but the easiest way to identify it is the piles it is left in because these animals use an outside latrine in order to keep their setts sweet-smelling, and also to mark their territory.

 Hedgehogs – Cylindrical hedgehog droppings are shiny and black and will measure no more than 5 cm in length. It might be possible to distinguish insects and worms in it.

 Rabbits and hares – Both issue grassy bullets which will appear in clusters, with hares' deposits being larger and flatter than those of a rabbit.

 Weasels and stoats – Dark brown or black, the tubes they leave are single, slender and twisted at each end. A stoat poo measures about 4 to 8 cm while a weasel will be smaller.

- **Deer** – All deer will leave smooth, shiny, dark clusters of excrement. As ruminants they regurgitate their food and chew it for a second time so there will be little evidence of what it looked like originally.
- **Owls** – There's two chances here, as owls issue pellets that contain hair, feathers and bones – all the indigestible parts of their prey. There will also be white liquid droppings under their favourite perches.
- **Otters** – Correctly termed a spraint, black otter poo at between three and ten centimetres in length is likely to have in it visible remnants of their fish dinners. It's left on river banks and waterside rocks, also to mark territory.
- **Green woodpecker** – Remarkably, being a white cylinder about 30 mm in length and six to eight mm in diameter with a tan-coloured tip, this looks something similar to a discarded cigarette.
- **Squirrel** – At eight millimetres in diameter and brown or red in colour, the most likely spot to find it is beneath a bird table.
- **Water shrew** – Poo contains white fragments of exoskeleton.

 Fungus foray

HAIR ICE

On a nippy morning look out for hair ice growing on twigs or sticks beneath a hedgerow or on the forest floor. Initially, it looks a bit like frost although on closer inspection this stunning phenomenon is more akin to a small explosion of fine silk thread. And there doesn't need to be weather-induced ice around for this to occur so, bright white against leaf brown, it snags on your vision. Hair ice only grows in very specific conditions, involving a temperature of slightly less than 0 degrees Celsius, humid air, a piece of rotting wood and the presence of the fungus *Exidiopsis effusa*. In 2015 scientists realised it was the fungus being there that led to a process called 'ice separation', when water in the rotting weed is squeezed out to the side by the formation of ice. It's thought an inhibitor in the fungus helps to preserve the ice floss, with each strand about 0.01 mm wide, for several hours.

Sunrise and sunset times for Britain's capital cities

31st March	☀ Sunrise	☀ Sunset
Belfast	06.56	19.58
London	06.36	19.32
Cardiff	06.48	19.44
Edinburgh	06.44	19.49

APRIL

The natural world is fizzing with activity this month. Some birds and animals are still involved in the rituals that are a precursor to finding a partner. Others are further down the track, involved in frantic food gathering because they have hungry young mouths to feed. Whatever the cause, there are visible commotions breaking out in habitats up and down the country. The need to feed can sometimes lead to the most appealingly vulnerable becoming targets. *Springwatch* viewers have often watched from their armchairs in helpless horror as nestlings are plucked from safety and gulped by bigger birds. For the most part there's a 'doomed surplus' among newly born wild animals that means overall population sizes are not unduly affected by such losses. Nor do the invertebrates that provide such a chunk of birds' and animals' diets garner public sympathy in the same way. So it's crucial that observers accept this apparent savagery as part of the circle of life and follow the mantra of *Springwatch* presenters, empathising with the prey, but not demonising the predators.

Sunrise and sunset times for Britain's capital cities

1st April	☼ Sunrise	☼ Sunset
Belfast	06.54	20.00
London	06.34	19.34
Cardiff	06.46	19.46
Edinburgh	06.41	19.51

Gowks and nosegays

In Scotland, April Fool's Day (1st) is Hunt-the-Gowk Day. A gowk is a cuckoo, the symbol of a foolish person, and to hunt-the-gowk was to be sent on a fool's errand. Maundy Thursday, or Royal Maundy, is on the Thursday closest to Easter, when the Queen and family, together with the clergy in attendance, carry nosegays. It is said to be the only day the Duke of Edinburgh consents to carry flowers. In the past, these sweet-smelling bouquets were supposed to ward off plagues and other diseases, when the sovereign came into contact with the poor. The following day, Good Friday, is the day to plant potatoes and other vegetables. There is many a yarn explaining why, but one version holds that agricultural labourers who lived in tied cottages on a landowner's estate were worked so hard that they only had time to plant their vegetables on their one day off between New Year and Easter – Good Friday.

> Cock snipe pipes & hums in the air. Is the latter sound ventriloquous or from the rapid motion of the wings? The bird always descends when that noise is made & the wings are violently agitated.
>
> Gilbert White, 6th April 1772

 ## Year of the Fox

On a warm day in April fox cubs will venture into the outdoors for the first time. It's certainly time to leave the earth, which by now is littered with rotting food and faeces. A noisy fly population is usually testament to that.

At this time fox cubs love nothing more than to chase and brawl with one another, finally flopping down in a weary pile. The mother vixen takes full advantage of their increasing independence in the morning and evening by foraging for food herself. Meanwhile, the dog fox is likely to stay close to the cubs for fear of predators. The most likely threat comes from a stalking domestic cat which, given the opportunity, might kill a cub when small.

Pleased to meet you … again

WALKING TALL

Cranes disappeared from Britain in the middle of the 16th century when the last recorded pair brooded in Norfolk. The population had been squeezed by hunting and the draining of the wetlands they called home.

Happily, extinct wasn't for ever in this case as three cranes turned up in the same county 400 years later and liked it so much they decided to stay.

It's impossible to know what drew the birds back to this country in 1979 but, at 1.2 metres (four feet) tall with a wing span measuring almost twice that, it was a welcome return for an iconic species.

Numbers grew in a continuing voluntary repatriation by the birds – some of whom have successfully bred – and the population doubled by 2015 when 93 birds were released in Somerset after being hand-reared at Slimbridge Wildfowl and Wetlands Trust in Gloucestershire.

Dubbed The Great Crane Project, eggs had been collected in Germany where cranes are abundant, over four years, to be artificially hatched here.

Springwatch viewers saw a video diary of how they were raised, with keepers disguised in baggy white suits using litter pickers made to look like crane heads, teaching the young birds to feed and exercise at arm's length so the birds didn't form an attachment to humans.

Although there are only some 50 pairs across the country in a population of less than 200 birds, they are breeding in Norfolk, Suffolk, Cambridgeshire, Yorkshire and East Scotland and they have now been re-introduced to Somerset, Wiltshire, Oxfordshire and Gloucestershire.

So the extraordinary trumpet call of the crane, produced when the white, black and grey bird throws backs its head and hollers, can now be heard echoing around those areas again. But that isn't the most remarkable aspect of their behaviour.

A lucky few will see the courtship dance between couples involving wing spreading, head dipping and long-legged posturing which occurs in spring. Together they canter around to the bugling soundtrack of their love calls.

Although they bear a resemblance to both herons and storks, cranes are more closely related to dumpy moorhens. As if to prove it, both birds have a crimson flash on their faces.

In flight cranes keep their necks in a straight line, like geese, while herons fly with an S-bend silhouette. On the ground herons keep statue-still while cranes pace around.

Populations are being closely monitored but, at the moment, there's optimism that they are the foundation for the future.

 ## Highest and lowest rainfall in millimetres recorded for April since 1910

	Highest		Lowest	
England	136.5	2012	6.7	1938
Wales	193.9	1920	8.8	1938
Scotland	191.1	1947	14.0	1974
Northern Ireland	144.2	1961	8.2	1938

April arrivals

Using information from four key birding sites – in Dorset, Wales and the Isle of Man – the British Trust for Ornithology can reveal the birds that are heading to Britain this month, in the order they are likely to appear. This is the April schedule for Portland, Dorset:

- Redstart
- Tree pipit
- Yellow wagtail
- House martin
- Grasshopper warbler
- Common sandpiper
- Whitethroat
- Sedge warbler
- Whinchat
- Cuckoo
- Pied flycatcher
- Garden warbler
- Turtle dove
- Lesser whitethroat
- Swift
- Spotted flycatcher

This month Britain says a seasonal farewell to scaup, merlin, purple sandpipers, Jack snipes, water pipits, great grey shrikes, redwings and bramblings.

 ## Tweet and greet

April marks the return of the cuckoo, a graceful bird with pointed wings folded across a dove-grey back and stripy, barred underparts that, at a glance, make it look like a sparrowhawk.

But its distinct call announces that, without doubt, it's a cuckoo rather than a bird of prey, although that's scant comfort for smaller birds as the cuckoo poses just as much peril to them as any predator.

Rather than devote time to the labour-intensive matter of hatching chicks, it squats in a nest belonging to another bird and departs after laying an egg.

Research carried out at the Norwegian University of Science and Technology has revealed that female cuckoos smuggle the egg past the host mum by laying an egg the same colour, specialising in the nests of specific species. So she can lay brown, speckled or blue eggs, depending on the birds she targets for foster care. Although the cuckoo egg is slightly larger, it looks about the same.

Only the female cuckoo carries the gene that affects the colour of eggs. A male may mate with several females so, if his input had an effect, the resulting egg could stand out as the work of an intruder. With the female cuckoo in control of the colour, the fledglings have the best possible chance of survival.

This subterfuge causes detriment to the unwitting host in two ways. Firstly, the cuckoo tips out one of the eggs already laid in the nest to make room for its own. Then, after the cuckoo chick has hatched, the new mother has to find food for this outsized family addition, inevitably at the expense of her own young. The hefty hatchling might even tip out rival birds itself to get maximum benefit of the food supply.

According to the RSPB, it is diminutive species like meadow pipits, dunnocks and reed warblers most likely to be left 'holding the baby'.

Still, being a brood parasite hasn't spelled success for cuckoos, whose numbers in Britain have gone down by half in the last 20 years according to the BTO. The decline is mirrored by a fall in the population of large moth species, which provides food for cuckoos.

In a bid to find out what happened to cuckoos after they left Britain in the summer, the BTO ringed some birds that spent spring here so they could satellite track their journey.

One, dubbed Selborne for naturalist Gilbert White who lived there, left the New Forest in Hampshire on 20th June 2017 and flew down the west of France to northern Spain then went on to Africa and was detected in Algeria, Mauritania, Mali, Burkina Faso, Benin,

Nigeria and Gabon on the west coast where it spent the winter. On its return journey it covered a distance of 2,115 km (1315 miles) in ten days, reaching Guinea in early February before skirting around the Ivory Coast and heading up through the Sahara Desert before arriving in Morocco in the middle of March. Selborne then flew across Spain and France to arrive back in Britain on 17th April 2018.

The cuckoo is notorious for its behaviour but it's not the only bird to take advantage of other nests. Starlings also deposit eggs in nests that aren't their own – but that do belong to other starlings. This is usually done by 'floaters', female birds that don't have a mate or a nest to call their own. Although she will likely go on to raise her own young she has probably taken this chance because early fledglings are more successful than those that come later.

 ## Highest and lowest average temperatures (°C) recorded for April since 1910

	Highest		Lowest	
England	16.9	2011	0.5	1917
Wales	15.8	2011	0.9	1922
Scotland	13.6	2011	-0.8	1922
Northern Ireland	15.5	2011	-0.3	1922

 ## Spot the difference

By now the swallows, swifts, house martins and sand martins have begun returning from their winter breaks in sub-Saharan Africa to bring up their families here. But as they fly past at speed, wheeling after flies and midges or skimming the surface of a river to snatch a drink, it's notoriously tricky to tell them apart. All have similar silhouettes and indulge in dynamic aerobatics as they snatch their dinner out of the air.

Swallows are the easiest to identify, given their distinctively elegant forked tails. They also have sooty heads and backs with a rust-red facial feature. Their flying patterns tend to be weather affected so if it is sunny and fine they will soar in the sky but if it is damp and chilly they fly low. Of course it is the effect the weather has on the insects they are pursuing that is key here.

By preference their cup-shaped, mud-constructed nests built by the male and lined by the female will be in barns or out-buildings. *Springwatch* presenters Kate Humble and Bill Oddie were once shocked to see film of a male swallow turfing five recently hatched chicks out of a nest after harassing the female. Experts explained the infanticide was probably carried out by a bird without a partner who had designs on the new mum.

The tail of the swift has a much shallower fork and this bird is brown rather than black, although it looks very dark against a bright spring sky. It has a loud shriek as opposed to the chattering of the swallow. Indeed, the two are not related. Nests tend to be in cavities with a small entrance. If you see similarly shaped birds gathered together on a wire, well, they're not swifts although they might be swallows or house martins. Swifts have tiny feet that are not built for perching.

House martins share the blue-black feather colouring of the swallow but are white from beak to tail underneath. Their mud-built nests are often found snug under eaves and they will struggle to complete it if nest-building coincides with a dry spell. Like sand martins, their tails have a more shallow fork, again when compared to swallows and swifts.

Sand martins are brown with white underparts and would, out of preference, choose the sandy banks of a river in which to nest. However, the risks of being flooded by a spring deluge have made gravel pits and quarries altogether more attractive. They are usually the winners of the migration race, arriving here before the others. Sand martins and house martins are cousins.

 ## Fungus foray

FOR ENGLAND AND ST GEORGE

It takes its name from England's patron saint as St George's mushroom reputedly appears each year on 23rd April, when the hero is remembered. The first of the edible fungi to bloom, sometimes growing in fairy rings, it has a smooth white cap which turns to tan as it ages. Beneath the cap the gills are white. It's long been a favourite among those who forage for food. However, there are two reasons to treat this chunky mushroom with caution. First, it is easily confused with the deadly Fibrecap, the latter having pink rather than white underskirts. Secondly, it is prone to maggot infestation that might not be apparent until the first bite has been taken.

 ## Beware the garlic eaters

Watch out for conspicuous orange-tipped butterflies on the wing this month, one of the first to emerge after winter. Having spent nine months in a camouflaged chrysalis suspended on a stalk, its first act will be to dry damp wings in the sun and wait for its blood to start pumping. Then it will need to find a nectar-rich food source to replenish its flagging energy levels. Garlic mustard – also known as jack-by-the-hedge – is its menu of choice.

Only the males have the easy-to-spot orange tips, designed to send a 'keep off' warning to predators after its pungent snack as it is a passing food considered distasteful for predators. As egg-layers, females live a more sedentary life and don't need the showy spots.

They could be mistaken for one of the white butterflies, but for the mottled wing undersides that they have in common with the males.

Look out for the dancing flight of the male as he wanders along meadows, hedgerows and woodland margins, intent on beginning the pressing business of reproduction. A female tends to lie low until she is found by the male. Once they have mated she lays tiny eggs which turn from green to orange and then hatch, although the larvae are smaller than a pinhead. After three weeks of continuous eating each will be 800 times heavier than when it first hatched and ready to build its winter home.

Ice Age IV

Curiously, although the wildlife found in Ireland is rich, there are species found in Britain that don't appear there. Both are near neighbours and enjoy similar climates. The answer to this mystery lies 10,000 years ago and with the movement of land and sea during the last Ice Age. That's when Ireland became an island and, with the disappearance of the land bridge, its ecosystem was complete.

Britain remained linked to Europe for hundreds of years more, so the northward spread of animals from warmer spots in Europe continued for longer.

Snakes: Folklore would have you believe that Ireland's patron saint drove snakes from Ireland. In fact, there were never any there. The tale grew out of common depictions of St Patrick battling with a serpent. Today it's thought that Christian St Patrick is shown winning the battle against paganism, depicted in snake form.

Weasels: Sometimes the Irish stoat is mistakenly branded a weasel but it is in fact an Irish native that differs from its

Scottish and English cousins by never changing its coat from brown to white in the winter. The smaller weasel is nowhere to be found.

 Moles: Irish farmers and gardeners count their blessings for not having the soil disruption caused by busy moles.

 Great crested newt: Protected by law in Britain, it has caused consternation to developers who encounter colonies on sites earmarked for development. Irish builders have no such headaches. There are three amphibians found in Ireland; the natterjack toad, the common frog and the smooth newt alongside one reptile, the common lizard.

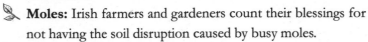 Britain's favourite flower

With flowers there's no doubting the nation's favourite. The naming of the rose as Britain's top scorer in numerous polls down the decades comes as little surprise. It's England's national flower as well as having infamous historical links with the once-warring counties of Yorkshire and Lancashire.

Roses are commonly associated with the English country garden, a ready target for bees and butterflies. They also have a language all of their own with red roses signifying love, pink meaning grace, orange for fascination and burgundy for beauty.

In 2017 a poll carried out by Monarch Airlines put the country's favourite flowers in the following order.

1. Rose
2. Lily
3. Tulip
4. Daffodil
5. Sunflower
6. Orchid
7. Carnation
8. Bluebell
9. Freesia
10. Poppy

Sensational seasonal spectacles: Britain's favourite wild flowers

1. Bluebell
2. Primrose (which claimed the top spot in Scotland, Wales and Northern Ireland)
3. Poppy
4. Snowdrop
5. Cowslip

When it comes to finding the country's best-loved wild flower it's a different story and in England it is bluebells that top the most recently devised chart. Research carried out by the charity Plantlife in 2015 reflected how springtime carpets of the vivid-violet arch of bells won special merit in the minds of the English public. More than half the world's bluebells are in Britain, transforming the British countryside in April on a major scale. But which bluebell?

At times like this people typically think of the native bluebell (*Hyacinthoides non-scripta*), which has a caustic colour and a distinctive scent. It favours woods but might be found in hedges and even on sea cliffs.

But in fact they may be encountering either Spanish bluebells (*Hyacinthoides hispanica*), with its larger, paler, odourless blooms. The Spanish bluebell was initially cultivated in Britain in 1690 and first appeared in the wild in 1909. With bees showing similar favour to both the British bluebell and its Spanish cousin, nature has taken its course and thrown up a third option. Now the hybrid bluebell (*Hyacinthoides hispanica x non-scripta*), which emerged in the wild after 1963, is also encroaching on the native variety.

With loss of habitat, the illegal collection of highly desirable native bluebell bulbs and these marauding competitors, England's

Bluebell

Cowslip

Snowdrop

Poppy

Primrose

most popular wild flower – which typically first flowers on St George's Day – is at risk.

See bluebells in all their glory at Ashridge Estate in Hertfordshire, Blickling Hall in Norfolk and Buckland Abbey in Devon. Check the Wildlife Trust's website for more suggestions.

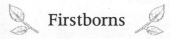

Firstborns

To their mums, all newborns are beautiful. But it's remarkable that the most besotted mother bird doesn't have doubts when her brood emerges from their eggs; blind, bald and incapable of moving or feeding themselves. The technical term for chicks like this is altricial, derived from a Latin word meaning 'to nourish'. Examples include swallows and blue tits. Indeed, all the passerine – or perching – birds are altricial.

By contrast, some recently hatched birds are up and about virtually straight away. Born with their eyes open and a coating of down, they are quickly out foraging for themselves. These chicks are called precocial, from the word 'precocious' which implies early development. Avocets, shelducks, swans, coots and ringed plovers are just a few types of precocial birds.

The difference between the two lies in the size of the yolk in relation to the egg laid by the mum. The yoke in a starling's egg accounts for 20 per cent of its size and it is altricial. In precocial tufted ducks the egg is 40 per cent yolk and, at twice the relative size, it takes far more energy from mother birds to produce.

Both have evolutionary advantages. While helpless chicks are easy meat for predators, the more developed precocial types can scatter in the face of a threat. However, altricial birds, born with smaller brains, seem to have a post-birth growth spurt that ultimately gives them slightly bigger brains than their precocial counterparts.

Walking on eggshells

Along path and alleyway, field edge and lane, there are signs of spring in the shape of fragments of discarded birds' eggs.

Immediately one thinks of the egg shell's occupant as a newly hatched chick straining for food from its diligent parents. But the shattered remains could have more serious undertones, indicating a hungry nest marauder pecking its way through to a helpless unborn.

A swift examination of the shell remains will help tell you its story. A chick opens its shell neatly by pecking an exit hole, leaving the rim of the shell pointing outwards. If you find a shell that fits this description bear in mind that the nest it came from may not necessarily be nearby. Nest-proud mother birds often fly some distance to dump the unwanted shell so as not to alert predators to their whereabouts.

Meanwhile, predators working from the outside will be altogether messier in their approach to breaking the shell, leaving remnants pointing inwards. They are likely to have consumed all the contents, including the membrane, while eggs from which birds have hatched will probably have traces of it left inside.

 # Rare sights

British birds have their fair share of success stories. But to counterbalance the good news there are numerous species that are still a major cause for concern. Here are ten birds that even the most dedicated bird watcher would consider themselves fortunate to spot these days.

1. **Nightingale:** It's an unobtrusive bird with a gorgeous voice. A nightingale is the size of a robin with a silhouette of a redstart, although its own plumage is an unremarkable

brown so expect to hear rather than see one. After arriving in southern England in April, male nightingales sing for about six weeks, primarily to attract a female. The older they get, the bigger their repertoire and the more attractive they are to the opposite sex. Thus age proves no barrier to romance in this bird's world. The chances of a nightingale singing in Berkeley Square, as per the famous Vera Lynn song, are remote, however. These birds favour woodlands, heathlands and scrub, staying away from urban areas. This nocturnal songster is loud and proud, singing at 95 decibels, a sound similar to a motorbike just 25 ft away from your ear. One recorded male made 600 different sounds and sang 250 identifiable phrases. Remarkably, every performance was unique. Nightingales seem to appreciate fine music too, as renowned cellist Beatrice Harrison noticed when she practised in her garden in Oxted, Surrey. At each musical phrase the bird piped up in concert with the strings. On 19th May 1924, just two years after BBC Radio began, a recording of cello and nightingale was broadcast to the nation, to popular acclaim. And it remains an inspiration for musicians who are among those now campaigning to protect the bird better. The nightingale population has decreased by an estimated 91 per cent in fifty years, with only an estimated 5,500 singing males left. It's thought over-grazing by muntjac and roe deer might play a part, as well as the disappearance of swathes of their favoured habitat. There's concern that housing development is eating into the nightingales' last strongholds in southern England and East Anglia. After a monitor was attached to one bird, *Autumnwatch* viewers learned that when nightingales left England in the summer months they took a staged journey before arriving in West Africa, a trip of some 5,000 kilometres. It means their winter quarters can now be investigated to see if nightingales are suffering from any environmental issues there too.

2. **Nightjar:** Another summer visitor that turns up in April or May, the nightjar – like the nightingale – is best heard at dusk or dawn. Rather than singing it churs, with the ability to turn out 1,900 notes per minute. During the day this mottled grey and brown bird stays motionless in its favoured woodland, heathland or moorland habitat and looks like a stone. But in flight at night hunting for moths it is more distinctive, with the body of a starling and the wing of a sparrowhawk. You might even hear the clap of its wings in flight. The birds use a serrated middle claw on their feet as a comb to preen their feathers.

3. **Pied flycatcher:** In a smart tuxedo, the male pied flycatcher with his chirping song is confident he is a good catch. So after mating with one bird in the Welsh oak woods that are his stronghold he flies back to the tree branches and breaks out into song once more, hoping to attract a second love interest. The agile black and white bigamist, about the size of a sparrow, is then condemned to feeding two nests of fledglings. Curiously, if he is going to neglect either of his brides it seems he usually chooses the second.

4. **Capercaillie:** The largest of the grouse family, all public attention focusses on the male with his iridescent black colouring, a white wing spot, a fan tail and a ring of red skin around his eye. He is also remarkable for clicking, gulping and popping noises that announce his amorous intentions. Females are far quieter in colouring, ideally suited for squatting on nests on the floor of Scots pine forests, where the needles are a source of food. Displaying males weighing in at about four kilos fight each other in forest floor arenas, like turkey gladiators. Memorably, Sir David Attenborough was once bowled over by a capercaillie when mistaken for a rival. The

present population, confined to the wilds of Scotland, came from Sweden in the 19th century after native birds were hunted to extinction. Once again, numbers are perilously small, standing at just a few thousand compared to 20,000 during the seventies.

5. **Lesser redpoll:** Once the lesser redpoll thrived on the birch and alder seeds freely available in British woodlands. After the Second World War this habitat declined, along with the lesser redpoll population. Now a different kind of seed appears to be supporting a welcome boom in the numbers. Niger seed on bird tables may be becoming a mainstay in the diet of these small, sociable finches which are named for the splash of red on their foreheads. When they make an appearance in a garden it's often in the company of siskins and goldfinches.

6. **Willow tit:** Black-capped willow tits are battling on all fronts. Their chosen nesting sites are damp and scrubby – and old industrial zones were a perfect fit. Today most of these brownfield sites are swiftly earmarked for development. When they nest, with females chiselling out a hole in rotten wood with her beak, there's a chorus of chirps which attracts the attentions of competing great and blue tits, looking for a quick eviction, as well as marauding woodpeckers. The main populations are now in the north of England. Willow tits are easily confused with marsh tits, who actually prefer dry woodland and have a glossier black cap with less prominent white cheeks.

7. **Spoonbill:** Gangly spoonbills used to feel more at home in southern Europe. Today Britain has small coastal breeding colonies with these handsome waders thought to have crossed the English Channel in a response to climate change. They have only been sporadic visitors to these shores after the domestic population disappeared in the middle of the

17th century. Standing tall on thin black legs, they use their spatula bill to sweep through the water in search of food. Breeding colonies have been establishing themselves in Britain for a decade.

8. **Spotted flycatcher:** With an apparent preference for vicarage gardens and churchyards where they catch insects on the wing this has long been dubbed 'the parson's bird'. Thirty years ago there were six times as many as there are today. The tree-bark-coloured birds arrive in April from wintering in sub-Saharan Africa, often returning to a familiar nesting site. In 2010, *Springwatch* audiences were thrilled by a spotted flycatcher family caught on film at Pensthorpe, where cameras established the parents fed their young 36 times every hour.

9. **Wood warbler:** After wood warblers arrive from Africa in April, they mostly head for Wales and the oak woods that proliferate there. But fewer are coming here each year, although the reason for the decline isn't clear. Wood warblers are distinguished by a yellow eye stripe, a white undercarriage and a trilling song. They are ground nesters, typically seeking shelter under fallen branches where their brood will be hidden from the prying gaze of predators.

10. **Hawfinch:** The largest of the finch family, they are a bit like buses. You wait for one for ages then several come along at the same time. So it was in the autumn of 2017 when flocks of hawfinches were sighted all over Britain. It's thought a poor seed harvest in central Europe, where they normally choose to spend the winter, propelled the birds to the UK. There is a small population that calls the UK home. An elusive bird that sings softly, feeds high in trees and has perfectly camouflaged feathers when it forages on the ground, the best guess says that it amounts to only 1,500.

Highest and lowest hours of sunshine recorded for April since 1929

☼	Highest		Lowest	
England	220.7	2015	88.9	1966
Wales	222.4	2007	97.4	1961
Scotland	202.1	1942	85.3	1937
Northern Ireland	206.9	2015	50.1	1937

 ## Bee, which?

The sound of merry buzzing and the sight of a yellow belly reveals that winter is finally over as the bees are back to perform their essential role of flower pollination. But which bee? Britain boasts a bewildering 270 species and it's not easy to tell them apart.

The country's favourite is surely the honey bee. There's only one species and it is recognisable for its tapered shape, coated with black and amber stripes. Honey bees are loved not only for producing the ideal spread for toast or crumpets but because they communicate inside the hive by dancing, telling the rest in 'Saturday Night Fever' fashion where the best nectar is to be found.

Hive life is strictly segregated into roles for the female queen bee, the male drone and the worker bees. Lucky larvae chosen as royalty have a diet comprising exclusively of 'royal jelly', protein-rich foodstuff produced by the saliva glands of worker bees, while the rest get nectar and pollen.

Bumble bees are louder and fluffier. There are 25 species in the UK but the most abundant are collectively known as 'the big eight'.

They are the ginger-brown **carder bee**; the **red-tailed bees** whose queens and workers are all black but for their fiery behind;

the smaller **early bee**, with its duller orange tail; the **tree bee** which has ginger, black and white sections; the white-tailed **garden bee**; the **heath bee** which is a petite version of it. The bigger **buff-tailed bee** and **white-tailed bees** are actually more distinctive for their lemon-yellow stripes. It's no comfort to know that whole training courses have been devised to help distinguish one from the next.

Within each species it's easier to tell females from males. Busy females go from one flower to the next, collecting nectar for the nest, while males will often take an idle moment in the sun while they patrol an area or look for a mate.

Bumble bees and honey bees live in communities but other bees prefer a solitary existence – and there are more than 220 different types of these! Depending on the species, solitary bees will live in old wood, masonry or in burrows. Sometimes they are close neighbours but they never share a nest. Females emerge in the spring to secrete about 20 eggs in sealed cells, which will hatch the following spring.

Although their life span is shorter than the better-recognised honey bee, it's solitary bees who haul the heavy load when it comes to pollination. A single red mason bee achieves as much as 120 worker honey bees, collecting pollen which is mixed with a dab of nectar to provide food for its young.

Solitary bees are best distinguished by habitat than shape or colour. First to emerge is the hairy-footed flower bee which can make an appearance as early as February. Its favourite flower is lungwort and when it hovers it beats its wings at 400 times per second. Seven varieties of leaf-cutter bees leave their unmistakeable mark on garden plants. As many as 40 pieces are necessary for a single nesting cell, which is why leaves are left looking like lace after they have visited. Burrowing bees frustrate gardeners by making holes in lawns. The biggest among them is the ivy bee.

If distinguishing one bee from the next wasn't already hard enough, there are some wannabees out there who are great impersonators. Bee flies share the same ginger colouring as some bees and even use bee burrows for their eggs. But they are parasites, with larvae that grow up feasting on stored pollen. Hoverflies wear their yellow and black stripes with pride, knowing it will deter predators. Like the bees they mimic, they are essential pollinators. Social wasps are often cursed in the height of summer but they are experts at both pollinating and pest control, feasting on garden aphids.

 ## Watch your step!

Tread carefully this month if you are walking in grasslands, among sand dunes or on the moors. Male adders fresh from hibernation will be basking lethargically in the sunshine and might take exception to getting a walking boot up their backside. Commonly referred to as 'cold-blooded', adders are in fact ectothermic, that is, they depend on external sources of heat to raise their body temperature.

A snake won't be active until its body reaches more than 25 degrees Celsius, which is why it is soaking up the sun. Only after that will it be energetic enough to hunt down its first dinner of a small mammal, a bird or an amphibian. Having slept all winter its last meal was probably September.

The adder, bearing distinctive diamond markings with an inverted V-shape on the back of its head, is Britain's only venomous snake. Although it has a hinged jaw and fangs, its bite is unlikely to cause premature death as its venom is designed to incapacitate small creatures like voles rather than humans. There have been only 14 fatalities recorded in Britain since 1876 and none in the last 20 years. Indeed, sometimes the snake delivers what's known as a dry bite, puncturing the skin but not delivering a poison. Whether or not venom is involved, the victim must seek professional medical help as it is likely to cause soreness, nausea and dizziness. In its advice on the subject the NHS strongly counsels against following old wives' tales such as making the bite bleed, sucking out the venom or applying a tourniquet. About 100 adder bites are recorded each year in Britain.

Although most people don't hang around to find out, all adders are differently patterned as amateur naturalist Sylvia Sheldon, from Wyre Forest in Worcestershire, showed *Springwatch* viewers. Years of carefully catalogued photographic observation led her to those findings.

It's not Britain's only snake, although the others are entirely harmless. Grass snakes may be olive-green, brown or grey with a yellow collar and relatively common in its favoured watery habitat. The female is generally larger than the male and, should you get close enough to compare, the grass snake's pupil is round while the adder's is slit-shaped. Although it won't bite, a grass snake will emit a noxious-smelling secretion by way of defence, or even play dead hoping to fool predators after live prey to leave it alone.

Rarely seen is the grey-brown smooth snake, only found in heathlands in Dorset, Hampshire and Surrey. Numbers are so scarce there's a real fear it will become extinct. They hide under stones rather than bask in the sunshine. Its black-marked back is far more subtle than that of the adder.

Little breeders

Anyone with access to a garden pond has a chance to witness newts and their unusual breeding routine this month. There are three different native species of newt in the United Kingdom: the palmate, smooth or common, and great crested. Common and palmate newts are similar in size and have inconspicuous crests with the common newt alone having spots under its chin. Sometimes the spots merge to form lines. Palmate newts have pale, unmarked throats and a dark stripe through their eyes. The males develop webbed feet during the breeding season. Dark-coloured great crested newts are half as big again, with an upright black crest apparent during the mating season. Its underside is orange with dark blotches. These newts and their eggs, breeding sites and resting places are protected by law. It means any excavation, ploughing and even pond renovation which may affect great crested newts needs a licence.

These three are amphibians with tails, not to be mistaken with lizards that are reptiles.

Newts mate at night under water so wait for fine weather and take a torch, aiming the beam at the pond mud to find newts shaping up for mating. It won't feel intrusive as they do not get as up close and personal as you might expect.

Females are attracted by the finesse of the male crest and the potency of his perfume. To ensure she receives the benefits of his smelly scent or pheromones, he elaborately flicks his tail through the water. In turn, she indicates her willingness to mate by touching his tail with her nose. He then deposits a sperm sac on the bed of the pond which she picks up, both using their sex organ or cloaca at this stage of the procedure. So the fusion usually associated with the mating process is entirely absent.

Newt eggs are difficult to discern, not least because the female, using her rear feet, wraps each jelly egg individually in a leaf from an aquatic plant to protect them. It takes several weeks for the eggs to hatch into larvae or newt tadpoles. As they mature, their front legs will grow before their back legs. In August, when their gills are fully developed, they leave the pond as newtlets or efts.

No matter how repugnant people find snakes, few could tear themselves away from the hypnotic adder dance, seen in April. It's performed by two males who become entwined as each tries to gain a height advantage over the other. This slithery wrestling match is presumably carried out to win the favours of a female snake nearby, or at least drive one away from the territory, and the winner is the snake with the most staying power.

When they finally mate, the bodies of both snakes are all a-quiver. By contrast, grass snakes form writhing balls as a number of males try to mate with just a few females, who will go on to lay eggs in the warmth of some rotting vegetation.

Little is known of the courtship rituals carried out among secretive smooth snakes, although males are known to go into aggressive combat beforehand.

Whose habitat?

MUCK HEAP

Farmers and stable hands not only have to feed their animals but must deal with what comes out the other end. The answer is a muck heap, something that might quickly assume substantial proportions.

Given time the poo and the bedding it's caught up in will rot down into usable manure. When you see smoke rising from the heap you know the transformation process is well underway.

Until then, it provides a fantastic habitat for birds. They feast on feed remnants as well as the invertebrates working hard to transform the waste products into valuable soil enhancer.

All kinds of field birds, like chaffinches, goldfinches, robins and yellow hammers, will scratch around the heap to scavenge worms, spiders and other insects. It's especially popular on chilly days as the heat given off when the contents are broken down means the temperature can reach anything between 35 and 77 degrees Celsius.

At dusk bats will visit, also targeting the insects here.

Beneath the muck heap there's another story unfolding with adders, grass snakes and slow worms opting for a well-heated home. Research relayed on *Springwatch* has shown 71 per cent of grass snakes' eggs laid in a muck heap will hatch successfully. With garden compost heaps the figure drops to 43 per cent while an artificial nest site for snakes didn't have any success at all.

Not all of us have sufficient animal waste to make a dung heap of significant proportions, but anyone with a small patch of land can build their own compost heap. Use boundary fencing to stop the contents spilling out – leaving a gap in it for foraging hedgehogs to use as an entrance and exit. Then put in all your grass cuttings, kitchen peelings and even some cardboard. Mix it thoroughly and leave for months – or even years. The result will be some magnificent compost for your tubs as well as the satisfaction of knowing you've improved biodiversity in a place it didn't exist before.

Sunrise and sunset times for Britain's capital cities

30th April	Sunrise	Sunset
Belfast	05.45	20.55
London	05.32	20.22
Cardiff	05.45	20.34
Edinburgh	05.29	20.50

MAY

This month hedgerows and gardens, parks and deciduous woods are cloaked in fresh colours, sharp enough to make the eyes ache. The acid in these new green garments will be gone before the month is out as the countryside settles into summer. But for now there's a newness that erases winter once and for all. It stretches to wildlife too, as the air is filled with the call of hatched birds. Young foxes will be romping and badger cubs careering around close to their setts. Every trip outside yields more information as other newly borns break cover.

Sunrise and sunset times for Britain's capital cities

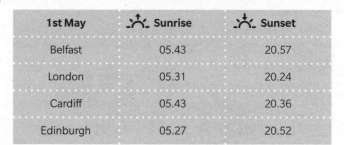

1st May	☀ Sunrise	☀ Sunset
Belfast	05.43	20.57
London	05.31	20.24
Cardiff	05.43	20.36
Edinburgh	05.27	20.52

May Day queen

The Loddon lily, known also as the 'summer snow flake' or 'summer snowdrop', is the county flower of Berkshire, but it was first recognised in Hampshire and the River Loddon, a tributary of the River Thames. It grows in wet soil beneath willow trees and in water meadows and has umbels of white, bell-shaped flowers with lime-green tips to the six tepals. The lily features in a tradition that has been revived at Long Wittenham in Oxfordshire. On 1st May, the local community crowns the May Queen, and posies carried by its participants are of wild flowers that include Loddon lilies. The flowers are prevalent along the Thames from Oxford to Maidenhead, including the banks of the River Loddon near Sandford Mill, but one of the largest sites is at Withymead Nature Reserve between Goring-on-Thames and South Stoke. It is open to the public on Sundays and Bank Holiday Mondays throughout April and May.

In some districts chafer swarm. I see none at Selborne. Cotton-blows from the willows & fills the air: with this substance some birds line their nests.

Gilbert White, 11th May 1788

 ## Going bats

Few animals are burdened with such mythology as bats, not least because they are creatures of the night.

Bats and witches go together in the public consciousness, with the first long thought to be a manifestation of the second.

If a bat flies around a house three times then it is supposedly a portent of death. Bats are associated with belfries where they hang upside down, with some manner of malign intention implied by their topsy-turvy presence. Indeed, the phrase 'like a bat out of hell' instantly puts them the wrong side of the line when it comes to religion.

And in European folklore they are infamous for attacking a victim's jugular and draining its body dry of blood. So there's a lot to untangle when it comes to bats.

They may choose to live in belfries but it is unlikely bats distinguish one high roost from the next. So a barn or cave will do just as well. There are no blood-sucking bats in Britain and those that do exist in South and Central America very much favour the blood of birds above the human kind.

Hanging upside down comes naturally to bats, whose toes and tendons are built to hold them safely even when they are asleep. Bats' knees bend backwards rather than forwards, to better accommodate this unusual sleeping position. The advantage of this repose is that they can unfurl their long wings without hindrance.

That our thoughts become entwined with witchcraft and bad omens says more about us than it says about the 17 different varieties of native British bats, who are mostly getting on with the sometimes challenging business of survival.

This month pregnant females gather together in warm, safe havens to give birth. These are called maternity roosts and might be used annually by the bat population. Depending on species and weather conditions, the female will be pregnant for between six and nine weeks before giving birth to a single pup. She suckles it for four or five weeks until it's old enough to fly and forage for itself.

Bats are the UK's only flying mammal, on thin wings that are effectively webbed fingers.

When you spot a flitting bat it's difficult to discern what type it is and sometimes behavioural clues are the best guide.

Most bats seen in the UK will be pipistrelles, the smallest European variety that accounts for 90 per cent of the bats in the UK with a population something in the order of 2.5 million. There are two sorts – common and soprano – which are so similar they were only classified differently in the 1990s. They have an erratic flight as they hunt, consuming a mighty 3,000 midges a night or one-third of their own body weight.

At the other end of the scale is the noctule bat, one of the largest varieties out early in the evening to pick insects from waterways, fields and even rubbish dumps, typically with a more arrow-straight flight. About the size of a starling, bird and bat are at loggerheads. Starlings will kill noctules or turn them out of their roosts. The current drop in the starling population may improve the outlook for noctules.

The second most common species in Britain is the brown long-eared bat which has a taste for moths that it may pull off tree leaves and bark and is thought to land on the ground more than the rest, making it vulnerable to predators.

If you are watching bat acrobatics over water then it is likely to be a Dabenton's bat in action, swooping unfeasibly close to the water's surface to catch its prey.

The fact is, it's easier to tell one bat from the next by the sound it makes. For humans the sound is almost impossible to discern but bats use echolocation for navigation and hunting, emitting a noise and listening for its echo to judge distances.

Echolocation allows bats to forage in darkness, when insects are abundant but predators are in bed. Individual bat species use specific frequencies and a bat detector that amplifies the sounds they make offers the best hope of correctly identifying which bat is nearby. Even those out of sight can be heard on the bat detector. It's not foolproof, though, and should properly be matched with bat libraries of known calls alongside habitat know-how. Although these are specialist bits of kit, the days of bat location by mobile phone app are fast approaching.

Although bats are protected by government legislation, that hasn't been sufficient to stem a radical decline in populations. Building and renovation work puts them at risk as does change in farming practice or anything that inhibits the supply of insects they need to feed on.

How can you get closer to your local bat population?

Install a bat box in your garden. You can buy or make bat boxes using untreated, rough-sawn timber. Do not include a removable lid. Remember, once it is in place it is an offence to disturb the occupants.

- Make yours a bat-friendly garden. That means including a diverse range of flowers and trees that will attract the insects that bats like to eat, including night-scented flowers. Also, remove artificial lighting, install a pond, create a linear feature like a hedgerow that bats like to use for navigation and let that garden go a little wild.
- Keep cats indoors at dusk.
- Go on an organised bat walk. Look out for events at your local National Trust sites or join your local bat group via the Bat Conservation Trust.
- Start conducting bat surveys on behalf of the BCT. Look up details on their website.

 ## Hail maybe

Since 1986 there's been a scale to measure the ferocity of hail storms.

Usually short-lived affairs, hail occurs when the updrafts of thunderstorms carry water droplets into a zone that's freezing. Each frozen droplet gathers more ice until the ball becomes so heavy it drops to the ground.

Records used by the Tornado and Storm Research Organisation to gauge how hail storms prior to the mid eighties should be categorised, found that Britain's 50 worst hail storms since 1650 occurred between the months of May and September, peaking in July.

But, singularly, the most severe happened on 15th May 1697 which, on a scale of one to ten, measured eight.

Centred on Hertfordshire, the hail stones were reportedly 20 cm in diameter and were variously oval, round and flat. A letter from the apothecary at Hitchin told how a lad minding sheep was killed after his eye was knocked out and his body was left chronically bruised.

Livestock died, trees were ripped up and houses destroyed in the storm, one of several intense episodes that happened within a year.

It's not the only startling weather to occur in May.

1911 – A ferocious thunderstorm erupted on the last day of the month after a spell of stifling warm weather. The worst effects were felt at Epsom, Surrey, where the Derby was being held and one estimate put the number of lightning flashes in one 15-minute period at 159. In a three-mile radius four people were killed, 14 were injured and four horses being used for transport rather than racing died. A further 13 people died as the storm progressed.

1935 – Hertfordshire recorded a night-time temperature of −8.6 degrees Celsius in the middle of the month while Yorkshire was paralysed by snow.

1944 – At Whitsun soaring temperatures of 32.8 degrees Celsius were followed by cloudbursts that killed three and left hundreds homeless.

1950 – On 21st May a tornado scythed along a 110 km trail in Buckinghamshire and Bedfordshire, leaving devastation in its wake.

2006 – On 10th May in eastern England people woke to find their cars covered in yellow dust which was at first thought to be Saharan sand carried by unusual wind currents. In fact it was a cloud of pollen from catkins on Danish birch trees that had blown over the sea.

Highest and lowest rainfall in millimetres recorded for May since 1910

	Highest		Lowest	
England	126.5	1967	13.6	1991
Wales	179.2	1967	15.5	1991
Scotland	191.4	2011	22.5	1984
Northern Ireland	156.1	1916	11.3	1991

Painted ladies vs hummingbirds

If you want to spot a painted lady butterfly in Britain then the last two weeks of May are the best time to do it. Figures gathered by Butterfly Conservation reveal that this is the most likely period for an influx of the orange, black and white butterfly, a member of the nymphalid family alongside red admirals, small tortoiseshells and peacocks.

Britain is the finishing point in a remarkable journey that starts at the desert fringes of Africa. Although some are now thought to overwinter in Britain, the majority have flittered over the Mediterranean Sea, then Europe.

Butterfly Conservation can speak with some authority, having carried out a decade-long study on painted ladies alongside hummingbird hawk-moths. It records sightings of both migrant species made by members of the public to get a better picture of how butterflies and moths are faring.

In 2017, 1,695 painted lady butterflies were reported across Britain throughout the year, a 20 per cent drop on previously.

Numerically, the hummingbird hawk-moth has the upper hand with 5,428 sightings. This moth, which flies and feeds like a hummingbird, spends its winter months in southern Europe.

It's the same story most years, culminating in ten-year totals for the hummingbird hawk-moth of 35,248 sightings compared to 23,563 for the painted lady. Only in 2009 – a boom year for the painted lady – was the trend reversed. In fact, 54 per cent of all painted lady sightings across the ten-year project came in that year alone.

According to Butterfly Conservation, the ten most endangered butterflies in Britain today are the large blue, high brown fritillary, chequered skipper, wood white, white letter hairstreak, black hairstreak, Duke of Burgundy, pearl bordered fritillary, Glanville fritillary and heath fritillary.

You can be a citizen scientist and report your sightings to Butterfly Conservation as it continues to gather data.

Hedgehogs need help!

Despite having a prickly coat, hedgehogs have earned affection over the centuries, not least because they are prodigious slug eaters.

Like other animals in the UK, they are known by various names depending on region:

- Hotchi-witchi – Romany
- Furze-man-pig – Gloucestershire
- Rock – Somerset
- Pricky back ochun – Yorkshire
- Grainneog – Ireland

It has around 6,000 spines on its back, measuring between two and three centimetres in length, which are regularly shed every 18 months or so, just as humans lose hair. By contrast its undercarriage is covered in coarse hair that keeps it dry and warm.

The prickles are a first-rate defence against predators. In the face of danger a hedgehog rolls into a ball, so protecting its head and vulnerable underbelly. Sadly, it's a flawed system when it comes to cars on the road and some 50,000 hedgehogs die under the wheels each year in Britain. Together with habitat losses, the hedgehog population is under pressure with numbers crashing in countryside and towns – and we could be down to our last million.

This month sees Hedgehog Awareness Week swing into action as the British Hedgehog Society tries to raise awareness of the spiky animal's plight.

It's notoriously difficult to obtain reliable figures for the populations of nocturnal animals, countrywide, as it's inevitably a mixed picture with hedgehogs holding their own in some areas while diminishing in others.

But one estimate has put the decline in the domestic hedgehog population at 97 per cent in 70 years.

According to campaigners at Hedgehog Street, a group aiming to arrest the drift in numbers, it seems certain that Britain has lost 30 per cent of its only spiny mammal since 2002. Its view is partly based on a reduction in sightings as well as a fall in the number of reported roadkill.

The group believes that hedgehogs in the UK are declining at the same rate as tigers globally.

There's a lot going against hedgehogs, not least a noisy and awkward reproduction process that starts around this month with a rut between competing males that generally features head butts and chasing. The subsequent wooing process, comprising snorting, grunting and circling, ends when the male mounts the female from behind, as she obligingly flattens her prickles.

Hedgehogs are best left alone during this delicate operation and after they've had hoglets, usually born in June or July. A disturbed nest might result in the agitated mother eating her own young. But there is a list of do's and don'ts that can help hedgehogs.

- **Do** cut a hole in your garden fence that will allow hedgehogs to roam more freely. It only needs to be about 13 cm wide or the size of a CD, but with a foraging range of several km a hedgehog won't enjoy being confined to a single garden. It will also help frogs and newts to progress through the neighbourhood. These are called 'hedgehog highways' and at least 4,500 have been introduced since Hedgehog Street initiated this strategy.
- **Don't** use slug pellets. They are rendered unnecessary if hedgehogs eat up slugs and snails.
- **Do** provide food, like chicken-flavoured cat food, left in an elbow pipe so it is protected from other animals.
- **Don't** forget to leave out a sturdy or sunken saucer or bowl of water as hedgehogs get thirsty too.
- **Do** cover drains that nosey hedgehogs could tumble into and become trapped.
- **Do** leave log and leaf piles to provide shelter or provide a specially made hedgehog house.
- **Do** grow a variety of plants to attract the insects that hedgehogs like eating.

Bloodsuckers' ball

In 2013, hedgehogs emerged as Britain's preferred mammal motif in a poll to find a national emblem, cornering 42 per cent of the vote.

The contest, held by BBC *Wildlife* Magazine, quickly became mired in controversy as supporters of invertebrates complained about a serious lack of representation in the voting line-up and pushed for an insect insignia instead.

Yet really everyone was a winner, as hedgehogs may be cute but they are also crawling with fleas. The magazine – and the country – were really getting two species for the price of one. The worst-known example of hedgehog infestation came from Guernsey where a creature was once home to 7,116 fleas.

The good news for us is that hedgehog fleas only live on hedge-hogs so won't be biting our ankles, no matter how close we get.

Fleas are regarded as a painful pest when, in fact, they are one of the wonders of the world. It's relatively well known now that fleas can jump 150 times their own height, the equivalent of a human leaping over St Paul's Cathedral, and can procreate at a rate of knots.

This incredible creature can also live for 100 days without food, pull 160,000 times its own weight and jump with acceleration 50 times greater than the space shuttle taking off.

The fact that we do know so much about fleas today is thanks to some remarkable and unlikely flea fans. Charles Rothschild, from the major banking family, was a city worker and a gifted entomologist who collected 260,000 fleas and described some 500 new species before his death in 1923.

The baton then went to Robert George, a Spitfire pilot during the Second World War and afterwards a biology teacher who made the study of fleas his life's work.

It all began when he caught 35 mice in Gloucester, where he lived at the time, and sent a dozen fleas he found on them to the Natural History Museum for identification. After he was told several had never been found in the area before it ignited a desire to learn more and he quickly became the eminent entomologist in a field that admittedly had little competition.

As a volunteer for the Biological Records Centre, he produced tens of thousands of notes on the whereabouts of the 60 flea species in this country. To do so he appealed to members of the public to send him the fleas they found on pets, soft furnishings and wildlife. With a large microscope set up in the sitting room of his home – which was in Bournemouth on the south coast before his death in 2013 – he could correctly identify 1,000 in a single evening.

In 2008 he produced *The Atlas of Fleas (*Siphonaptera*) of Britain and Ireland*, the country's first flea catalogue.

It proved what most of us already knew deep down, that cat fleas were the most abundant of the species and in Scotland fleas that live on dogs are likely to be cat fleas.

But he also discovered that squirrels, house martins and bank voles were prone to picking up the parasites. His contribution to the study of fleas in a society that abhors them earned plaudits everywhere.

With their flattened bodies, flightless fleas measure between 1.5 and 3.3 mm in length. They have four stages to their life cycles: egg, larva, pupa and adult.

They've been with us a long time. A fossil flea found in Australia – a ringer for modern descendants – was judged to be 200 million years old. Our Victorian ancestors were transfixed by flea circuses, where the tiny insects, viewed by a magnifying glass, appeared to be clothed and harnessed to tiny carts. The flea's strong legs permitted it to perform tricks like this. The unfeasibly small kit used was made by watchmakers and jewellers, keen to show off their precise talents.

Highest and lowest average temperatures (°C) recorded for May since 1910

	Highest		Lowest	
England	18.2	1992	4.1	1941
Wales	17.2	2008	3.9	1996
Scotland	15.4	2017	2.5	1915
Northern Ireland	17.3	2008	3.6	1923

Licence to thrill

Watching nature is an exhilarating joy that's open to everyone. But there are regulations to restrict other activities like filming and surveying that unduly intrude on the wellbeing of wildlife. This is particularly true of animals protected by legislation.

While walking through a wood armed with a camera, leaving animals undisturbed, won't break any rules, using torches near a known bat roost will. It's also against the law – without proper permission – to interfere with an occupied badger sett, otter holt or water vole burrow, to use an acoustic lure to tempt a protected species into the open or fly a drone in their vicinity.

A raft of legislation is involved, including the Wildlife & Countryside Act 1981 which protects all wild birds, as well as other animals. The following animals are on the list of European Protected Species:

 All species of bat, great crested newt, marine turtles, sturgeon, smooth snake, common otter, natterjack toad, dolphin, porpoises and whales, large blue butterfly, Fisher's estaurine moth, wild cat, pool frog, sand lizard and the lesser whirlpool ram's-horn snail.

Natural England gives free advice about when a licence is needed.

 ## Year of the Fox

The mother vixen starts to distance herself from her cubs as they become increasingly energetic. It looks like play but in fact it is pouncing practice, essential for young predators. These are the same moves that will keep them alive when they go it alone. Playtimes also establish a hierarchy that will last a lifetime. Peak activity comes at dawn and dusk.

To wean them off milk, she will bring back manageably small items of food on numerous hunting missions. Given the chance, she will no longer sleep with them during the day. Litters seen apparently unattended in the open are often mistakenly thought to have been abandoned when in fact their mother is just detaching herself as the cubs move into the next stage of development.

 ## Little breeders

Baby moles will all be born by the end of this month. Moles are largely solitary creatures renowned for excavating lengthy tunnels with their spade-like front paws and you can mark their route by the visible mounds they leave in the process. But look out for one mound that's bigger than the rest. That's the mole 'fortress' which is used both as a nursery for naked pups – usually between two and seven in number – and a larder for food. Although they will eat grubs, larvae and even baby mice, moles thrive on worms. One old-school estimate put the annual worm consumption of an average female mole at 21,900. And without regular meals moles will soon perish, which is why they organise a 'zombie' store of live worms that have been immobilised by a bite to the head. At seven weeks the young moles will be fully grown, covered in a rich velvety

coat and won't welcome the company of another until it's mating time again.

It's certainly easier to spot molehills than it is to see moles. They are rarely seen above ground as, being wholly unsociable, they are perfectly adapted for the life of a miner. Although they are cursed as a pest by gardeners for soil disturbance, 'little gentlemen in black velvet' were the toast of Jacobites after their nemesis King William III died in 1702 as a result of falling from his horse when it fell down a mole hole.

Five steps to fledging

1. **Feast:** Only the plumpest birds will have the energy to successfully fledge, with runts having a substantially smaller chance of survival. That means adults must remain busy to give their youngsters the best chance of survival. In 2017, *Springwatch* cameras recorded the parents of a brood of nine blue tits bring about 450 caterpillars a day back to the boxed nest. Although presenters feared that bad weather was affecting the number which would impinge on the overall health of the hatchling, eight of the nine successfully fledged.

2. **Flap:** When they are still confined to the nest, birds need to stretch those untried wings to start working out how to use them.

3. **Fearlessness:** It takes a measure of courage to step out of the safety of the nest and plummet into the unknown. Parent birds often appear on the perimeter of the nest with a beak full of food to tempt out young birds who are short on pluck.

4. **Contact call:** Fledglings can't feed themselves for about a fortnight after leaving the nest. So they need to alert their parents where they are in the nest neighbourhood. Hence, there's a contact call, made by the young and recognisable by parents who will bring food.

5. **Good fortune:** Once they have fledged, young birds will no longer be wiped out in numbers by a nest marauder. Yet a fledgling remains at risk on numerous fronts: from cats, other birds, traffic – and even humans. If you see a fledgling on the ground, resist the temptation to intervene. It may well be waiting for the return of a parent who is better fitted to feed it than any human. Keep an eye on the youngster to ensure it is being adequately cared for and only scoop it up if you are confident it has been deserted.

Highest and lowest hours of sunshine recorded for May since 1929

☼	Highest		Lowest	
England	268.9	1989	108.3	1932
Wales	265.4	1948	113.3	1932
Scotland	229.3	2000	99.3	1983
Northern Ireland	277.9	1946	112.5	2014

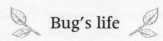

Bug's life

It's the month of the common cockchafer, otherwise known as the may bug, which announces its presence by clattering into electric lights and crashing into windows.

Never an accomplished flier, these bulky beetles can be heard as well as seen when they are on the wing as their stiff transparent wings and clunky wing cases generate a buzz. In flight they are trying to detect the pheromones of a nearby female before mating.

They also rejoice in the alternative names of doodlebug, Spang beetle and Billy Witch while their larvae are known as rook worms as they are apparently a delicacy for these birds.

Measuring some five centimetres in length and with a pronounced spike on their rear ends, the sight of a cockchafer has been sufficient to instil fear in generations of householders, especially as the bug has a habit of making an unannounced entrance down the chimney.

But there's no need for alarm. The gruesome-looking point is technically called a pygidium, a section of fused body segments that's only used by the female to push her eggs to safety in soil.

Cockchafer haters have far less to fear today than previously. Once they were prolific and, once every 30 years or so, appeared in swarms when a cyclical glut occurred.

Today population strongholds are restricted to the south of England.

Pesticides have decimated cockchafer populations, some of which were targeted specifically at the larvae.

The white grubs have a prodigious appetite, feeding on tubers like potatoes. Given that between 60 and 80 eggs are laid together in soil by a single female, a clutch has the ability to significantly damage a field's crop.

For enthusiasts who want to get up close to a cockchafer there are fine-feathered antennae to admire. You can distinguish the males, who have seven leaves on the end of the antennae, and the females, who have just six.

 ## Departures

Migrant birds that have already been recorded in southern Britain are starting to make an appearance in Scotland and its islands this month.

Saying goodbye to Britain are long-tailed ducks, velvet scoters, hen harriers and fieldfares.

 ## Thorn tree

It's traditionally in May that the hawthorn bursts into flower, giving hedges an enticing white or pink frosting which excites numerous insects.

That's why it is better known as the May tree and it is, perhaps unexpectedly, a tree of consequence in the British countryside. Its leaves are food for caterpillars of numerous moths, including the orchard ermine, pear leaf blister and lappet. Indeed, it's believed to support 150 insect species. Meanwhile the flowers are food for dormice. The fruit that emerges later in the summer, known as haws, provides for birds before they migrate as well as high-climbing small animals.

And its dense and thorny branches keep birds on their nests safe from predators.

Not all hawthorns are equal. The twice-flowering, much-propagated Glastonbury hawthorn is imbued with sacred meaning as it is said to have been carried here as a staff by Joseph of Arimathea, the man who buried Jesus.

Perhaps because of its unpleasant scent, it's thought May blossom in the house is a sign of death.

 ## Greening the grey

With nearly a quarter of all front gardens in Britain paved, a campaign to green-up grey areas like these promises remarkable results for householders. There are 5,000,000 homes that have been sucked into the concrete jungle as parking takes increasing priority over plants, according to the Royal Horticultural Society, three times as many as ten years ago. It's a vital statistic as gardens account for about 25 per cent of open land in most cities.

But a verdant 'welcome home' can have a restorative effect. As well as improving the possibilities for wildlife and air quality, trees, hedges and climbing plants help to insulate homes from extreme cold and heat. Rainwater bounces off impermeable paving stones while plants and soil soak it up, reducing the risk of flooding and taking the pressure from urban drains. There are a few simple steps people can take to bring back green to their daily lives.

1. Plump for permanent planting rather than lawns to save time and enhance the immediate environment.

2. If you can, remove a paving slab and fill the resulting hole with pollinator plants.
3. Sow seeds into crevices and cracks to make the most of every scrap of land.
4. Use safely secured plant pots on walls and windowsills.
5. If you have to lay paving, make sure it is porous.

 ## Spot the difference

A bird with white plumage or animal with a white coat is a rare and striking sight. There are two reasons it might happen. One is leucism, an inherited condition, when the feathers or fur lack the melanin pigment necessary to make colour.

Alternatively, albinoism could be to blame, when the bird or animal is unable to produce any melanin pigments at all due to a genetic mutation. Only the creature with albinoism has pink eyes.

Both conditions present a problem. The pigment reduction associated with leucism may cause weakness in the feathers which in turn might hinder flight. There's evidence too that leucistic birds find it harder to mate.

Albino birds and animals have poor eyesight which is likely to bring about an early demise. Indeed, any white-coloured animal is likely to be a subject for predation as they are so conspicuous.

 ## Small but beautifully formed

Only a lucky few will spot the increasingly rare Duke of Burgundy butterfly this month as it takes flight during a five-day life span.

With a total wing width of just three centimetres, a passing resemblance to the Burnet Companion moth and a critical shortage of numbers, it's a butterfly that often goes unseen as it flies around the woodlands it calls home.

Although during its lifecycle it is dependent on primroses, it is a butterfly more likely to be seen perching on leaf than flower. The female tends to stay out of sight altogether, lying low on the ground.

It has dark brown wings patterned with bright orange markings and white dots on its wing fringes. Once it was classified as part of the fritillary family and was even known as 'Mr Vernon's Small Fritillary'. Now 'Your Grace', as it is sometimes dubbed, is in a series called 'metalmarks', more typically found in tropical America.

Female butterflies lay spherical eggs, either singly or in batches of up to five, beneath the crinkly leaves of the primrose. Once the egg has hatched, the hairy caterpillar devours the leaves by night, moulting four times in six weeks before entering the lengthy chrysalis stage.

Close observation will reveal that only the female has six fully functioning legs while the male, with shortened forelegs, has just four.

Changes in woodland management seem to be having a positive effect on population strength but there's still a long way to go.

It's only found in England and, with the exception of colonies in the Lake District and North Yorkshire, its remaining strongholds are restricted to the south.

Sensational seasonal spectacles: Mayfly hatches

The calm of a gently flowing river is shattered this time of year by one of nature's understated marvels, when a host of primitive insects emerges from the water and takes flight.

Clear air is clouded by millions of creatures whose only purpose is to seek a mate and lay eggs. Time is not on their side. Those that are not swallowed by predators will soon die, within days or even a few hours.

Of the 3,000 mayfly species in the world there are 51 in the UK. As an olive-coloured three-tailed nymph it spends months or even years under the water feeding on algae and plants, using feathered gills to take oxygen from the water.

Then a phalanx of them rise to the surface for one moult, quickly followed by another. The result is a fully fledged mayfly with its stubby antennae, large eyes and lacy wings.

In the air they might be joined by midges and other small flying insects. But it is the beating upwing of the mayfly that dominates.

The hatch – which doesn't always happen in May – brings frantic life to the river with birds swooping in from above and fish jumping from below, capitalising on the easy pickings being presented to them. At dusk bats will fly in to feast on the insects.

In July 2014 one mayfly hatch from the Mississippi River was so intense that it showed up on radar, appearing the same way as a rain shower.

There's an evolutionary explanation for this sudden emergence, called predator swamping. More mayfly survive this hazardous spell simply because there are so many for predators to target. Numerous studies have shown that the risk of being eaten is lessened when the number of prey increases, not least because those feeding on mayflies must spend time catching, consuming and digesting them, all of which imposes an upper limit on the total number taken.

Another remarkable aspect of the event is how mayflies help to clean up polluted waterways. The nymph absorbs pollution that settles on the muddy floors where it eats. When it bursts forth as an adult mayfly it takes the contamination out of the water with it.

In flight, the males go up and down, hoping to encounter a female flying along its path. The swift mating process ends with a female laying eggs. Soon afterwards, she dies.

Whose habitat?

DRY STONE WALLS

In remote locations, where the soil was thin, our ancestors turned their talents to building dry stone walls, knowing hedgerows would not flourish.

Among the first to appear – as far as we know – was in the village of Skara Brae in the Orkneys, which was built around 3,200 BC.

Later they were embraced by religious orders to mark land boundaries, then by the wave of incoming Vikings. In the Middle Ages farmers used locally found stones to build walls. And once land became enclosed by Parliament as the feudal system gradually unfurled, stone walls were used to define field ownership.

Techniques differ but they are usually constructed over a narrow trench and are essentially two walls built close together, with the resulting gap filled in with small stones. Builders must choose their stones well as no mortar is used to glue the stones together, leaving numerous cavities.

According to the Dry Stone Wall Association, they are linear nature reserves as, if one side is windswept, the other is sheltered and warmer. The core of the wall stays dry along the lee side although there may be a helpful trickle of water from the most exposed face for those who choose to make this their habitat.

A host of mammals will make their homes in dry stone walls, including shrews, field mice, voles and stoats. They are small enough to weedle their way into tiny openings where they remain well protected from weather and predators.

At the base of the wall there may be hedgehogs and hares, tucking under at ground level. The damp crevices will be a welcome bolthole for toads, frogs, lizards, adders and slow worms.

And there are an array of insects that make themselves at home, alongside spiders, slugs and snails.

Perhaps because of this rich insect life, it's not unusual to see a bird taking advantage of the wall's apertures for nesting purposes. Expect to see smaller varieties here like blue and great tits, wagtails, sparrows, spotted flycatchers and wheatears.

Plants, too, take advantage of conditions on the wall, particularly if it is made of limestone. Look out for lichens, mosses and liverworts, with protruding ferns alongside.

 ## Tweet and greet

Devoted music lovers may have already tuned in to the fact that the first Sunday in May is International Dawn Chorus Day. The symphony of bird song that happens at daybreak, billed by enthusiasts as one of the exquisite wonders of the natural world, is missed by most of us as we snooze under our duvets. To make the most of the occasion means a 4 am alarm, so you can either join an organised event or alternatively simply step outside into the nearest garden or park. Choosing this day to celebrate the dawn chorus is credited to writer and broadcaster Professor Chris Baines who, back in the eighties, asked pals to a birthday celebration at his Midlands home that centred on the frenzy of bird song. Later, he explained: 'The dawn chorus is a simple and beautiful way of sharing nature with lots of people.' Rather than a larynx birds have a syrinx that permits them to sing as they both breathe in and exhale, while humans can only vocalise as they breathe out. Birds strike up at the earliest opportunity precisely because there is no one else around to drown out the sound. Robins, blackbirds and thrushes are usually the first to hit the high notes, and it is almost exclusively the males that are striking up. Usually, the sweet singing has sinister undertones as within it there is a dire warning to rivals to stay away. However, in certain months it is to attract a mate and females are drawn by the complexity of the song. Research has proved that male birds tone it down once they are paired up, while single males continue earnestly singing. Other birds like the wrens, chaffinches and species of tit join in a little later, avoiding the attentions of any patrolling owls and filling time before the insects that will provide their breakfast stir. Indeed, the dawn chorus fades away when the birds involved are distracted by the main business of the day, feeding.

 ## Sunrise and sunset times for Britain's capital cities

31st May	☼ Sunrise	☼ Sunset
Belfast	04.55	21.47
London	04.49	21.07
Cardiff	05.01	21.19
Edinburgh	04.35	21.45

JUNE

There are great expectations for June; that the days are languid and long, that the strawberries will be piled high and that flowers will still be radiating vibrant colour. Of course, there are no guarantees when it comes to weather although, when it does appear, the sun will be tracking in its greatest arcs in the sky. The hottest day of the year is likely to follow weeks or even months later, in the seasonal lag that means land masses and oceans warming up much more slowly than we do. Still on high alert for intruders, bird song continues to crescendo at dawn and dusk.

Sunrise and sunset times for Britain's capital cities

1st June	Sunrise	Sunset
Belfast	04.54	21.49
London	04.48	21.08
Cardiff	05.00	21.20
Edinburgh	04.34	21.46

Midsummer Day

The second of the four English 'quarter days', Midsummer is close to the time of the summer solstice, the longest day and the shortest night of the year (on 20th June or 21st, and occasionally 22nd). Midsummer Day, however, is on 24th, another fallback to the Julian calendar. Midsummer's Eve was always a magical time, when witches and fairies were abroad, so folk used to light bonfires partly to burn them up, and partly to strengthen the sun, which was perceived to be getting weaker as the days begin to shorten. Roses were also important. At midnight on

Midsummer's Eve, young girls were advised to scatter rose petals and chant:

Rose leaves, rose leaves
Rose leaves I strew.
He that will love me
Come after me now.

If they did that with sincerity, their true love would come knocking at the door on Midsummer Day. And, if you picked a rose on Midsummer Day, it was said to keep fresh until Christmas.

> Hardly any shell-snails are seen; they were destroyed & eaten by the thrushes last summer during the long dry season. This year scarce a thrush, they were killed by the severe winter.
>
> Gilbert White, 8th June 1776

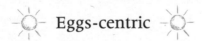 Eggs-centric

It's difficult to see a sand lizard these days, and not just because of its cunning camouflage.

It's the rarest lizard of the trio that lives in Britain, with the common lizard and the slow worm, a legless lizard, existing in far greater numbers. Sand lizards are also the only one of the three to lay eggs, with the others giving birth to live young.

Habitat loss decimated the sand lizard population so acutely that its colonies became restricted to heathlands in Surrey, Dorset, Hampshire and the sand dune systems in Merseyside.

Happily, matters have improved thanks to a captive breeding scheme that's brought populations back to Devon, Cornwall, Wales and West Sussex.

By June the colouration of males is returning to a plainer brown as they lose the lime green that electrifies their appearance during the mating season – although even when they are not trying to attract a partner their spotted skins are attractively decorated.

Meanwhile, female sand lizards are laying eggs in sand that's exposed to the sun. One tell-tale sign a sand lizard has been at work in the vicinity are small holes poked in the sand along south-facing slopes. She heads in about eight centimetres, testing for heat and humidity, and selects the most promising spot in which to deposit between five and 15 small white eggs. Given the British weather and other obvious hazards only a few will hatch, sometime between August and October, when baby lizards using an egg tooth break through the shell, burrow out of the sand and dash for cover.

Sand lizards are subject to predation from foxes, falcons, gulls and corvids and to counter this they have a fascinating self-defence tool. Thanks to autotomy, or self-amputation, they will shed their tail if it is in the grip of a predator. Furthermore, the tail will spontaneously lash around, hopefully keeping the attention of the hungry hunter while the lizard makes good a getaway. It happens via a weakness in the upper tail vertebrae. In conjunction with the parting of the bones, blood vessels constrict to stop it bleeding to death. Given time the tail will grow back.

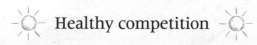

Healthy competition

With *Springwatch* 2018, the cameras were trained on raptors living in close proximity. Kestrels, buzzards and red kites were nesting in different parts of the same estate while peregrine falcons on Salisbury Cathedral were some 70 miles distant, well within flying distance.

Red Kite

Buzzard

Kestrel

Yet there were no raptor wars, with each species barely impinging on the next. They happily co-existed because they all hunted and ate differently, something called niche separation.

The kestrel, with its range of about ten square kilometres, hovers to spy its prey on the ground, with its favourite meal being a field vole.

Buzzards have a similar range but soar through the air to swoop, by choice, on rabbits. Red kites also wheel around the sky with an even bigger range at their disposal. However, for preference they aren't looking for live prey but carrion, meat that's already dead that they can take back to their nests. This is because their feet are too weak to wrestle with wriggling bodies.

Streamlined peregrine falcons have vast ranges of up to 150 sq km. Their priority is avian prey which they take out of the air, achieving speeds of up to 200 mph. Small cones in their noses help break up the impact of fast rushing air when they dive and a membrane covers their eyes to protect them from damage.

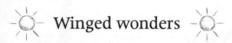

Winged wonders

Bugs are beautiful. At least eminent Victorian actress Ellen Terry thought so.

When she played Lady Macbeth opposite Henry Fielding in 1888, she wore a dress made of cotton mesh embellished with hundreds of iridescent beetle wings.

The outfit caused a sensation although history hasn't recorded the type of beetle that provided its inspiration. When the emerald-green dress was restored in the early 21st century, wafer-thin tissue paper was used to mend broken wings while replacements came from an antique dealer who had a collection of naturally discarded ones.

The Royal Entomological Society is keen to encourage the view that insects are exquisite – although not by divesting little creatures of their wings. Instead it holds National Insect Week every other year in June to help the British public see what they commonly call 'creepy crawlies' with new eyes.

Not all grubs in the undergrowth are insects. Those that are will have six legs, three body parts, a pair of antennae and a hard shell or exoskeleton on the outside. They have compound eyes, made up of thousands of receptors that means clarity is poor but angle of vision is broad. Thanks to the structure of their eyes they are also able to detect rapid movement, which is why flies usually win in the war waged by fly swatters. Most insects have wings and also experience three or more stages of a life cycle.

With 24,000 species of insects to contend with, entomologists tend to divide them into 12 different categories for ease of classification. These are beetles, butterflies and moths, bees, ants and wasps, true bugs, true flies, crickets and grasshoppers, dragonflies and damselflies, earwigs, lacewings, mayflies, silverfish and firebrats and stoneflies.

It's an uphill task, persuading a reluctant population to love bugs. Although many are involved in vital pollination work and are also pillars of the ecology system, being on the menu for more appealing-looking animals further up the food chain, they seem largely unloved.

But there's plenty about insects to pique our interest, if not our affection. Researchers in New York have just discovered that wasps communicate the whereabouts of food and its quality by banging on their stomachs.

For years this signal was taken as a sign of hunger. But scientists at LaGuardia Community College in New York realised the gastral drumming was a method of communication that explained why, after one wasp turned up at a summer picnic, they were usually followed by a crowd.

Courting lacewings serenade each other with low-frequency songs, generated when they vibrate their abdomens while green shield bugs are also known as stink bugs for the foul smell they

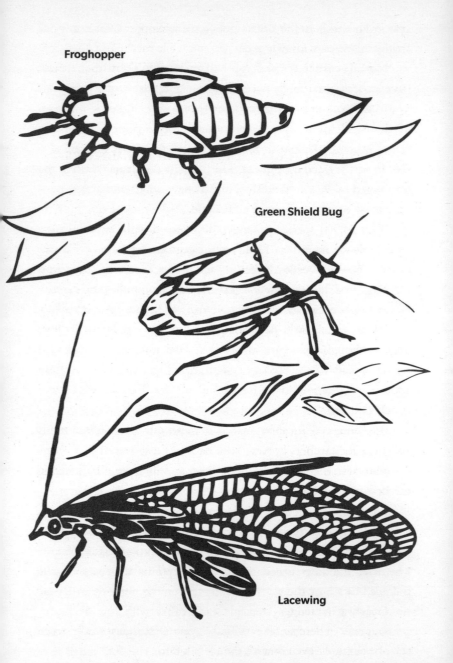

Froghopper

Green Shield Bug

Lacewing

trail over leaves and fruit. Rarely seen froghoppers leave a white frothy calling card known as cuckoo spit while earwigs – which definitely do not enter people's ears to burrow into their brain – have other more endearing names including arrywinkle, furkin, forky-tail, gewlick, scotch bell, twinge and clepshires.

Highest and lowest rainfall in millimetres recorded for June since 1910

	Highest		Lowest	
England	147.9	2012	4.3	1925
Wales	219.1	2012	2.1	1925
Scotland	157.9	2017	30.1	1988
Northern Ireland	179.0	2012	11.5	1921

 # One for sorrow

A magpie is distinctive for its black, blue and white markings, having an acquisitive eye for shiny things and being the subject of wide-ranging superstition.

Part of the crow family, it is known by different names across the country. In Norfolk and Somerset it's called chatterpie while it's a maggot in Lincolnshire, Worcestershire and Gloucestershire; a pyenate in West Yorkshire; a ninut in Nottinghamshire; a pyot in Scotland and a Cornish pheasant in the far west of England.

Items like keys and an engagement ring have been found in magpie nests over the years although it's now thought that they are not unduly attracted to glittering objects.

But everywhere similar fallacies have arisen; that it's unlucky to see one singly or even that it's the Devil's bird.

A well-known rhyme has fuelled the idea of it being bad luck.

'One for sorrow, two for joy, three for a girl, four for a boy,' the ditty insists.

In other parts of the country it goes: 'One for sorrow, two for mirth, three for a wedding, four for a birth.'

It's unlikely any number of magpies will materially affect forthcoming pregnancies. But it is remarkable how many people believe they are warding off bad luck by saluting a single magpie.

Since childhood many have uttered: 'Good morning, Mr Magpie, how is Mrs Magpie and all the other little magpies?'

The salutation may well be accompanied by hat raising in Staffordshire and spitting, if possible three times over the left shoulder, in Dorset.

In other regions the sound of a magpie is enough to engender bad luck – unless those that hear it respond with the words: 'Magpie, magpie, flutter and flee, turn up your tail and good luck come to me.'

Unfortunately for the magpie it is said to have refused to enter Noah's ark and later sat on the cross when Jesus was crucified. A chattering and an undeniably aggressive bird, it is perhaps these characteristics that have attracted so much folklore.

In general terms they are unpopular birds, often blamed for carnage among songbirds.

To find out if they were culpable, the RSPB commissioned the British Trust for Ornithology to analyse its records. With 35 years of observations duly investigated, it was found songbirds were declining at the same rate in places with few magpies as they were where they were many. Availability of food and nesting sites among declining populations have far greater relevance.

-☼- Beetle mania -☼-

To hear that a creature with antlers and wings takes flight on warm June nights hunting for a mate sounds both bizarre and alarming, like something from a children's book.

But the male stag beetle, with its shiny horns, is best observed when airborne, being secretive and increasingly scarce. Females are mostly ground based, eyeing up likely ground in which to lay eggs.

Stag beetles can measure up to a mighty 7.5 cm. Only water beetles can beat them for length in Britain. The protruding jaws make the insect look fearsome but those impressive mandibles are only used in anger to see off competitors during mating.

These insects are both entirely harmless and protected by law, such is their growing rarity.

Stag beetles have black heads and middles while their wing cases are chestnut brown. The smaller female is sometimes mistaken for the lesser stag beetle.

Most of their lives are spent underground as an orange-headed white larva, a stage that can last between three and six years. During this time the larva's staple diet is rotten wood and it's the tidying up of landscapes that's deprived it of its favourite habitat.

As it grows it sheds its skin four times before cocooning itself in earth for the final transformation, to adult beetle. This happens in the autumn and the beetle stays below ground for months before appearing mid-summer the following year.

Now all thoughts of food are banished as the hunt for a mate begins. If it takes anything on board at all it will be tree sap or fallen fruit or a drop of water, lapped up with its furry orange tongue.

Male stag beetles patrol in circuits to protect their territory so if you've seen a stag beetle once, there's a chance you will get a second opportunity.

But it's also the moment in their lives when they become vulnerable to predators. There's a theory that the rise in magpie and crow populations correlates with the fall in the number of stag beetles.

They are also weather affected, with extremely wet or dry weather compromising larvae while rain and wind hinders their flight.

At home in urban environments, stag beetles are most likely to be found in the south east of England.

Three ways to assist stag beetles:

- ☼ Leave a vertical wood pile in your garden to give them shelter.
- ☼ Make an artificial nesting site by drilling holes in a bucket, filling it with chippings and burying it in the garden.
- ☼ Record stag beetle sightings so experts can get a better idea of what's going on.

Best places to see a stag beetle:

- ☼ Colchester gardens, Essex
- ☼ New Forest gardens, Hampshire
- ☼ Wimbledon Common, London

Highest and lowest average temperatures (°C) recorded for June since 1910

	Highest		Lowest	
England	22.0	1976	7.1	1916
Wales	20.4	1940	6.7	1972
Scotland	18.8	1940	5.1	1927
Northern Ireland	19.6	1940	5.9	1927

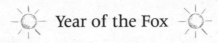

Year of the Fox

Ringing the changes for the fox cubs, it's time to look for a new home. The earth where they were born was chosen for its warmth in the winter nights. Now it is not only soiled but probably too hot. Litters may even be split between two dens at this point as while the cubs are no longer taking milk from their mother, the parents are still providing food. With both parents out hunting, the youngsters are left in what's termed a play area. If you spot a group of noisy fox cubs together, it's almost certainly a set of siblings. Dominant vixens will have killed the cubs born to subordinate females long ago.

It remains a dangerous time. During the breeding season about 425,000 cubs are born each year, although the overall population remains constant. This implies numerous cubs will lose their lives on roads or as prey to other animals before reaching adulthood.

Spot the difference

One of Britain's least-known animals, the Scottish wildcat, closely resembles one of the country's most familiar pets, the tabby cat. But there are striking differences between household or even feral cats and the secretive and resilient wildcat. At a glance it is not easy to observe the wildcat's more powerful jaws and its lush coat that's 50 per cent thicker than that of domestic cats. It also has a larger brain.

Markers that are more apparent are its thick-set appearance around face and neck, more powerful hind legs and thick, ringed blunt tail. Nor will a wildcat bear any white markings, common to tamer tabbies. Wildcats purr but they don't miaow like lap cats, nor are they so fearful of water.

Still, the chances of ever having to distinguish one from the other are remote. The several hundred-strong population of

Scottish wildcats abhor human contact, living in the most secluded parts of the Highlands. In fact, for once it's not humans who pose the greatest threat to the survival of the species but roaming feral cats, of which there are untold thousands, as interbreeding has diluted the Scottish wildcat genes.

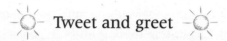

Tweet and greet

June is probably the last chance to hear the curious call of the woodcock as it flies circuits, looking for a mate.

Woodcock are cautious and coy birds about the size of a pigeon that spend their days lying low on a forest floor. Their plumage, which looks like crushed autumn leaves, provides ideal camouflage.

A domestic population is joined by a far bigger number of migrants in the winter months but all effectively disappear from view into the undergrowth, even in the north of England where they are comparatively numerous. There are significant populations in eastern England and northern Scotland, but few are to be found in Wales or the South West.

Migrant woodcock have normally left Britain by the end of March, largely heading north-east to breeding grounds in Finland, Sweden, Denmark, Norway, Russia, Belarus, Latvia and Poland.

From April the resident birds begin their courtship rituals. Woodcock only become active at dawn and dusk and that's when the breeding display flight above the tree line, called roding, might be spotted.

These patrols may overlap with those of another woodcock.

Listen for a two-part call, a high nasal 'psiek' whistle followed by several low, pig-like grunts. Receptive females will move to a clearing to call back and flash the white tips of their tails. It's likely the birds roding at the moment have already fathered one brood and are backing their chances for a second.

It's not just the call that makes woodcock an oddity. This bird is built like a wader, with a long beak, but chooses to live among trees, earning itself the name of 'snipe of the woods'.

Populations have been falling away, with woodcocks found in just one-third of woodlands surveyed in 2013. Then the British population was put at 55,000 breeding pairs, a contraction of 29 per cent over a decade. However, in 2016 there was a substantial increase in the number of roding males recorded, matching the levels of 2008. It's thought a mild winter previously helped more birds than ever to survive.

See resident woodcock in the New Forest, Thetford Forest, the Forest of Dean and Kielder Forest.

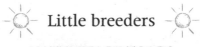 Little breeders

NATTERJACK TOADS

While the breeding season is drawing to a close for many animals, the natterjack toad can still be heard shouting for females from the edge of a pond. It is the country's smallest but loudest amphibian, with a rasping call that travels for up to a mile. But it is not the most numerous, with natterjack populations having been hit hard by a decline in the warm pools amid the sandy dunes it likes to call home.

The natterjack is quickly distinguished from the common toad by a yellow stripe down its back. Overall, it is green rather than brown while its numerous warts are tipped in reddish orange which, with its hooded iridescent eyes, lend it an exotic appearance. It has shorter legs than a common toad and is a poor swimmer. In self defence it will puff up its body and stand on four legs, to look bigger than it really is, while its larger warts secrete poison. Perhaps most eye-catching of all is the way it runs rather than hops when it chases prey, reeling in an unfortunate bug on its long, sticky tongue.

Natterjack males are now mostly likely to strike up following summer rain, when the pools required for spawn are replenished. A female natterjack will lay between 3,000 and 4,000 eggs. Natterjack spawn appears in one fine string rather than two, like the common toad, and tadpoles develop a white chin.

The breeding season starts as early as April but spawn and tadpoles are at risk during a dry spell when their typically shallow pools dry out in the sun. Even this ability to respond to optimum breeding conditions hasn't made the natterjack population buoyant in Britain. Natterjack breeding sites are measured by the score rather than by the hundreds, with more than half being in Cumbria. A protected species, carefully monitored re-introduction schemes have helped to increase numbers.

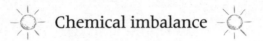

Chemical imbalance

For farmers and gardeners, aphids pose a threat to harvests. But for ants they are a bringer of food and the two insects appear to co-habit happily on leaves and stalks, both benefitting from one of nature's bizarre relationships. Look in a garden or park for a plant that's laden with greenfly or blackfly to witness this in action. Aphids kill a plant when they feed on its sap, so the piece of greenery will probably be wilting. However, when they've done so they produce a sweet, sticky secretion called honeydew that's a mouth-watering, sugary treat for ants. In return for their treat the ants protect the aphids from predators. It's possible to see ants using their antennae to gently drum on the backs of aphids which, for years, was thought to be a way of 'milking' in smaller insects. However, there could be a more sinister aspect to the attentions of the ant bodyguards. Scientists have not only proved that ants occasionally bite the wings off aphids to stop them departing, but research by three British universities (Reading, Royal Holloway and Imperial College) has revealed that ants use tranquilising chemicals issued through their feet to subdue the aphids, eliminating an element of choice in order to keep their honeydew colony intact.

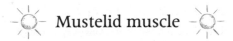 Mustelid muscle

As *Springwatch* cameras watched a stoat mum relocating her growing kits during the 2017 series and, afterwards, moving her larder to the new home, some clever mathematicians went to work to put her immense strength into context. Lithe and agile the stoat, weighing in at an estimated 210 g, made 15 trips incorporating a distance of some 900 metres. The five kits she transported were nearly the same size as she was and at least one of the bits of stored prey, a fully grown rabbit, was bigger. The equivalent in human terms would be a person weighing 62 kilos carrying a polar bear for 265 km.

Sunrise and sunset times for Britain's capital cities

21st June	Sunrise	Sunset
Belfast	04.47	22.04
London	04.42	21.21
Cardiff	04.55	21.33
Edinburgh	04.26	22.03

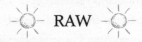 RAW

June is devoted to Random Acts of Wildness, thanks to a campaign by the Wildlife Trusts to get more of us enjoying the outdoors. The aim is to get people to pledge to doing something wild every day of the month. The good news is that the Wildlife Trusts have a vast reservoir of suggestions to make life as easy as possible. They include trying wildlife photography, lifting a log to investigate the wildlife beneath and pond dipping, to see for yourself what lives in the depths of the river. Your personal RAW hitlist might include something sensory, like smelling wild flowers or something swift, like hugging a tree. Sign up with your local Wildlife Trust to take part.

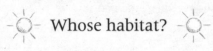

Whose habitat?

RIVERS

Rushing rivers offer an oxygen-rich environment in which plants will flourish. Thriving plant life attracts a raft of insects, whose consumption will in turn support small fish, birds and mammals. These creatures can't afford to be complacent as they may well become a meal for the alpha predators. But the abundant life that characterises British rivers begins with fresh water.

There are about 90,000 km of rivers all over the UK and there's general consensus that the quality of water has improved in the 21st century.

Many river habitats were at their worst in the middle of the last century when factories and fields discharged noxious effluent. But a new impetus for nature has helped transform many of the worst examples.

It's not just the centre of the river that's important, but its margins, known as the riparian zone. Rivers might also create wetlands when they flood and feed ditches.

The plants found there could include purple loosestrife, great willowherb, yellow flag iris, marsh marigolds and watercress.

Look for the water boatman, an oval-shaped bug with red eyes who swims upside down below the surface of the water, in

Kingfisher

Freshwater Shrimp

Minnow

contrast to the pond skater who skims along above. There may be freshwater shrimps, dragonflies, mayflies, damselflies plus two kinds of snail. In chalk rivers it might be possible to see the shy white-clawed crayfish.

Its population is suffering along with those of pearl mussels, now thought to be living in just 66 viable populations in the UK. Even in Scotland, where the mussels should be thriving in beds of clean and fast-running rivers, the outlook is bleak. First recorded in the 18th century, the pearl mussel was duly over-exploited. The species became extinct from two Scottish rivers a year on average between 1970 and 1998, when the mussel got legal protection.

Freshwater pearl mussels look like their salt water counterparts but grow far bigger and live more than 100 years. As larvae they attach themselves to the gills of salmon and the collapse in salmon stocks had a profound effect on their numbers, alongside pollution and river engineering. They feed by drawing on river water, filtering more litres per day than most people use in a shower, to access fine grains of organic matter. Only occasionally will they produce a pearl.

Minnows are an indication of river health and a buoyant population will help support populations of bigger fish. Anyone pond dipping this month, using a jam jar tied to a piece of string, might think that males in their vivid-red spawning colours are an entirely different species. Females stay in their winter greys.

Alongside otters, mink and water voles, there is the water shrew that lives in and around stream banks. Dark brown or black above, pale beneath, it is the biggest of the shrew family but nonetheless won't break the 100 mm mark. It has a long snout, small eyes and poisonous saliva with which it stuns its prey.

Kingfishers are synonymous with river life, although they are sometimes spotted in harbours too. Their striking blue plumage arrests the eye as they dart down the river. These are birds of habit; if you see one flying a particular route, you may well see it a second time in a similar spot. They also like to perch while they peruse for prey. If you spot the perch they favour then you may enjoy more than just a glimpse of this orange-breasted bird.

Indeed, they might retire to that same perch to beat their recently caught fish into submission before swallowing it, head first.

Should you get close enough, you can identify a female by the orange colour in the lower half of her beak. The male's beak is solid black.

Another cherished river bird is the dipper, that dives and swims underwater like a duck. In fact, it's a passerine or perching bird which can ably grip boulders in a river while water rushes past.

It's a small, stout, short-tailed bird beloved for its distinctive bobbing action. It can also walk underwater on riverbeds, looking for food. It has a special gland that waterproofs its black back and white throat feathers and nasal flaps that enable it to stay underwater for 30 seconds or more.

The health of the river has a direct impact on dippers that lasts into adulthood, as research at Lancaster University has shown.

Highly territorial birds, dippers sing all year round to ward off encroachment. When the song of one bird, raised on the rich pickings of a healthy river, was analysed it revealed a rich and complex construction featuring numerous syllables. Another bird which grew up on more frugal offerings from a stream had a much simpler song.

Greater quantities of food had allowed the first dipper to invest energy in developing its song which in turn would permit it greater reproductive success and the means to defend a better territory.

The other had to devote its energy to physical development alone. This meant it would be less attractive to females and consigned to a less fruitful stretch of river.

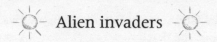 Alien invaders

Despite recent improvements, statistics from the European Water Framework about the quality of water in British rivers still make sober reading.

While 43 per cent of waterways across the continent are regarded as being in ecologically good order, that figure for Britain falls to just 17 per cent. A tiny 0.08 per cent are judged to be in high order.

Nonetheless, Britain's waterways are still the healthiest they've been for decades and, to prove it, wildlife like otters and salmon are being seen again in numbers.

But they are not alone in relishing the improved cleanliness of rivers and canals across the country. A number of invasive species from overseas are thriving too, causing difficulties for native varieties. It costs the government about two million pounds a year to combat the spread of these alien invaders. Some successes have been notched up, including those against the fathead minnow in 2008 and the bullhead catfish in 2014. The Environment Agency urges river users to remain vigilant and report sightings. Here's a top eight of the worst offenders.

1. **Killer shrimp:** Although it won't be more than 30 mm long it has a voracious appetite and will scoff freshwater invertebrates and small fish in quantity. Larger than our native shrimp, it is often stripy and has two tell-tale cones on its tail.

2. **Water primrose:** This five-petalled yellow flowering floater, a native of South America, clogs waterways and crowds out native plants.

3. **Floating pennywort:** The source of this plague was probably a discarded pond plant. It has been rampant since 1990 and can grow 20 cm a day, choking flowing water with its thick matted growth.

4. **Signal crayfish:** A North American import, this clawed creature menaces native crayfish as well eating fish eggs and invertebrates, thus skewing the natural ecology.

5. **Topmouth gudgeon:** Once a popular aquarium fish, it went rogue and has been reported in 30 lakes and ponds since 1996. Apart from spreading disease and soaking up all the available food, they can strip the scales from a larger fish unnoticed and start nibbling the exposed flesh.

6. **Himalayan balsam:** Its pink flowers were prized as an ornamental garden addition during Victorian times but swift seed propagation has seen this tall plant colonising river banks where it can impede the flow of water.

7. **Parrot's feather:** Found in slow-flowing or still waters, it's a prolific plant once sold in garden centres. Its propensity to cause flooding by blocking watercourses has led to it being banned from being grown in the wild.

8. **Mink:** Dark and glossy mink were first introduced to Britain in 1929 and kept on fur farms. Some escaped and more were released by those opposed to the fur trade, and since they've had the run of the British countryside they've attacked all kinds of native wildlife. There are signs that a more buoyant otter population helps to control mink.

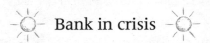 Bank in crisis

Generations of children have been charmed by the wit and wisdom of Ratty in *The Wind in the Willows*.

The home-loving Ratty in Kenneth Grahame's book is, in fact, a water vole, smaller, chestnut-coloured and chunkier than a brown rat, with furry ears and tail. Its common name of water rat was coined in the 16th century, before the arrival of the brown rat.

But it's a species that may soon be consigned to the pages of a book in Britain as a sharp decline that began in the second half of the 20th century continues apace.

Back in the nineties it was estimated that 94 per cent of their favourite habitat had been lost. More recent figures by the Wildlife Trusts reveal a further 30 per cent reduction was recorded between 2006 and 2015 in England and Wales.

It's notoriously difficult to speculate about exact numbers but, according to one set of figures, there were 8,000,000 of them at the turn of the 20th century while, 120 years on, that figure has plummeted to just 100,000.

These alarming statistics have earned the water vole the unenviable title of Britain's fastest declining mammal.

Habitat loss and pollution have played their part, but it's predation by the American mink that has proved critical. As this ruthless hunter colonised Britain's waterways, water voles became increasingly at risk, with the nimble mink small enough to enter the burrow of this, its chosen prey. Now the population of mink is thought to be greater than that of water voles. A small revival in water vole numbers, helped by several re-introduction schemes, doesn't – for the moment – seem sufficient to reverse the fortunes of water voles.

Landowners can help by leaving river banks and pond edges to grow wild so the water vole can burrow in relative seclusion. Fencing stock so the banks don't get trampled will also aid water vole chances.

You can help by surveying a 500-metre strip of riverbank annually between April and June to monitor water voles in a study being orchestrated by the People's Trust for Endangered Species. The National Water Vole Monitoring Programme represents a determined effort to inform conservationists about what to do next.

Clues that a water vole is in residence nearby include a pile of plant stems, nibbled off at a tell-tale 45-degree angle. Water voles are voracious plant eaters, having to consume 80 per cent of their body weight each day in vegetation.

Look out too for the water vole latrine; a pile of green or brown pellets shaped like a cigar with two blunt ends that happily doesn't smell. By contrast a rat's excrement is found singly rather than in a heap and does smell. Make sure not to touch the excrement with your hands. Use a stick instead, and always wash your hands afterwards.

Burrows, which tend to be wider than they are long, may have a lawn outside the front. And if you see a water vole, rather than just hear it plop into the water on your approach, it will swim higher in the water than a brown rat.

 ## Pleased to meet you ... again

WHITE-TAILED EAGLES

These statuesque sea eagles vanished from British shores while national attention was distracted, focussing on the First World War.

They had been shot in their droves at the behest of anxious sheep farmers who were losing lambs to the birds. Only decades later was the loss so keenly felt that young birds were re-introduced to replace the population.

In 1975, 82 juveniles from Norwegian nests were brought to the Island of Rum in Scotland's Inner Hebrides. A waiting game ensued and it was a painfully slow process. As a consequence a further 58 young birds were brought in, also from Norway, in the mid-nineties to underwrite the success of the scheme. Now the goal is to quadruple the number who have made their homes in western Scotland, from 50 pairs to 200. It's estimated their presence is worth five million pounds a year to the local economy and has created 110 jobs.

Standing at one metre in height and with a wingspan of two and a half metres, the white-tailed eagle, also known as an erne, is the largest eagle in Europe. Alongside golden eagles, the only other variety you can see in Scotland, they are larger with a shorter, paler tail and a golden bill. Their talons are smaller and more curved, ideal for scooping up aquatic prey. Both have the same remarkable eyesight that can pinpoint a rabbit from three miles. Humans would need eyes the size of oranges to have similar capabilities.

In Finland there's been an unexpected bonus to hosting white-tailed eagles as they pick North American mink from the water, thus lessening the impact this intruder species has on native wildlife.

Highest and lowest hours of sunshine recorded for June since 1929

	Highest		Lowest	
England	284.3	1957	117.1	1987
Wales	286.2	1957	110.7	1987
Scotland	240.1	1940	99.0	1966
Northern Ireland	258.9	1940	91.4	2012

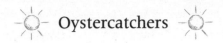

Oystercatchers

Fifty years ago, a sharp-eyed teacher in Aberdeen spotted oyster-catchers nesting on his school's flat roof.

For Alastair Duncan it signalled the start of a long study of these black-and-white birds who are usually more mudflats than high-rise when it comes to favoured habitats.

When he first observed the distinctive orange-beaked birds taking to the city roof tops, Aberdeen had just undergone a building boom.

By smothering new roof tops with gravel, builders had unwit-tingly mimicked the natural nesting sites of oystercatchers – a rudimentary scrape on a shingle beach. Only the penthouse height offered birds an added protection against predators like foxes and cats, who were restricted to ground level.

Although there was a range of tower blocks accessible to oyster-catchers, there seemed a preference for schools. The attraction was the proximity of a playing field, replete with juicy earthworms.

Fortunately, oystercatchers bring food back to their young, rather than expecting newly hatched chicks to follow parent birds to food sources. Thus, untimely plunges for youngsters were never a problem.

Oystercatchers are territorial birds who return year after year to the same nesting site. Renovations to the city's flat roofs – which saw gravel being replaced with a smooth and durable surface – put the success of the skyline colony in doubt until Mr Duncan inter-vened by placing gravel-filled seed trays at strategic intervals; that seemed to satisfy the instincts of the home-coming birds.

Today there are more than 200 pairs of oystercatchers living the high life in Aberdeen. And these are the trend-setters, with oyster-catchers now making roof-top homes on venues across the country.

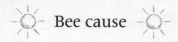

Bee cause

The plight of bees in Britain has been gaining greater traction, as an understanding of how bleak a bee-less future will seem sinks in.

According to Friends of the Earth, 13 species of bee in Britain are extinct and a further 35 are at risk.

It is encouraging everyone to take part in an annual bee count which begins in the middle of May and runs throughout June. There's a phone app that helps identify and record bees. After all the data has been collected it is verified, then sent to the National Biodiversity Network Atlas, an online library that is available to ecologists, academic researchers and environmental policy-makers.

In the meantime, if you want to help there are some simple steps you can take:

- Make a bee banquet. All this entails is planting pollen-rich flowers outside in the garden, in patio tubs or window boxes. Wise choices will mean bees are given options almost all year round. Try planting lungwort, sedum, crocus, phacelia, chives, lavender, honeysuckle, comfrey and ivy.
- Buy a bee box, commercially produced homes for solitary bees, and witness nesting progress first hand.
- Put marbles in a dish and then add water to create a safe drinking station for bees.
- If you have a lawn, raise the mower blade and let the grass grow a tad longer so bees can shelter there.
- Leave a corner of the garden to go wild. That way nesting bees will be undisturbed.
- Avoid using pesticides.
- Make a simple bee hotel by tying hollow bamboo canes and other sticks in bunches. Poke the bundle into a hedge or hang it in a tree so solitary bees can find it.

☀ If you see a struggling bee, provide it with a shallow saucer containing sugary water. Ensure the depth isn't sufficient to drown it. Never use honey as it won't help, commercial honey being subject to additives.

 ## Sunrise and sunset times for Britain's capital cities

30th June	☀ Sunrise	☀ Sunset
Belfast	04.51	22.03
London	04.47	21.21
Cardiff	04.59	21.33
Edinburgh	04.31	22.01

JULY

High summer is the time for exploration – rock pools, sandy beaches and surf, but it's also the time for insects. Just lie back in a field and listen. When the sounds of cars and aeroplanes have faded, drink in the drone of bees going about their everyday business. Everything on six legs and with one or two pairs of wings is making the best use of the warm summer temperatures, and anything that eats them is not far behind!

Sunrise and sunset times for Britain's capital cities

1st July	☀ Sunrise	☀ Sunset
Belfast	04.52	22.02
London	04.47	21.20
Cardiff	05.00	21.33
Edinburgh	04.31	22.01

St Swithin's curse

On 15th July 971 CE, the body of Swithin, Bishop of Winchester, was exhumed. The intention was to rebury him in a new cathedral, but plans were scuppered when the British weather intervened. Unusually heavy rain delayed the ceremony from taking place. It led to the belief that if it rains on St Swithin's day, it will rain persistently for another 40 days.

The pair of flycatchers in the vine are preparing for a second brood and have got one egg. This is the first instance that I remember of their breeding twice.

Gilbert White, 12th July 1785

Day of the mini-triffids

We know of plant-eating animals, but what about animal-eating plants? July is the month that the carnivorous sundew bursts into white and surprisingly pretty flowers for an assassin. It lives in boggy heaths and peaty moorlands, where nutrients are less abundant in the acidic soils than in other parts of the countryside, so it gains an edge over its rivals by trapping insects. Its leaves are covered with scarlet tentacles, each tipped with glistening, sticky, sugary mucilage. When an insect is attracted to sup at the sweet, seductive solution, it is doomed. It becomes stuck to the goo. Within seconds, the sundew's leaves curl around it, secreting digestive juices that break down the victim into a nutritious soup. The sundew absorbs the nutrients through its leaf surface, and then unfurls the leaf ready to lure in another unwary victim.

Sundew is found amongst sphagnum moss on bogs throughout Scotland, Wales and Northern Ireland, but is confined to north west and south west England.

Flowers of the Month

The poppy is not a native British flower. It arrived in Neolithic times, probably carried here by our Stone Age forebears at about the same time as farming got underway. Its seeds are extraordinarily resilient, and can lie dormant for over a century. Today, poppies are often seen on disturbed ground, such as arable land; the gaudy red flower of the common or field poppy often contrasting with swathes of pale blue cornflowers. The base of each petal usually has a black mark, as does the deeper-red petals of the less common rough poppy, but this is absent in other species. The long-stalked poppy is a paler version, with orange-red flowers, which can be found in rural gardens and on wasteland. The less abundant prickly poppy grows on chalky, lime-rich soils, its name referring to its prickly seed capsule.

Highest and lowest rainfall in millimetres recorded for July since 1910

	Highest		Lowest	
England	128.6	2009	13.2	1911
Wales	241.4	1939	20.7	1911
Scotland	185.6	1940	32.7	1913
Northern Ireland	186.2	1936	19.7	1919

 # Refuelling stop

July is a busy month for insects. The air on these warm, long days of summer is filled with the incessant drone of bees, flies and the many other flying insects that jostle for prime position on the season's blooms. Centre of attention are the flowers of buddleia, thistles, knapweed and honeysuckle, all of which are reaching their peak this month. The visitors availing themselves of their sugary nectar, among many others, include a colourful array of day-flying moths. Watch out for the stunning hummingbird hawk-moth hovering like a hummingbird in front of the pink tubular flowers of viper's-bugloss, and the extravagantly patterned jersey tiger with its black wings and creamy-white stripes, visiting buddleia. Black and red six spot burnets are active in the sunshine. They have a slow, buzzing flight, and alight on thistles and knapweeds to refuel.

The thistles, which are a big attraction for moths, are considered weeds by many people: after all, they do tend to spring up on poorly looked after grassland and wastelands. They can be controlled, but only if you know when to cut them back. A traditional country diary rhyme sums it up:

Cut thistles in May – they'll grow in a day
Cut thistles in June – that is too soon
Cut thistles in July – then they will die.

And, if you leave them until August, their fluffy white seeds float away to be spread far and wide by the wind.

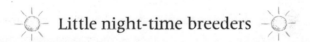 Little night-time breeders

July is also the best month for night-flying moths. When they break out of their chrysalis and take to the air, their only purpose is to procreate. Some, like the poplar hawk-moths, do not even feed at night. Female poplars rest by day with their hind wings held in front of their forewings and the rear part of their abdomen curved upwards. They start to fly just before midnight, the males joining them shortly afterwards.

The pink and olive-coloured elephant hawk-moth relaxes by day amongst rosebay willow herb, one of the foods of its caterpillars, and is active at night, sipping the occasional energy boost from honeysuckle flowers. The dark brown male oak egger moth, recognised by its feathery antennae, flies in an erratic zigzag fashion along hedgerows by day in search of resting females, the light brown females joining the party after sunset. Many of these moths will come to lighted windows, like the instantly recognisable plume moths with their feathery wings that are rolled up tight when at rest.

It is the peak time for nocturnal moth watching, and one simple way to entice them to visit you is to hang up a white sheet and shine a light on it. They are more active on mild, still nights, so avoid rain and strong winds and they'll be more likely to be attracted to your light on moonless nights. Alternatively, simply leave the curtains or blinds open, switch on the light and they'll flock to your window.

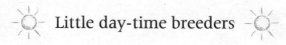

Little day-time breeders

During the day, butterflies dominate, especially the gatekeeper, which has topped the annual Big Butterfly Count three times in recent years. The chalkhill blue can be seen on chalk or limestone downs where there is an abundance of rabbits. Bunnies keep the grass trimmed so chalkhill caterpillars can feast on horseshoe vetch. Female ringlet butterflies drop their eggs into the grass instead of attaching them to leaves as most other butterflies do. They are easy to spot because when they land, they have distinct yellow-ringed spots on the underside of the hind wings. They'll fly in all weathers, even when it is dull and drizzling, refuelling on the nectar of bramble flowers.

In woodlands mainly in southern England, the swooping flight of the fast-flying silver-washed fritillary propels it through glades, the brighter orange-brown and black males searching for the paler females, but the pièce de résistance of English woodlands is high up in the canopy of oak woods – the magnificent purple emperor butterfly. During the first two weeks of July, males can be seen gliding around their treetop territories, seeing off rivals or attracting potential partners. Their 'majesties', as purple emperor aficionados call them,

Chalkhill Blue

Silver-washed Fritillary

Ringlet

Purple Emperor

Gatekeeper

are so aggressive that they have been known to chase anything that flies into their airspace, including buzzards. Up there, in and above the canopy, they refuel on oozing oak sap or honeydew secreted by aphids, but occasionally drop down to the forest floor, particularly in the early morning, to supplement their diet with salts and minerals from animal droppings, rotting corpses and the edges of rain puddles.

For most butterfly watchers, the purple emperor is the ultimate in butterfly watching, and hotspots in central southern England include: Shotover Country Park, Oxfordshire; Wellington Country Park, near Reading; Knepp Castle Estate and Bookham Common, Surrey; The Mens, West Sussex; Chiddington Forest, Surrey; and Bentley Wood, Wiltshire. But be quick: by the end of July all the adult purple emperor butterflies will have died.

 # Highest and lowest average temperatures (°C) recorded for July since 1910

	Highest		Lowest	
England	25.2	2006	9.2	1919
Wales	23.1	1983	8.9	1922
Scotland	20.3	2006	7.2	1922
Northern Ireland	21.8	2013	8.2	1922

 ## Botanical vampire

This month, a scoundrel of our British flora is more visible than usual. Dodder is a parasite, and, although it relies on its host plants for sustenance, it still has to produce its own flowers in order to reproduce. One species of dodder invades gorse, occasionally heather and wild thyme. As a plant, it is unimpressive.

A mature dodder consists of a tangled mass of pink spaghetti-like stems, its leaves reduced to tiny scales. It gains water and essential nutrients with root-like structures that penetrate the host's xylem and phloem tissues. Its flowers, which appear in July, are in globular clusters. Each has five white, triangular petals, tinged with pink, with a beetroot-red base. Some people have noticed the flowering plant gives off a stench reminiscent of rotting fish, which may be one reason it's called 'Devil's Guts' in some areas. The smell probably attracts blowflies, which help in pollination. Seeds are small but plentiful, and they can germinate without a host plant, but the sapling needs to find one within five to ten days, for with its limited ability to photosynthesise, it would quickly die. It does this by 'sniffing out' a host. It then twirls in an anti-clockwise direction until it hits a stem and taps in, like a vampire penetrating a blood vessel. Its roots then die and it is totally dependent on its host.

Look out for dodder on heaths, chalk downs and fixed dune grasslands, mainly in the southern parts of England from Cornwall across to East Anglia. There are several species and they do invade gardens. They can be removed by judicious pruning, and try to remove the dodder before it sets seed.

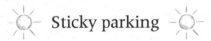

Sticky parking

The sweet chestnut is a late-flowering tree; often well into July. Male and female flowers are on the same tree, the small green rosettes of female flowers sitting at the base of the long golden male catkins. The tree can be recognised instantly from the horse chestnut as the leaves differ. The sweet chestnut has long leaves with prominent veins and a pointed tip, and the edges are serrated like a saw. Later in the autumn, the nut is contained within an extremely prickly, leathery case, which differs from the less prickly case of the horse chestnut.

Also flowering late is the small-leaved lime. Its trusses of champagne-coloured flowers stand erect or lie horizontal, which differs from the dangling flowers of the more common lime seen in cities, but for the rest of the annual life cycle to continue the weather must be warm. This lime only sets seeds during a hot summer. The tree is relatively scarce these days, but it was once the dominant species in the native forests that sprung up in the British Isles after the last Ice Age, and specimens today can be more than 2,000 years old. One word of warning, though: the leaves of lime trees, including the large leaved lime and common lime, attract aphids and they secrete honeydew, so don't park your car underneath a lime tree!

Beetlemania

It's a good month for beetles too. The most formidable is the green tiger beetle. This large metallic-green, long-legged ground beetle is a fast-moving hunter – one of our fastest running insects. It pursues its prey like a cheetah and has formidable sickle-shaped jaws to crush and cut spiders, ants and caterpillars.

Humid days bring out rove beetles. The largest is the Devil's coach horse, which is found in woods and gardens. When cornered it exudes an evil-smelling liquid from a pair of glands at the tip of its raised tail, and watch out for the other end – it bites!

Smaller rove beetles sometimes land in your hair and they are so light that they are wafted high into the sky by thermals where they become part of the aerial plankton that is scooped up by swifts, swallows and house martins. They can also be spotted on the flat umbels of cow parsley, but, as July progresses, it is replaced by the taller hogweed and one beetle that homes in on its nutritious nectar is the very conspicuous red soldier beetle, also known as the 'hogweed bonking beetle'. Usually you see them in mating pairs and,

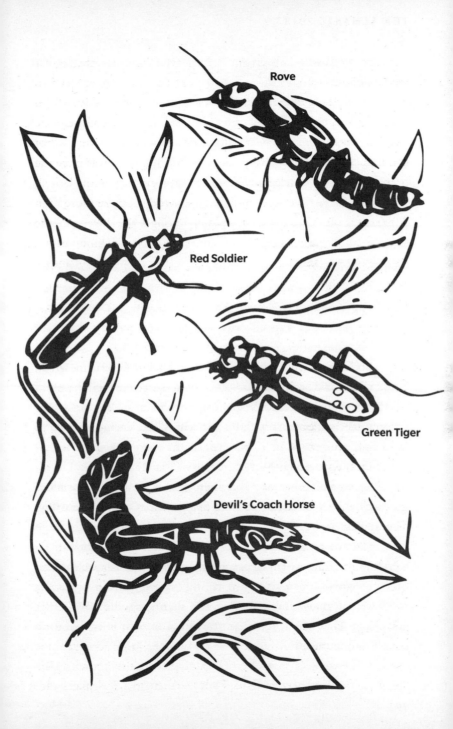

Rove

Red Soldier

Green Tiger

Devil's Coach Horse

between copulating and drinking, they grab and consume smaller passing insects.

Ground, rove and soldier beetles are a gardener's friends, for they prey on many garden pests. You can encourage them with piles of wood, compost heaps and leave a little leaf litter in flower borders. Soldier beetles also predict the weather: if a thunderstorm is approaching, they take shelter underneath leaves.

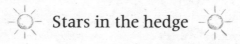

Stars in the hedge

At night, it is worth checking out grassy banks and woodland rides for signs of glow-worms. They are not worms, but female beetles, and they glow to attract a mate. The female is wingless, so she must climb up plant stems to advertise her location, and she does this with some illuminating chemistry. The cells in the last two segments of her abdomen contain the light-emitting chemical luciferin, which glows when oxidised in the presence of the enzyme luciferase and the energy-transfer molecule adenosine triphosphate. It is an astonishingly efficient process with 98 per cent of the energy emitted as 'cold light', compared to 90 per cent of the energy of an incandescent light bulb lost as heat.

The female arches her abdomen until it shows off her bluegreen glow to best effect, and the flying suitors come a-courting. The males are ordinary light brown beetles, but with large light-sensitive eyes, whereas the females closely resemble their larval stage. Glow-worm larvae, recognised by the spots at the end of each segment, can also glow faintly, but they hide away under rocks, where they catch, paralyse and then consume small slugs and snails. They might remain at this stage in their life cycle for a couple of summers.

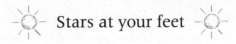

Stars at your feet

Rather than look up at the stars, look down at your feet, especially when walking on a sandy beach in La Rocque Harbour at the south-east tip of Jersey. When it is dark, with no moon, and where there are no streetlights nearby, rake the sand and then watch it glow with hundreds of tiny pinpricks of light. The bioluminescence comes from a small polychaete worm, *Caulleriella bioculata*. Unfortunately it's without a common English name but, when disturbed, it glows for about twenty seconds. It could be a display aimed at startling any would-be predator, but nobody knows for sure why it behaves in this way. Jersey Walking Adventures organise night-time rambles to see the phenomenon, and the guides believe there could be more beaches around the British Isles that are home to the worms. It's a global species; so, if you're on a beach at night, keep your eyes peeled.

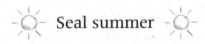

Seal summer

Summer is the time common or harbour seals are dropping their pups. In Scottish sea lochs, especially in the Hebrides, Orkney and Shetland, in and around Strangford Loch and on the shores and sandbanks of the Wash, seal mothers are giving birth between June and August. A pup enters the world without the white coat or lanugo that many other newborn seals wear. It has already moulted it in the womb. It is also born with unusually large hind flippers because, unlike other baby seals, it will be swimming almost immediately, its mother suckling it at sea rather than on land. It grows quickly on its mother's fat-rich milk, doubling its weight in just a month. Its ability to swim so soon after being born means the mother can leave her pup on a gently shelving shore that is inundated at high tide, a strategy that reduces the risk from shore-based predators, such as foxes. The common seal, despite its name, is less common than the grey seal, distinguished by its longer snout. The common seal, by contrast, has more of a snub nose and it often rests, rather comically, with its body in a banana shape, the head and tail in the air at the same time. It spends most of its life close to shore, but when it does dive for food it can remain submerged for ten minutes or so and reach depths of more than 50 metres on average.

Blakeney Point in Norfolk and shorelines stretching eastwards to the Wash host the UK's largest concentration of common seals. Look around at the birds too. Four species of terns – common, sandwich, little and Arctic terns – nest here, and there are ringed plovers, turnstones and dunlin.

Grey seals give birth later, in the autumn (see page 290).

Shark central, UK

Basking sharks first appear off the south-west coast of England, such as the Lizard in Cornwall, in April, and by July, they can be spotted from headlands around the entire coast of the British Isles, including Scotland and the North Sea. They are enormous. With a maximum length of 12 m, they are the second largest fish in the sea after the tropical whale shark, and everything about them is big. Their large gill slits almost encircle their head and their dorsal fin stands erect, like some extra from the Hollywood movie *Jaws*, but the long snout sticking out of the water at the front end and the tail fin slicing languidly through the water surface at the other end is a dead giveaway that you are watching a basking shark and not a great white!

That's not to say great white sharks do not visit these shores. Every summer, during the newspaper 'silly season', there's a killer shark story, like the great white shark supposedly seen repeatedly for the last couple of years off Hayling Island, in Hampshire. The reality, though, is that despite our healthy seal populations, there is still not enough easy food to be had for the world's largest hunting shark to bother swimming our way and, to date, there have been no authenticated sightings. The closest one got to our shores was the northern Bay of Biscay, about 270 kilometres south of Lands End, although there was a story a few years back of an injured seal being brought to a seal sanctuary in south Wales. An Australian shark expert happened to be on holiday in the area at the time. The bite marks on the seal, he suggested, had been made by a great white shark.

WORLD'S FASTEST SHARK

Three of the great white's closest relatives are most definitely frequent visitors. The fast-swimming short-fin mako shark, with a fiery attitude to match its speed, enters British waters in summer and is often seen off the coasts of south west England, Wales and Ireland. The largest ever caught off the British coast was a 227 kg specimen, which grandmother Joyce Yallop hooked near the Eddystone Lighthouse. Now, that is a sizeable shark, with a mouth overflowing with seriously sharp teeth but, fear not, they are designed to snag slippery fish not bathers.

- ☼ **Stout-bodied bruiser:** The porbeagle could easily be mistaken for a great white, because of its size and shape. Like the great white and the mako, its swimming muscles are kept warmer than the surrounding water, so it can live in cool, temperate waters all around the British Isles. UK porbeagles have been caught with lengths up to about three metres, and particularly large specimens have been caught off Dunnet Head, at the northern tip of mainland Scotland, and near Boscastle, on the north Cornish coast.
- ☼ **Fox shark:** Another great white relative is the thresher or fox shark. It is instantly recognised by its exceptionally long, sickle-shaped tail. Scientists have long wondered why it should be this shape, but recent research has revealed that

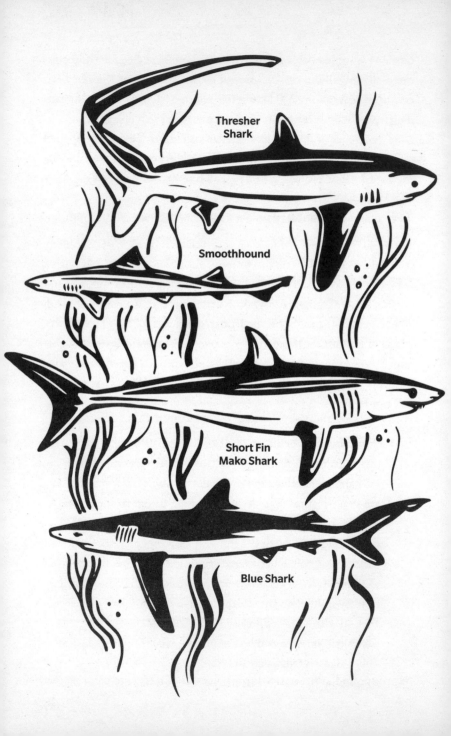

Thresher
Shark

Smoothhound

Short Fin
Mako Shark

Blue Shark

it uses it like a whip, thrashing shoals of fish in order to disorientate or even kill them. A thresher hotspot is south of the Isle of Wight, where the sharks chase herring and mackerel inshore, but the largest ever found in British waters was hauled up in a fishing net off Lands End. When landed at Newlyn fish market it was found to be a staggering 9.7 metres long, half of its length consisting of tail.

Fish markets, such as those at Newlyn, Brixham, Plymouth and Portsmouth, are great places to go fish spotting. The trawlers, day boats and crabbers bring in all manner of strange fishes, including such exotics as the smooth hammerhead shark, a rare visitor. A specimen washed up on the beach at Portreath in 2004, and others have turned up at Yarmouth, Isle of Wight, Carmarthen Bay, Banffshire and Ilfracombe.

- ☼ **Ancient shark:** The bluntnose sixgill or cow shark is more usually encountered by manned submersibles in the deep sea, but this primitive species makes occasional forays into shallow waters, perhaps to breed, and, off Ireland's west coast shark anglers have hooked these monsters. In May 2017, a 7.5-metres-long sixgill, weighing an estimated 680 kg, was caught off Loop Head in County Clare, the largest known shark to have been caught by an angler in Europe in recent times. Occasionally these sharks venture into the English Channel, the UK record holder being a 444 kg specimen caught off Penlee Point, near Plymouth.
- ☼ **Ubiquitous blues:** Many shark watchers consider the blue shark to be the most beautiful of all the sharks. This transoceanic migrant, with long glider-like pectoral fins, sashays into our waters in the summer months and might well be spotted at the surface from pleasure boats quite close to the

shore. Most are relatively small, but occasionally a giant turns up like the 2.7-metres-long blue shark that was hooked and released about 15 km off Penzance on the south Cornish coast in August 2017.

☼ **Miller's dog:** The summer visitors mentioned above are just a few of the 40 or so species of sharks that frequent our shores. Twenty-one of them stay with us all year. One of our larger residents is the tope or soupfin shark, known also as Penny's dog or Miller's dog. Large tope can be up to two metres long and they remain offshore in British waters all year round. Small tope, sometimes known as 'dog-tope', form packs and chase small fish into water only a few feet deep. They are common in Morecambe Bay, the Thames Estuary, the Bristol Channel, off the Cornish coast, and in Luce Bay in south west Scotland. Some tope migrate. A tagging programme off the north west coast of Scotland revealed that British tope range widely in the north east Atlantic, migrating as far south as the Canary Islands, and as far north as Iceland.

☼ **Rock salmon:** The spiny or spur dogfish travels too, all around the British Isles. It roams in packs, in deep water for most of the year, but will come into shallow water to feed, and is particularly common off the west coast of Scotland in summer. However, if you should come across one, be careful. It has venomous spines at the front of each of its dorsal fins. You might also be invited to eat one at a fish and chip shop. It is often sold as 'rock salmon', 'flake' or 'huss', but, with our population threatened by overfishing, these species have been assessed as critically endangered by the IUCN.

☼ **The dogs and cats:** Of the smaller British sharks, the smoothhound and starry smoothhound are very shark-like, but in miniature, about a metre long, and the 80-cm-long small spotted catshark and the slightly larger nursehound have an exquisite pattern of spots all over their bodies.

Unless you snorkel or scuba dive, you are unlikely to see them in their natural habitat, but they are often kept in seaside aquaria, and you might see dogfish egg cases washed up on a beach. They are known as 'mermaid's purses', and each consists of a rectangular, light brown leathery case with horns at each corner ending in curly tendrils. These catch in seaweeds and anchor the egg case so it doesn't get washed out to the open sea. If the egg case you find is large and black, it is more likely to be that of a skate or ray, rather than a shark.

So, get out on those headlands and see if you can spot a shark. Hotspots for basking sharks include Skye, Mull, Isle of Man, Malin Head, and all around the coasts of Devon and Cornwall. And, if you see one, be sure to report it to the Basking Shark Project of the Shark Trust: www.sharktrust.org/en/sightingform

 ## Highest and lowest hours of sunshine recorded for July since 1929

☼	Highest		Lowest	
England	291.9	2006	113.1	1944
Wales	297.6	1955	110.7	1987
Scotland	239.8	1955	83.8	1931
Northern Ireland	247.6	1955	82.2	1986

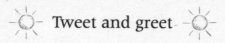 Tweet and greet

Most songbirds have stopped singing by now, but not all. The corn bunting is a sparrow-sized, streaky 'little brown job' that can still be heard singing well into July. You might spot it on top of a bush or fence post singing its jangly song. It breeds late in the season so its nests may be destroyed during harvesting, making it a vulnerable species in the UK. It is found on open farmland mainly in England and the east coast of Scotland.

Also active at this time is the turtle dove, especially in south east England. It is more colourful than its cousin, the collared dove. It has an orange-brown back with a tortoiseshell pattern in black, a blue-grey head, and black and white or blue lines at the sides of the neck. Its purring call, which sounds like 'turrr-turrr-turrr', differs from the familiar 'hoo-hoooo-hoo' of the collared dove. It is our only migrant pigeon and heads to Africa in winter.

Sensational seasonal spectacles: Seabird cities

Towering sea cliffs are like enormous vertical cities, with different species of birds living in different neighbourhoods on the sheer rock face. They nest on the precarious ledges, because, believe it or not, it's the safest for their offspring. No fox worth its salt is going to risk balancing on these narrow slivers of slippery rock, so, apart from any skilled aerial predator that might swoop in, such as a herring gull or a stoat or weasel that braves the cliff face to grab an egg or chick, the city is like a fortress. In high summer it's a place of intense activity. Time is running out. All the parents have to get their offspring fit and able to survive the autumn storms that may be just weeks away.

Nesting closest to the sea are the cormorants and shags. They occupy the lower ledges, where they build nests of seaweeds and

Kittiwake

Puffin

Razorbill

Cormorant

Guillemot

sticks in which their eggs and chicks are safe from falling out. They're careful to stay well out of range of the surf at high tide.

Next up are the razorbills that tuck themselves away in ravines and rocky places at the base of the cliff. They fly in at tremendous speed, pulling up at the last minute with wings and feet out to crash land. They are more used to being at sea. They are great divers, pursuing fish down to 20 m, and have even been spotted by submersible crews hundreds of metres from the surface.

Guillemots are also deep divers, almost flying underwater in pursuit of fish. They occupy the narrow ledges on the cliff face above the razorbills. They pack closely together, but they don't build a nest. Their eggs and later their chicks perch on bare rock. Each pair tends to its single chick, but just three or four weeks after hatching, in early to mid-July, the chick does the most extraordinary thing: encouraged by its male parent, it has to leap off its cliff-side ledge and flutter helplessly to the sea. Some crash onto the rocks below, to be swallowed whole by voracious great black-backed gulls. Even so, many chicks survive and they can dive as soon as they hit the water. It is then up to the father alone to escort his offspring away from the coast and to deeper water, where he will protect it and provide it with fish until it can fly and dive for its own food. The mother, meanwhile, remains at the nest site for a couple weeks, until she too heads out to sea, to where she will spend the winter.

Sharing the guillemots' mid-level ledges are the kittiwakes, the most sea-loving of British gulls. They are recognised by their 'kitti-wake' call. They make nests with seaweed glued together by their own droppings. They are skilled flyers, twisting this way and that in the wind. Out at sea, they are surface feeders, barely dipping below the sea's surface.

Higher up still are the fulmars, recognised by the stiff way they hold their wings. You can watch these skilled flyers ride updrafts, like going up in a lift, barely flapping their wings, to return to their nest sites near the top of the cliffs. Related to the albatross, they have a distinct tubular nostril on top of the bill from which they not only smell fish oils on the sea's surface from up to 25 km away, but also get rid of excess salt. Salt-infused 'snot' dribbles from the nostrils, along to the end of the bill where it drops to the ground well clear of the bird's plumage. As a defence, the fulmar and its chick can regurgitate evil-smelling stomach oil that can gum up the wings of predatory birds and send any terrestrial predator running.

At the top-most nest sites are the puffins. Their wide, multi-coloured bill, at least in summer, has led to them being dubbed the 'clowns' of the bird world. Often as not, they nest in old rabbit burrows or in burrows they have dug themselves, as on Skomer in south west Wales but, where the rocks are hard, they find cracks, crevices and holes in the cliff, as at Bempton Cliffs in Yorkshire. The further north they live, the more likely they are to be chased by skuas, which harass them to such an extent they drop their catch. This means they have to turn around and head back out to sea to catch some more, or their offspring will go hungry.

During July, the puffin colony is reaching peak activity, with parents constantly bringing back sandeels for their youngster. Each bird is able to carry several fish at once as it has a loose fold of soft tissue between the upper and lower halves of the bill. A firm grip is maintained on a row of fish, holding them between the tongue and the bill. The bird can then grab another fish without losing the others. This frantic bustle continues until early August, when parents abandon their chick. It lives off fat deposits until it embarks on its first adventure out on the ocean.

The best seabird cities are on the coasts of Wales, northern England and Scotland. One of the largest seabird colonies on mainland England is at Bempton Cliffs, Yorkshire; and there are others at the Farne islands, Northumberland; Isle of May, Fife; Scottish Seabird Centre, North Berwick; the Treshnish Isles, Mull;

and the coasts of Orkney and Shetland, which have some of the tallest sea cliffs in the British Isles.

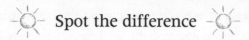

Spot the difference

Razorbills and guillemots look superficially like penguins, but the two species are easily confused. The simplest way to tell them apart is that the razorbill has a thicker bill with white markings, whereas the guillemot has a totally black head with a narrower bill. There are exceptions: a variety known as the bridled guillemot, which is found in the more northerly colonies, such as on Orkney, does have white markings, in particular, a white line from the corner of the eye.

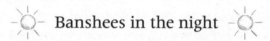

Banshees in the night

On Welsh islands, such as Skomer, puffins are joined at the top of the cliff by Manx shearwaters, but you'll hear rather than see them and only at night. During the day, the shearwaters head out to sea to fish, returning at night to avoid predators. Puffins dominate the cliff tops before dark. Apart from the momentary panic during attacks by peregrines or black-back gulls, the seascape is relatively quiet. At night, however, the noise is extraordinary. The incoming shearwaters fly out of the darkness over the ocean screaming like banshees in the night, and each new arrival is guided to its burrow by the less strident sounds of its partner inside.

The adults leave in mid-August, the chicks remaining in their nest burrows for another week or so. They emerge occasionally, flapping their wings and getting used to life outside, but they have to watch out for those pesky gulls. Then, one night, with ample fat reserves, they head out to sea. They fly all the way to their winter home off the coast of southern Brazil and northern Argentina, a 10,000 km journey that they complete in less than a fortnight.

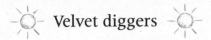

Velvet diggers

July is the one month that you might spot a mole. These velvet-furred characters, with shovel-like front feet and tiny eyes, spend much of their lives underground, so most people would never have seen one, although you can see the results of their digging activity as molehills on your lawn. At this time of year, however, young moles must leave their mother and find territories of their own, so they have to come above ground. You might see them crossing a road.

Once underground, they dig tunnels and catch earthworms. The tunnel is, in effect, an exceptionally long trap. The earthworms drop in and the mole scrabbles along and grabs them. Its saliva contains a toxin that does not kill the worm, but paralyses it, so the moles can store fresh food, sometimes many hundreds of worms, for when times are hard. The mole also has a special kind of haemoglobin in its red blood cells, which enables it to function normally even when the carbon dioxide levels in its tunnel are high enough to knock out other animals. It's a very specialised little mammal.

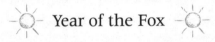

Year of the Fox

After weeks devoted to caring for the young, adult foxes are, by now, looking the worse for wear. Finding sufficient food for the brood during the previous months has left them thin. It's also the time of year when their fur coat moults, so they appear rundown and ragged. As a consequence they stop feeding the cubs, although the parents do lead instructive hunting expeditions. Often the dog fox will take three cubs in tow, and the vixen, too. It won't be long before the adults expect their cubs to be self-sufficient. In the meantime, there's still plenty of time for play for the youngsters on open ground near their earth.

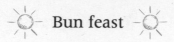

Bun feast

In the summer there's one animal that's on the menu for a host of others. Rabbits are a mainstay for birds of prey, swooping from above, as well as foxes, badgers, pet dogs, pet cats, weasels and stoats, sneaking up from behind. Even other rabbits can be killers, if youngsters unwittingly contravene established territorial rules.

Evolution has helped keep them alive, with rabbit eyes placed on each side of the head to best monitor predators. Their ears are long and act like radars, detecting an enemy as it approaches. But why are bunnies such a tasty treat? The answer probably lies in the way they have been brought up. Rabbits give birth underground in the chambers of warrens. Mum pulls out the fur from her stomach to make the nest protectively warm. But what is surprising is how mums leave baby bunnies for hours at a time. She returns for them to suckle for as little as three minutes in every 24 hours. The fact is, rabbit milk is very nutritious, rich in both fats and proteins, the most protein-rich milk known. Milk produced by the rabbit on a plant-based diet is all it takes to transform the deaf, blind and bald scrap that's born weighing just 30 g to a 'mini me' that's ready to explore the outer reaches of the warren just three weeks later. And the goodness in the mother's milk is what makes babies so darned tasty. Only about one in ten baby rabbits will survive to see its first birthday.

Nature has its own way of lending a helping hand to rabbit populations, of course. If rabbits are famous for anything, it is breeding at an incredible rate. Mother rabbits will mate soon after the birth of a litter, while she is still feeding the babies. Here, timing is of the essence. Baby rabbits are fully independent within 30 days. Her gestation period is between 28 and 31 days. The nest isn't left empty for long.

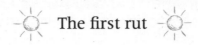

The first rut

Roe deer bucks start their rut during July, and they look magnificent. Gone is the grey to dull brown winter coat, to be replaced by a bright red-brown pelage for summer. Bucks have small three-pronged antlers, and they joust for the right to mate with the does, but the females do not let the males have everything their own way. Lengthy chases ensue before the doe is ready to mate, during which the two animals whistle and rasp to one another.

The roe deer is one of two native British deer, the other being the red deer. It has been here since Mesolithic times, arriving directly after the last Ice Age, but it was hunted and numbers fell to such an extent it became extinct in England, but hung on in Scotland. After re-introductions during Victorian times, the population has bounced back, except for Kent and some parts of the Midlands. Roe deer are most active at dawn and at dusk and, if you should startle one, it will probably bark a warning.

Deer, however, are notorious for spreading the ticks that are responsible for Lyme disease. They wait on leaves and grass for you to walk by, then latch on to your skin and suck your blood. So, after a walk in the country, where you have brushed against foliage, always check for ticks. NHS choices website has advice on ticks and Lyme disease: www.nhs.uk/conditions/lyme-disease

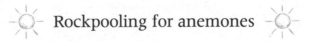

Rockpooling for anemones

No seaside holiday is complete without exploring rockpools. Whether you're three or eighty-three, it's the most absorbing pastime imaginable. When the tide goes out, it leaves behind pools filled with fresh seawater and they contain a remarkable bunch of creatures that are battered by waves for half the day, then trapped in a placid saltwater pond, where the temperature can soar, the salinity oscillate and the oxygen deplete for the other half.

Sea anemones are best equipped to deal with this twice-daily cycle. They simply adhere to the rocks so they can't be washed away. The most stunning must be the snakelocks anemone, with its flowing tresses of bright green, snake-like tentacles with purple tips. Symbiotic algae, known as zooxanthellae, live in its tissues, produce food that supplements its diet, and provide the vivid colours. As these tiny organisms are photosynthetic, the snakelocks anemone tends to position itself in the sunniest parts of the pool. In some places, such as Babbacombe Bay and Swanage Pier, the anemone is also home to a shrimp that appears to be immune to the anemone's stings. Humans are not immune. Touch the tentacles with your finger and they'll appear sticky, as the anemone's sting cells try but fail to pierce the thick skin, but if you brush them with your arm, or, when swimming, they touch your abdomen, then it can raise a severe rash that can last for a month or more. The snakelocks is found along shores in the south west of England and Wales, and as far to the east as Worthing on the south coast.

The dahlia anemone is the largest British anemone, its broad, squat body reaching up to 12 cm across. Its shorter, thicker tentacles can also have purple tips, like the snakelocks, but it is fussier about where it lives. If a rock pool warms to over 22°C, on the next tide it will loosen its grip on the rock and let the currents move it to a new location. It is found all around the British Isles, and is often buried under sand or gravel.

The plumose anemone is only seen at very low tides. In water it has circles of fine, feathery tentacles, but out of water the anemone deflates and looks rather bedraggled. It is usually white or orange, and is often seen on wharves and pontoons in harbours.

The commonest sea anemones are the beadlet and strawberry anemones. You can see both in and out of water on rocks close to the low tide mark. If the tide should go out and leave them high and dry, they haul in their tentacles and form red, brown or green blobs that minimise the loss of water until the tide returns, when they open up again. The strawberry anemone is slightly bigger than the beadlet, and it has a dark red body with pale spots that make it look like a strawberry. The beadlet has blue beads at the top of its body, beneath the tentacles, and a brilliant blue line around its base. Both are to be found on rocky shores, beadlets all around the British Isles, but strawberry anemones are absent from North Sea coasts.

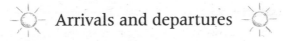

Arrivals and departures

For some animals the breeding season is already over and they are beginning to prepare for winter. In mid to late July, before the nights are cool, swifts start to depart for Africa. They do not roost en route, but simply fly almost non-stop. One young swift left Britain on 31st July and was found in Madrid on 3rd August. By mid-August they will all have reached Central Africa.

Passing through the British Isles and following the swifts to warmer climes are several waders, often still in their breeding plumage. Curlew sandpipers, with an unusually reddish tinge to their plumage, travel from the Arctic to Africa, and spotted redshanks leave their northern Scandinavia breeding grounds and head south. If a spotted redshank should stop off, its breeding colours are unmistakable: jet black with white spots over the back and wings.

Arrivals include the first bar-tailed godwits and sanderlings, some also still in their breeding plumage. The godwits from northern Scandinavia and Russia have their summer chestnut breasts instead of the more familiar winter grey, and the normally monochromatic silver-grey sanderlings from Svalbard, an archipelago to the north of Norway, have chestnut-red backs and breasts. Both of these high summer arrivals spend our uncertain winter with us, when they revert to their winter colours. You can spot the godwits in estuaries, such as the Thames, Dee, Humber and Wash, but check out long, sandy beaches for sanderlings.

Sunrise and sunset times for Britain's capital cities

31st July	Sunrise	Sunset
Belfast	05.33	21.26
London	05.23	20.50
Cardiff	05.35	21.02
Edinburgh	05.16	21.21

AUGUST

The dog days of summer are those hot and humid days, with the occasional thunderstorm, which the Greeks and Romans thought were influenced by Sirius, the dog star. It's sometimes an uncomfortable time of the year, both for people and wildlife. Sultry weather sees large animals scurrying for shade and shelter, including birds that have stopped singing, are moulting and are more difficult to spot, but there are many others to see. Generally, wildlife populations have reached their highest numbers. As the breeding season for many comes to an end, there are more animals about this month than in any other, but not all creatures have stopped reproducing. Some have only just started. Insects are active all day and some into the night, whatever the weather, because conditions are right for them to bring on the next generation.

 ## Sunrise and sunset times for Britain's capital cities

1st August	Sunrise	Sunset
Belfast	05.35	21.24
London	05.25	20.48
Cardiff	05.37	21.00
Edinburgh	05.17	21.19

Old Lammas Day

Lammas lands are mediaeval flood plain meadows that the lord of the manor traditionally divides into 'lots' or 'doles' and sells the right to local farmers to cut and collect hay. On 12th August, known as Lammas Day, after the crop has been harvested, the livestock of certain commoners is allowed to graze the meadows until Candlemas at the beginning of February. It's a form of land management that has protected meadows from exploitation and damage for over 800 years, so they are rich in wildlife.

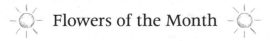

The male and female ants of the little dusky sort come forth by myriads and course about with great agility.

Gilbert White, 6th August 1773

Flowers of the Month

If you go down to the woods today, you might well find one of the last orchids of the year. In amongst the brambles, often beneath a beech tree, is the rare violet helleborine. Its 60-cm-long purple stem supports a spike of 50 or more large pale green flowers with white lips, tinged with pink. They attract insects, especially wasps. They sip the nectar, but afterwards they fall about and fly erratically, appearing to be drunk. Several stems might grow together in a small cluster, the underside of their large lance-shaped leaves showing a distinct purplish hue. The violet helleborine can be found in woodland, mainly in the south of England and parts of the Midlands, but occasionally as far north as Cumbria.

British scabious are in flower this month. The field scabious has delicate lilac pompoms, which gave rise to its alternative name 'lady's pincushion', and the Devil's-bit scabious resembles a darker purple-blue pincushion, because of its protruding red anthers. Its common English name of the latter arose because it has short, stubby roots. The Devil was said to have bitten them off during one of his rants, because the plant has curative properties. It's used to treat scabies and other itchy afflictions, and was once applied to the sores from plague. Both species are found throughout the British Isles, and are very attractive to insects.

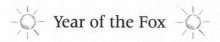 Year of the Fox

As the dog days of summer draw to a close, playful young foxes still find the energy to practise a 'mouse pounce'; high-jumping to secure small prey. Cubs pair up to go hunting at dusk. When food is bountiful they stay within earshot of a parent who will emit a sharp bark to warn if there's danger.

A long, dry summer takes its toll as the youngsters range further into unknown territory to find sufficient food. This increases the hazards they face, particularly from busy roads.

Adults are recovering their coats and proper body weight. One surprising facet of fox diet comes into play this month, with a crop of ripening blackberries hanging from the bush. If you spot some purple poo on the ground, well, it's probably the work of a fox that's indulged in some hedgerow hunting.

Highest and lowest rainfall in millimetres recorded for August since 1910

	Highest		Lowest	
England	261.4	1947	9.6	1995
Wales	274.5	1917	14.7	1995
Scotland	216.5	1985	5.1	1947
Northern Ireland	201.4	2008	12.4	1947

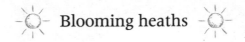

Blooming heaths

And the wild mountain thyme
Grows around the blooming heather

Two lines from the Scottish folk ballad 'Will Ye Go Lassie Go' celebrate the romance and spectacle of the heaths and moorlands at this time of the year. The heathers put on the last big floral spectacle of the year. Common heather or ling dominates in the late summer and autumn, distinguished from the spring heather by having larger scale-like leaves in pairs rather than whorls of three to five. There's also bell heather, with its bell-shaped flowers, and amongst the strong purples are the more subtle lilacs and pinks of wild thyme; including the strong-smelling large thyme and the less common Breckland thyme only to be found on the Breckland heaths of Norfolk.

Look closely amongst the heathers and thyme and you might also see the moss-like stems of stag's-horn clubmoss, not a true moss, but a diminutive descendent of an ancient group of plants that grew to the size of trees 350 million years ago and died en masse to form coal. In July, spore cones, which look like pairs of antlers, appear on its little brush-like shoots.

And, should you lie back amongst the heather, thyme and ancient clubmoss, just take a moment and listen: you're sure to hear the frantic buzz of honey bees collecting the vital ingredients that make some of the best honey in the world.

There's one plant, however, whose nectar is not what it seems. On the boggy edges of moorland, the grass of Parnassus or bog star is not a grass. It gets its name from the way cattle on Mount Parnassus developed a taste for its leaves, and it became an 'honorary' grass. In early summer you'd probably miss it, but in August its tall stem is topped with an ivory-white flower, with prominent light green veins, which smells of honey. Within the flower

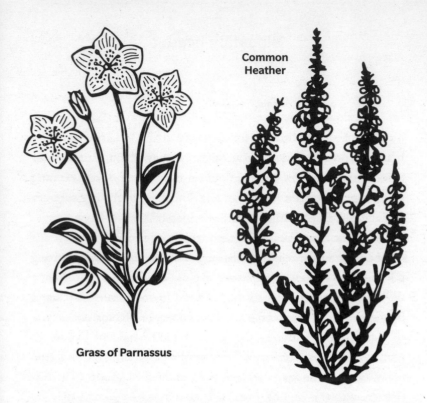

Common Heather

Grass of Parnassus

are what looks like drops of nectar but they're not; they're decoys. They attract insects, but there's no reward. By the time the insect has realised it's been cheated, the flower has been pollinated. It is not a common plant in the UK, but is found in upland areas, as well as the long wet depressions between sand dunes, known as dune slacks, along the Lancashire coast. It is the county flower of Cumbria and Sutherland, appearing on the county arms of the former, and is the clan badge of Clan MacLea (Clan Livingstone).

 Reptile hatches and births

Early on a sunny morning is the best time to spot reptiles this month. On heaths, in rough grasslands and woodland, adders, common lizards and slow worms head for their favourite basking places to warm up. Lowland heaths in the south of England also have smooth snakes, and sandy heaths and dunes in Lancashire have sand lizards.

The slow worms are usually more difficult to see, as they hide under sun-warmed rocks, logs and corrugated metal, rather than bask in the open, although they usually return to the same place everyday. In early evening you might see them hunting slugs, especially after a spell of rain. Pregnant females give birth from mid-August. Although they resemble snakes and are named 'worms', they're neither. They're legless lizards, and can discard their tail, like other lizards, to escape predators, such as badgers and hedgehogs.

Common lizards give birth about now too, each offspring a miniature but darker version of its parents, while sand lizards are the only native lizards to lay eggs. Their hatchlings emerge from burrows in sunny spots in the sand, and every single offspring counts as the species is nationally rare. They have been reintroduced to Devon, Cornwall, north Wales and West Sussex, and there is even a small population that was introduced to the Scottish Isle of Coll in 1970, to see if the lizards could survive so far north. It seems they're doing fine.

Emerging from your compost heap, hay-rick or a pile of reed stems beside a pond, you might see baby grass snakes. Up to 40 of them will have been incubating inside their eggs in the warmth of their nest site since June, and during August they hatch and go their separate ways, leaving behind their thin, leathery eggshells.

Baby adders are born this month, litters of nine on average. Their patterning could be mistaken for fern fronds. They too bask in the sun, but they do not feed. They survive on yolk until they hibernate in autumn and then re-emerge next spring ready to face the world.

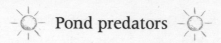

Pond predators

Active in the pond this month are water boatmen. Of the four British species, the most abundant and widespread is the light brown-coloured backswimmer or great water boatman. It swims upside down on the underside of the water surface, and often looks silvery from the air trapped against its body. When hunting, it propels itself along with its long hairy hind legs that are flattened like oars. It is a formidable hunter, tackling prey as large as tadpoles and small fish. Beware of ever picking one up: its mouthparts can inflict a wound that has been likened to being 'stabbed with a hot needle'. They also fly and, during August and into the autumn, they travel between ponds.

Joining it might be another bug – the large and formidable water scorpion, recognised by its long, curved pincers for grabbing prey and a long breathing tube coming from the tip of the abdomen that is used like a snorkel. It flies at night and may be attracted to the light from windows.

The largest insect predator below the surface is the great diving beetle. It has a streamlined beetle shape, is dark brown with yellow legs and a yellow border around the head and thorax. These beetles also fly to colonise new ponds. They leave the water on evenings with little wind, and take off like giant ladybirds. Nowadays, though, they are often confused. Instead of a pond, they have been known to land on the shiny roofs of cars, garden cold frames and wet roads, mistaking them for water. Its yellowish-brown aquatic larvae possess huge jaws, so don't pick one up!

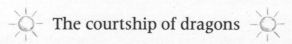

The courtship of dragons

Dragonflies are abundant this month because the insects on which they feed have also emerged en masse. They are an ancient group

whose forerunners lived during the Carboniferous period, about 325 million years ago. There were even giant relatives that had a wingspan of up to 75 cm. Today's largest dragonflies are closer to 12 cm, and they have evolved some remarkable skills. Scientists, for instance, have recorded seeing dragonflies perform an Immelmann turn, named after Max Immelmann, the World War I flying ace. It's an ascending half loop with a half roll at the top, which effectively reverses the direction of horizontal flight. They can also hover and fly backwards, and the males put these aerial manoeuvres to good use in dogfights with rivals and to impress females.

At this time of year, they gather at ponds and lakes to mate, and the first to arrive at a new garden pond is likely to be the lime-green southern hawker. You can spot the male, as he has blue markings on his long abdomen, and he's very territorial. He'll likely come and check out who you are. He has excellent vision, all the better to spot a potential mate. When successful, he grabs her and clasps her 'neck' with two appendages at the tip of his abdomen, and the two fly together in tandem. The female bends her abdomen forwards, forming a heart-shaped wheel. Some pairs mate on the wing, others on a perch.

If you don't have a pond in your garden, the hotspots for dragonflies in the British Isles include: RSPB Loch Garten, Abernethy; Pocklington Canal, Yorkshire; Wicken Fen, along with British Dragonfly Society groups in many other parts of the country; Barton Broad, Norfolk; Cornhill Meadows Dragonfly Sanctuary, Epping; Basingstoke Canal, Hampshire; Kenfig National Nature Reserve, Bridgend; Brackagh Bog Nature Reserve, Northern Ireland; and Glen Affric, Highland Scotland.

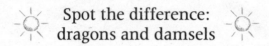

Spot the difference: dragons and damsels

Dragonflies are more heavily built than damselflies, the former with hindwings slightly shorter and broader than the forewings, and the latter with all four wings the same size and shape. When at rest, most dragonflies hold their wings out horizontally, at right angles to the body, whilst damselflies tend to fold their wings above or along their abdomen. In flight, dragonflies are fast and agile flyers, up to 30 mph (although 60 mph has been claimed), whereas the damselflies have a weaker, fluttery, daintier flight.

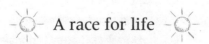

A race for life

The land can become parched during the summer months, but a late summer or early autumn deluge can see the formation of vernal or temporary pools. These can be the trigger that causes ancient creatures to emerge from the earth. Eggs lie dormant throughout the drier months, but when the warm rain falls and the pool fills, their inmates suddenly hatch out. It's the start of a frenetic few weeks during which they must reproduce before the pool dries up again.

The stars of this vernal pool are tadpole shrimps, a type of primitive crustacean that was alive millions of years ago; in fact, the species found in the UK today appears to have changed very little from tadpole shrimps seen as fossils in Upper Triassic period rocks dated 220 million years old … they are just as rare. Only two ponds – a vernal pool in the New Forest and more permanent water in the Caerlaverock Wetlands of south west Scotland – are known to harbour them.

Tadpole shrimps look prehistoric. They have a shield-shaped carapace that resembles that of the horseshoe crab, another 'living fossil'. They breathe with leaf-like extensions of their legs, and have heightened levels of haemoglobin, which gives them a pink hue and enables them to survive in low-oxygen conditions. They feed voraciously on anything they can find, until they double in size and turn green. They must deposit their eggs before the pool dries up and, as the water recedes and food is harder to find, they turn on each other, becoming cannibalistic.

When all the water has gone, the eggs are safely hidden away in the soil. They dry out and development is put on pause. They can survive in this state for up to 27 years. They can also endure high and low temperatures, being carried by the wind, and even eaten and egested by animals without coming to harm. All they need to rehydrate is another rainstorm and a vernal pool, and their crazy lifecycle starts all over again.

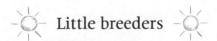

Little breeders

This month, the little breeders really are little: they're ants. When temperature, humidity and wind speed are right – often during hot, thundery weather – the winged male and female ants leave their colonies and take to the air; and the breeders from many colonies do so at roughly the same time. The first sign is sometimes the sudden appearance of large numbers of gulls flying in an erratic manner.

Unlike swallows and house martins, which simply scoop up the flying ants as they swoop through the swarm, gulls must flap about a bit before they can catch one.

The colonies swarm at the same time to ensure a good mix of genes, and so avoid inbreeding. During the flight, the virgin queens produce pheromones that entice the males to follow. They fly high and then mate with a male that can match their fitness, mainly on the wing but sometimes on the ground. With the nuptial flight completed, the tiny males die, and the larger females – the new queens – fly to the ground, rub off their wings, and scrabble about looking for a place to start a new colony. Many don't find it and perish.

Contrary to popular belief, there's not just one flying ant day per year. There can be many over several weeks in high summer, often after a thundery downpour, and the prominent flyer you'll see in the city is the black garden ant. It likes building its nests under patios and paving stones, where there is soft sand, and you see them navigating successfully to and from their nests across seemingly featureless bricks and concrete in the constant search for food. Large nests can have up to 20,000 workers, their queens living for up to 28 years; thought to be the longest life span of any adult insect.

 # Highest and lowest average temperatures (°C) recorded for August since 1910

🌡	Highest		Lowest	
England	24.3	1995	8.9	1912
Wales	23.4	1995	8.5	1912
Scotland	20.7	1947	7.0	1912
Northern Ireland	22.1	1995	7.2	1912

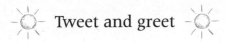

Tweet and greet

Some of the loudest sounds in August are not from birds, but from insects, and standing out from the crowd are the bush-crickets and grasshoppers, the former recognised by their long antenna and the female's sword-like egg-laying organ, and the latter with short antennae. While their chirpy, buzzy sounds seem very similar, the two groups produce them in different ways. The crickets rub their wings together, while grasshoppers rub their long hind legs against their wings, a sound-making process known as stridulation. Crickets tend to be noisier at dusk, while grasshoppers are out and about during the day.

Mole crickets are especially loud because they use an amplifier to blast out their song. They have large front feet, like a mole, and dig a burrow shaped like a double horn with twin openings on the soil's surface. Half an hour after sunset, the male mole cricket blasts out its song for about an hour. A female flying past is able to hear it from about 30 m away, and the most successful singers might attract up to 20 females in one evening.

While grasshoppers are widespread throughout the British Isles and crickets in the southern half of the country, the mole cricket is rare, with small populations in the New Forest and Guernsey, and isolated individuals found in other parts of the country – Oxfordshire, Bedfordshire, Cheshire, Essex and Dorset – having been brought in as eggs or nymphs on imported plants.

Young crickets mature in August, and one you might come across in southern Britain is the bright green and rather delicate oak bush-cricket, which is often found in parks and gardens and is attracted to the light from windows. Another character to watch out for is the larger great green bush cricket. Don't pick it up – it's another one that bites!

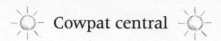 Cowpat central

Cow dung is a magnet for some insects. Dung beetles are not only in Africa. We have about 40 native species in the UK and, like their more exotic cousins, they work hard burying and shredding dung; food for their larvae, which pupate and emerge as adults in summer. They are dark, quite stocky insects with feet designed for digging, and four species are relatively common. The iridescent dor beetle has a preference for cow dung, while the glossy-black minotaur beetle likes rabbit droppings, and the wood dor beetle will tackle anything from fox scat to the droppings from deer and domestic animals. One species, the night-flying dung beetle, is attracted to artificial light, so if you should hear a mysterious tapping against your window, it's probably him.

Cowpats also attract yellow dung flies. Golden, hairy males congregate on the splat of dung like gladiators in an arena. The smaller females, less hairy and tinged with green, tend to be else-where, visiting the dung primarily to mate. They approach from downwind, and the males joust for the right to mate with them. The dung then becomes a nursery. It's also an adult feeding site. The males capture other insects attracted to the dung, and suck them dry, and the flies, in turn, are a favoured prey of lesser horseshoe bats.

Rove beetles are also attracted to cowpats, and they feed on the insects and larvae in the dung community, which might include black scavenger or ensign flies, stable flies, water scavenger beetles, wood gnats, soldier flies, drain or sewer flies, hoverflies and clown beetles. It's dung heaven.

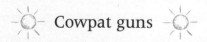 Cowpat guns

A gentle hint that autumn is slowly approaching is the appearance of fungi. The yellow field cap grows on cowpats, as do the little orange-red discs of the cup fungus *Cheilymenia granulata*. They are just two of many fungi that live on dung and some of them have something in common: they distribute their spores with what amounts to a high-pressure 'squirt gun'. With this they propel their spores at high speed and over considerable distances. They need to do this because the spores must be eaten by and pass through the gut of herbivores in order to grow, and animals tend not to eat close to their own dung, so the fungus must shoot them away. The acceleration is phenomenal. One moment the spore is on the cowpat, and, one-millionth of a second later, it is travelling at 25 m per second, with an acceleration of 180,000 g. By comparison, fleas experience 200 g when jumping, astronauts 4 g at take-off, and jellyfish sting cells fire at 40,000 g in water. Dung fungi achieve the fastest known acceleration in the natural world.

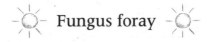

Fungus foray

The most charismatic fungi at this time of year must be the puffballs and stinkhorns. One of the largest fungal fruiting bodies in the world is that of the giant puffball. A schoolboy from Yorkshire stumbled across the UK's biggest specimen. In 2010, he found a giant puffball nearly 1.7 m across. More often, they are about as big as a football; even so, there are up to seven trillion olive-brown spores inside, which means this fungus produces more progeny than any other living thing. Aside from being gigantic, it is also of pharmaceutical importance: it is the source of a drug for treating cancer.

The giant is one of 18 species of puffballs growing in the UK, and they're all edible, as long as you get to them early. They tend to yellow with age and are then inedible. However, beware. There are fungi that resemble puffballs that are deadly poisonous.

Earthballs account for the second highest number of mushroom poisonings in the UK, because they're mistaken for puffballs. The outside is tough and pitted and, when cut in half, the inside is purple or black, although there are exceptions: some are white like puffballs. If you're unsure of the identity, don't eat it. The amanitas, which include the death cap and destroying angel, have white 'eggs' protruding from the ground like small puffballs. Inside is the traditional mushroom cap, ready to grow up. Whatever you do, don't eat it. Just half a death cap mushroom can kill an adult human by causing liver and kidney failure. The Roman Emperor Claudius ate it and died in CE 54, and the Holy Roman Emperor Charles VI succumbed to it in 1740. Don't be the next.

You'll probably smell a common stinkhorn before you see it. The stench it releases attracts flies, especially bluebottles. They gather, sometimes in large numbers, on the olive-green slimy cap or gleba, and help distribute the yellow fungal spores that stick to their feet. They eventually strip away the gleba and underneath is a raised white honeycomb texture, which is usually what most people find – unless you're up really early, before the flies. The fungus tends to grow in groups close to rotting wood, so look around and you might find the white 'egg' stage, four to eight centimetres across, just poking above the ground. From here the phallic-shaped fruiting body develops. The shape of the fungus disgusted some Victorians, including Charles Darwin's granddaughter, Etty. She destroyed them at dawn, before any gentlefolk could see them!

There are at least two other common stinkhorns: the smaller dog stinkhorn, with a slender stipe, whose tip turns orange when the flies have removed the gleba; and the dune stinkhorn found exclusively on sand dunes.

Warning: if you cannot identify a fungus accurately, don't eat it.

Highest and lowest hours of sunshine recorded for August since 1929

	Highest		Lowest	
England	291.9	2006	113.1	1944
Wales	270.8	1947	92.5	1944
Scotland	293.3	1947	78.6	1942
Northern Ireland	261.4	1947	70.7	2008

Fruits and berries and birds

Another indication that autumn is just around the corner is the appearance of the first wild fruits. On the danger list, however, is deadly nightshade. By late summer the purple bell-like flowers will have developed into shiny black berries, each set like a deadly precious stone in a bed of five pale green sepals. Song thrushes and black caps eat them with impunity, but for us humans they're fatal. Like many poisonous plants, however, they have had a medical use. Opticians have used a refined extract to dilate the pupils during eye examinations.

Fear not, however, for not everything is out to get you. There are plenty of fruits appearing in August that we can consume, albeit some need a bit of preparation. The bright red berries of rowan, which makes a wonderfully bitter rowan jelly, an accompaniment to venison, game birds and lamb, and elder berries, to brew elderberry wine that is said to rival that of the grape (but cook them both properly; they're mildly poisonous if eaten raw). Aside from human gastronomes, they also attract thrushes and blackbirds, and, when wild cherries ripen you might well see the shy, but handsome, orange-hued hawfinch, a rarity in the UK. This bird has a stout, powerful bill, quite capable of crushing a cherry stone. Field mice also nibble at the stones, gnawing a hole in the seed coat in order to get at the kernel inside.

Brambles give us wild blackberries, and picking them in hedge-rows across the land is an ongoing pleasure for many city folk, as well as dyed-in-the-wool countryphiles. They are not berries, but drupes and when birds have plucked them and carried their seeds to distant places, they establish thickets in no time at all. The fruits feed pheasants, blackbirds, field mice and foxes, and, when they become a little mushy, peacock, red admiral and small tortoiseshell butter-flies come to suck up their juices, along with wasps and a multitude of flies, so spiders weave their webs across bramble patches with the certainty of a catch. During the course of the spring and summer, the plant has entertained all manner of insects – the caterpillars of green hairstreak butterflies and oak eggar and emperor moths have fed on its leaves, while the nectar and pollen from its flowers has fortified many species of bees, along with day-flying moths, such as the silver Y.

On moorlands from Cornwall to Scotland, the small white bell-shaped flowers of the hardy cowberry, lingonberry or partridgeberry are giving way to bright red berries, a treat for grouse, and probably partridge and cattle if the alternative common names are to be believed. On acid woodland, moors and upland heath, mainly in the north and west of the British Isles, you'll find the small black-purple bilberries, also known as whortleberries, huckleberries and wimberries. They are the principal ingredient of 'wimberry tarts' on the Welsh Marches and 'mucky-mouth pies' in Yorkshire. The lantern-shaped green-pink flower is the county flower of Leeds, and was a favourite of the Brontë sisters.

The wild cranberry is also fruiting now. Much smaller than its North American relative, it can be seen spreading across sphagnum bogs, first noticeable by its pink cyclamen-like flowers and then

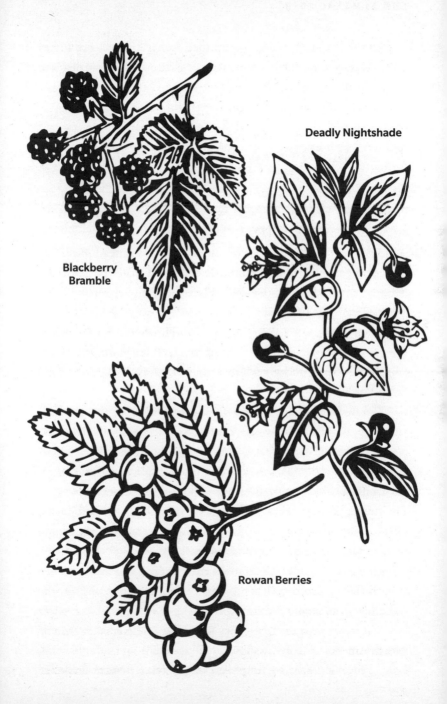

Blackberry Bramble

Deadly Nightshade

Rowan Berries

small bright red and sometimes mottled fruits. And let's not forget the wild raspberry. Aside from tasting delicious, albeit smaller and a little seedier than our supermarket varieties, the juices, it is said, dissolve the tartar on your teeth.

Birds of prey: the new generation

High summer is the season for young birds. Many species are fledging now, and finding their own way in the world; albeit with a little help from Mum and Dad.

As one of our most common and widespread birds of prey, you can hear young buzzards calling in many parts of the country, their 'klee-oo, klee-oo' calls slightly higher-pitched than the mewing calls of their parents. They can even be heard in the middle of cities, such as on Hampstead Heath and Hyde Park in London. Most pairs will have raised two or three youngsters from eggs laid in April, and the whole family are out looking for a meal – dead or alive.

The fledglings rely on their parents to find food, such as voles and mice, for about six weeks, but then they begin to be an irritation and a territorial threat and they're chased away. They gather together with other novices, and camp out in places where there is a reasonable food supply, even something as basic as earthworms. Their parents are probably looking a bit worse for wear at this time of year, but the young birds can be recognised by the light fringes on their spanking-new wing and tail feathers.

Young hobbies hunt alongside their parents for a short while after fledging, but they have a very different challenge from the buzzards. Resembling a giant swift – with a dark grey back, white face and red around the legs – they are exuberant flyers that are able to catch anything from swallows to dragonflies and other insects, even crane flies. These flying sessions are just a rehearsal for the mega-journey to come. The young hobbies, like their parents, must soon depart for Africa, where they spend the winter.

While buzzards can be spotted almost anywhere in the British Isles, including stretches of many motorways, hotspots for hobbies include Lakenheath Fen, Norfolk, New Forest, Hampshire, Lee Valley Country Park, Hertfordshire, Westhay Moor and Catcott Lows, Somerset, and Upton Warren Nature Reserve, Worcestershire.

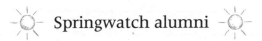

Springwatch alumni

Five very special birds of prey families featured in the 2017 *Springwatch* and *Autumnwatch* series from Sherborne Park Estate in the Cotswolds. Kestrels were nesting in the local church tower, while barn owls had made their nest in an old metal barn on the estate. Both families had chicks of very different sizes, and it was touch and go as to whether the runt in each family would survive; but, survive they did!

All the chicks in both families fledged. During the fledging period the male kestrel continued to look after his fledglings for about 18 days, after which the family dispersed. It is thought individuals might have travelled as far as 100 km in a southwesterly direction to find their own patch. The barn owls didn't fly so far, remaining within about 12 km of their nest site, although Chris revealed that some birds from Cornwall have actually pitched up in Germany. He also pointed out that this period in the birds' life cycle can be their most dangerous. Up to 50 per cent of barn owl deaths occur during dispersal, half of them killed on our roads. The birds' habit of flying low when quartering the roadside verges brings them in direct contact with motor vehicles.

Buzzard and red kite chicks fledged successfully, both dispersing some distance from the nest site. In 1997, one kite, Chris revealed, had been ringed in Inverness and was recorded later in Iceland.

However, when the birds mature and it's time for them to breed, both species return to their natal neighbourhood, the buzzards little more than 12 km from where they hatched, the kites within 22 km.

The fifth nest of the 2017 season was a peregrine's, high up on Salisbury Cathedral. The parents had a single chick, but the RSPB introduced a foster chick. Both birds were fed well and fledged. The male birds remained close to the nest site. The female parent, which was fitted with a satellite-tracking device, changed her behaviour after her chicks had fledged. While feeding them, she hunted in an area of about 36 sq km, but afterwards she roamed much wider, over an area 197 sq km, reaching as far north as Stonehenge.

All five nesting parents had been successful in raising all their brood.

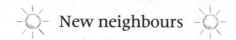

New neighbours

European bee-eaters appear occasionally in the south of the country. Some are thought to be 'spring overshoots', probably inexperienced birds that fly past their normal breeding areas, cross the English Channel, and end up in the southern half of England. Some even breed here. Two chicks from a brood of five in Bishop Middleham Quarry, in County Durham, survived and flew south in August 2002, but most breeding attempts have been unsuccessful. In summer 2017, Michaela and the *Autumnwatch* team went to see seven birds at East Leake Quarry, in Nottinghamshire. They had dug three nest holes, each nest with a pair of adult birds, with one bird – probably the offspring of one of the pairs that bred somewhere else the previous year – acting as helper. The area was cordoned off and a designated viewing area set up for bird watchers, and about 10,000 turned up. The birds were catching bees, dragonflies and other flying insects (they need a staggering 225 a day), and everything seemed to be going well, but then a kestrel came along and poked its head in the nest holes and that was that. By August, no chicks had fledged.

 ## Seasonal spectacle: The big moult

Shelduck are goose-like ducks that look black and white from a distance but, on closer inspection, have a glossy, dark green head and neck and a distinct brown band around the chest. In summer, enormous numbers of shelduck – up to 100,000 – fly to Germany's Waddenzee to moult. They come from all over Europe, including the British Isles, but many Irish birds don't go that far. About 4,000 visit Bridgwater Bay, on the north Somerset coast. They cannot fly for the four weeks they are here because, when they moult, they replace all their flight feathers at the same time. At low tide, the mud can be covered in feathers, like snow.

In north west England, on average 14,500 shelduck have abandoned the migration to Germany, and moult in the Mersey Estuary, probably the largest flock in the UK. On the east coast, there are smaller gatherings in the Wash and the Firth of Forth.

The Wash is also a spring and summer breeding site. Although many pairs now breed inland, some breed on the north and south sides of the Wash, and when the adults have set off for Germany on their moult migration, the youngsters are left behind, but they're not totally abandoned. They gather into crèches, some-times numbering up to 200 ducklings. Some are less than a week old, while others are able to fly, and they are looked after by several adults, probably birds that failed to breed or those that have yet to. If you disturb them, the escorts take off and quack loudly. At the first call, the youngsters dive below, almost simultaneously, each one leaving just a small jet of water behind. Having completed their moult the adults return at leisurely pace, arriving back in Britain by October.

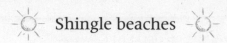

Shingle beaches

On the coast, beaches and banks of shingle, hammered regularly by salty sea winds, are probably the most forbidding places for wildlife to make a home, but there are a few plants that have gained a toehold, and they flower in summer. The yellow-horned poppy has almost-golden flowers atop fleshy blue-green foliage, which give rise to horn-like seed capsules, up to 30 cm long and very different from the little barrel-shaped seed containers of field poppies. It's found mainly along southern coasts, Slapton Sands in south Devon being a known hotspot. Be careful not to touch the leaves. If damaged, the veins exude yellow latex, which is poisonous.

Another shingle specialist is the sea kale, a member of the cabbage family. It can survive here because it has a long taproot that anchors the plant and pushes down vertically to find any rainwater that has percolated down between the stones. At this time of the year, the tough, waxy, grey-green leaves are decorated with a cushion of small white flowers. In the 19th century it was a popular vegetable, one of the few we can call our own, and in recent years it has been seeing something of a revival with British chefs. It is still common on the south coast, and parts of East Anglia, Cumbria, North Wales and south west Scotland. Elsewhere, the construction of sea defences has destroyed its natural habitat.

Shingle beaches on the south and east coast also have the sea pea, a legume whose low-lying stems cover large patches of shingle. It has purple and white flowers in short spikes. In the autumn, it produces pods containing slightly bitter seeds that were, nonetheless, eaten by folk in Suffolk during famines in the Middle Ages.

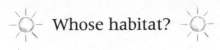

Whose habitat?

ROCKPOOLS

During the course of a year, adults in the UK make over 300,000,000 visits to the seaside. Add in the children who accompany some of them and, potentially, there are a lot of people scrambling about on the shore. Rockpools can be blitzed, so, rather than plunge that net you bought at the souvenir shop into the still waters and disturb everything living there, why not simply sit, watch and wait? You'll probably see a lot more.

First to appear are usually starfish and crabs. They are relatively slow movers so they must be out and about quickly to find something to eat before the tide turns and the churning ocean returns once more. There are several common species of starfish, particularly in pools closer to the low tide mark, the aptly named common starfish being the species you're most likely to encounter. It feeds on mussels by wrapping itself around the two shells and pulling them apart. It then slips its stomach in the gap and digests the mussel in situ. The shorter-armed cushion star scavenges on dead animals.

Several species of crabs hide in rock pools. The shore crab is the most common, hiding under rocks and amongst seaweeds, and the velvet swimming crab the most aggressive: watch out for its pincers. Its back legs are flattened like paddles. The little broad-clawed porcelain crab is found on the underside of muddy rocks, but it's well camouflaged and sometimes difficult to spot.

Of the swimmers, you might miss a semi-transparent brown shrimp unless it moves, and tiny fish move too fast. Gobies and blennies are present in rock pools, although they are well camouflaged against the rocks and weeds, and down by the low-water mark you just might get a glimpse of a pipefish. This relative of the seahorse is long and thin, with an elongated, horse-like head. It

Pipefish

Crab

Blenny

Starfish

seems to glide through the water propelled by its dorsal fin, and, like its close relative, the male retains the eggs in a pouch until they are 'born', rather than the female.

If you're really lucky you might witness another birth this month. Most sea snails release their eggs into the sea, where they are at the mercy of the currents, but, back in the spring, the dog whelk glued egg capsules to the undersides of rocks. They resemble rows of tiny yellow skittles. Each capsule contains up to 600 eggs, most of which are unfertilised, and they provide food for the dozen or so tiny survivors developing inside each capsule. In August, they hatch out, and when they grow into pointed-shell adults, they become formidable predators, drilling into other shellfish by using a toothed tongue or radula and some strong chemicals to get at the soft parts inside.

Whatever you do, don't be too engrossed. Keep a close eye on the tide and don't turn your back on the sea. Rocky coasts are like they are because powerful waves have pulverised them, and the sea is unpredictable. In an instant a rogue wave can swamp the shore and sweep unwary rockpoolers out to sea. Keep safe.

 ## Rockpool hotspots

- Wembury Bay, near Plymouth
- Tunnels Beach, Ilfracombe
- West Angle Bay, Milford Haven
- Cemlyn Bay, Anglesey
- St Abbs and Eyemouth Voluntary Marine Reserve
- Flamborough Head, Yorkshire
- St Mary's Island, Tyneside
- Bembridge Ledges, Isle of Wight
- Roome Bay, Fife
- Longis Bay, Alderney

☀ Hope Gap, Seven Sisters, Sussex
☀ Polzeath Beach, Cornwall
☀ Kimmeridge Bay, Dorset
☀ West Runton Beach, Norfolk
☀ Porth y Pwll, North Wales
☀ Creswell Shore, Northumberland
☀ Gyllyngvase Beach, Cornwall
☀ St Agnes Beach, Cornwall
☀ Dunseverick Harbour, County Antrim
☀ Calgary Beach, Isle of Mull

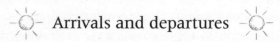

Arrivals and departures

One of the most unexpected arrivals must be leatherback sea turtles. They swim more than 7,000 km from their breeding beaches on the northern shores of South America to be in temperate waters when jellyfish are abundant, their favoured food. You might see a reptilian head poking out of the water when the turtle takes a breath, a strong candidate for sea serpent sightings on the west coast of the British Isles.

Other arrivals include red admiral butterflies from the Mediterranean, and a procession of waders, including greenshanks, spotted redshanks, wood sandpipers and juvenile turnstones either passing through on their way south, or arriving to spend the winter here.

By early August, adult swifts are already leaving, their youngsters not far behind. Sand martins abandon their tunnel nests and gather in reed beds before heading off. They're the first of the swallow family to appear and one of the first to leave. Even so, swallows and house martins are beginning to congregate on telephone wires and rooftops, although, in a good year, juvenile house martins might be helping parents to feed a second brood. The rest of the young swallows, house martins and sand martins take advantage of the abundance of insects, honing their flying skills before they join the procession southwards, but they'll not be alone. They're shadowed by hobbies all the way to Africa.

Sunrise and sunset times for Britain's capital cities

31st August	☀ Sunrise	☀ Sunset
Belfast	06.30	20.17
London	06.12	19.49
Cardiff	06.24	20.01
Edinburgh	06.16	20.09

SEPTEMBER

Autumn has arrived. The days are getting noticeably shorter and the nights longer. During the day, sunlight is exceptionally clear and bright, and the shadows long, and, at night, there's a distinct chill in the air. Most plants and animals are winding down after a frantic spring and summer of procreation, some preparing for a long and well-earned winter sleep, but not all. Fungal fruiting bodies are popping up all over, hops are ripening, and bats are swarming. Some of our smaller eight-legged beasties and fluttery winged ones are moving indoors with us, while the progeny of some of this year's breeders are leaving the country, heading south for sun, sea and a winter Shangri-La.

Michaelmas Day

Michaelmas Day is on 29th September and Old Michaelmas on 10th October. Michaelmas is the 'quarter day' closest to the autumn equinox on 23rd, and, in the traditional farming cycle, harvest should be completed by now, marking the end of the growing year. In Scotland, it was celebrated with an unusual custom. Women would go to the vegetable fields on the Sunday before Michaelmas and look for a fork-shaped carrot. It was a fertility symbol to be given to a 'muckle-man', the name for a boy who's reached manhood and is eligible for marriage. However, whatever you do, don't eat a blackberry after Old Michaelmas Day, for that was when the Devil was expelled from Heaven and landed in a bramble bush. He cursed the blackberries, spitting and stamping on them. Michaelmas is a special day, though, for Michaelmas daisies, a North America plant brought to the British Isles in the 18th century. They traditionally flower now and continue well into November.

This morning the swallows rendezvoused in a neighbour's walnut [sic] tree. At dawn of the day they arose altogether in infinite numbers occasioning such a rushing with strokes of their wings as might be heard a considerable distance. Since that no flock has appeared, only some late broods and stragglers.

Gilbert White, 22nd September 1771

Sunrise and sunset times for Britain's capital cities

1st September	☀ Sunrise	☀ Sunset
Belfast	06.31	20.15
London	06.13	19.46
Cardiff	06.26	19.58
Edinburgh	06.18	20.06

Flowers of the Month

With the harvest in, the stubble fields are dotted with colour. The bright red scarlet pimpernel opens only in sunshine, so it's known as 'the shepherd's weatherglass', and on the spent fields there are the delicate white stars of corn spurrey and the pink flowers, like miniature snapdragons, of weasel's snout; it's name coming from the shape of its hairy green fruit.

Damp meadows may hide meadow saffron. Its leaves go unnoticed during the spring and summer but, when they wither, the pink crocus-like flowers are left, so-called 'naked ladies'. Beautiful and

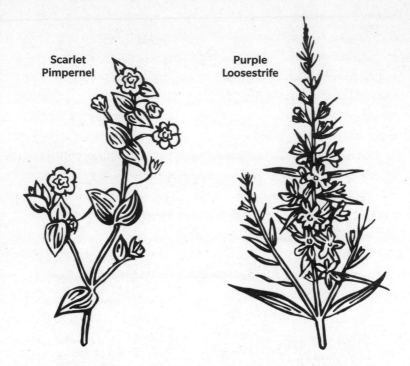

Scarlet Pimpernel

Purple Loosestrife

elusive this flower might be, but every part of it is poisonous, even to livestock, so don't confuse it with the saffron crocus, an escapee from gardens and nurseries. Meadow saffron is rare, but you'll find it growing around the Sheltered Lagoon in the London Wetland Centre.

With flowers becoming gradually fewer as the season changes, the drying mud at the edge of ponds, lakes, rivers and canals is a place to look for the season's blooms. Clusters of yellow flowers of the celery-leaved buttercup brighten these waterside places, along with the vivid blue flowers of brooklime, the four-petal yellow flowers of creeping yellowcress, the pink flowers of amphibious bistort and the impressively tall spikes of the magenta-coloured flowers of purple loosestrife.

Purple loosestrife is a valuable feeding station for bees, moths and butterflies, especially those with a long proboscis like red-tailed bumblebees and elephant hawk-moths. Other nectar sources are the clusters of pink flowerets of hemp-agrimony, known popularly as 'raspberries and cream', a favourite of small tortoiseshell and red admiral butterflies. Late season butterflies and moths are also attracted to the clusters of pink flowers of wild marjoram, the same species as the Mediterranean herb oregano, although with a slightly different scent.

Sand dunes and calcareous downland are the backdrops for the spirals of white flowers of autumn lady's tresses, a small orchid that looks uncannily like braided hair. It relies on an underground fungus to provide the nutrients and mineral salts it needs to bloom. Dunes and grasslands are also home to autumn gentian or felwort, its purple flower spikes a favourite of bumblebees, while salt marshes take on a distinct purple hue thanks to the tall mauve flowers of sea lavender.

Highest and lowest rainfall in millimetres recorded for September since 1910

☁	Highest		Lowest	
England	169.3	1918	7.9	1959
Wales	293.1	1918	11.7	1959
Scotland	267.6	1950	31.7	1972
Northern Ireland	193.9	1950	9.7	1986

 ## Late flyers

Despite the general drop in temperature, sunny September days will see several species of butterflies on the wing. Rough pastures have the wall brown, which gets its name from its habit of landing on bare surfaces and basking with its wings two-thirds open. It is tawny-orange with a large white eyespot on each forewing and smaller ones on the hind wings. Those flying in September could be the third generation of the year. The second generation of holly blues is among the late flyers. This species makes a seasonal switch in the food plant for its caterpillars, laying eggs exclusively on holly in spring and on ivy in the autumn. Woodlands are graced by the spectacular white admiral, a black butterfly with white patterning, which beats its wings in short bursts and then glides, much like a purple emperor, with which it can be confused.

A few of Britain's smaller butterflies are also about, like the fast and erratic-flying small copper, the brown hairstreak basking in the tops of bushes and trees, and the brown argus, which resembles a female common blue butterfly except that it sports a fringe of orange spots on the topside of the wings.

Other species are already preparing for winter. You might well find peacocks and small tortoiseshells hiding behind bedroom curtains, having found what they consider the ideal hibernation site. Unfortunately, central heating may cause them to wake and flap about, using up valuable food reserves, so try to move them to a sheltered outbuilding with access to the outside.

 House guests

As the nights draw in and house lights are switched on that little bit earlier, the illumination attracts green lacewings, and they are more than happy to enter our homes and stick around for the winter. Take a close look and you'll see their eyes are little nuggets of gold and their wings a lacy green, but not for long. During hibernation lacewings change colour, turning brown. In spring they turn back again to green. If you don't mind them lodging with you, they will eventually reward you by feeding on aphids. They are voracious predators, so horticulturalists are breeding them to patrol commercial greenhouses.

 Daddy longlegs

Autumn is most definitely the time for crane flies. The largest of the 300 known species has translucent wings, up to seven centimetres across, and even longer legs, and it's active now. Male and female can sometimes be found mating tail to tail, the male with the clubbed end to its abdomen and the female with a sharp tip. She can then be seen flinging herself into short grass or moss repeatedly, attempting to stab her egg-laying tool into the ground. The hatching larvae become grey leatherjackets that eat grass roots, so the bare patches they create in the lawn makes them unpopular with gardeners. Like many night-flying insects the adults are attracted to lit windows and will not hesitate to come indoors, where they fly about in an erratic, gangly manner.

Crane flies are more commonly known as 'daddy longlegs', an English name that has been given to several species of totally unrelated long-legged creatures. Harvestmen look like spiders, but they're not. They differ in having the body in one fused piece, and they don't produce silk or venom, whereas the spider has two parts to its body. With their eight long, slender legs, harvestmen are also called daddy longlegs, and they too are commonly active in the autumn. They can be found in damp corners and amongst the leaf litter. Many species are all legs and little body, what one scientist referred to as 'sultanas on stilts'! They may look delicate, but they have a range of effective defences. They can secrete a foul-smelling fluid, and if that fails to deter an aggressor, they can detach a leg, which continues to twitch because of a special 'pacemaker' in the first long segment of the leg.

Cellar spiders are also called daddy longlegs. When disturbed, they have the strange habit of vibrating rapidly, so the spider just becomes a blur. Despite its gangly appearance, it is an efficient predator. It is one of the few creatures that can take on a large house spider, and win, so with house spiders joining the autumnal procession of mini-bugs that want to spend the winter with us, cellar spiders are good to have about the house.

Highest and lowest average temperatures (°C) recorded for September since 1910

	Highest		Lowest	
England	20.8	1919	6.3	1986
Wales	19.3	1959	5.9	1986
Scotland	16.9	2006	4.5	1918
Northern Ireland	18.0	1959	6.0	1918

Fungus foray

Autumn means mushrooms and toadstools. Although fungi can be found throughout the year this is their big season, and the shapes and colours of their fruiting bodies are legion. Highly valued by mushroom aficionados are the cep porcini or penny bun and the chanterelle or girole.

The cep has a brown cap, like a crusty bread roll, with a white edge and its white stalk bulges, but you have to get it while it's young. Insect larvae and slugs like it too. It tends to pop up after a warm period with rain, after the soil temperature has dropped. The chanterelle has a funnel-shaped cap with a wavy margin, and can be from a pale yellow to a deep egg-yolk colour. The raised veins on the underside of the funnel distinguish the 'golden' chanterelle from the false chanterelle, the latter having tightly packed, forked

Fly Agaric

Cep

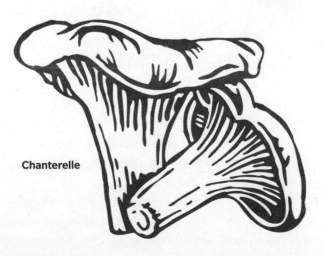

Chanterelle

gills that are more brightly coloured than the cap. The false chanterelle is bitter to eat. The cep is found mainly on woodland edges, close to oak, beech, birch and coniferous trees, while the chanterelle can be found in broad-leaved and coniferous woodland, often in a cushion of moss.

 ## Fatal fungi

One fungus you don't want to eat is the fly agaric. It's easy to identify, with its red cap and white warty spots, the quintessential toadstool frequently seen in fairy story illustrations. If eaten it causes stomach cramps, hallucinations and even death. Likewise, the white-coloured destroying angel and the olive-tinged death cap are two definitely to avoid. The death cap resembles a small puffball at first (see also page 225), before flattening out into a greenish or yellowish-coloured cap with a bulbous base to the stalk surrounded by a white sac, which is sometimes tinged with green inside. If eaten, there is no known antidote. The initial symptoms of vomiting and diarrhoea can last for several days before going away. What seems like a recovery changes dramatically, ending in death from kidney and liver failure. The only known remedy is a kidney or liver transplant.

Both these fungi can be confused with edible species. The field mushroom and wood mushroom occur in the same locations. Unless you are sure of a mushroom's ID, don't eat it. Stick to the mushrooms in the supermarket.

 ## Hedgerow temptations

Mushrooms are not the only autumn delicacies that foragers need to be careful with. The scarlet-red berries of white bryony or Devil's turnip, Britain's only native member of the cucumber family, are poisonous. The plant is recognised by its lobed cucumber-like leaves and tendrils. The shiny red berries of black bryony, which confusingly is not related to white bryony but is in the yam family, are poisonous too. Similarly, the red berries of bittersweet or woody nightshade are to be avoided. They are often on the plant at the same time as its mauve and yellow flowers are still blooming.

One of the more interesting berry producers is the spindle tree, a relatively small tree in hedgerows. Its dangling, glossy pink fruits have an extra, fleshy layer called an aril. This is more common in tropical plants than in temperate ones, but is a feature shared with the yew. Inside, the seed itself is bright orange. Like the others, spindle berries are poisonous.

However, we are not necessarily the target species for these plants to distribute their seeds. The brightly coloured berries are to attract birds. When the seeds inside the berries pass through a bird's gut and are ejected when it defecates, the seed is probably some considerable distance from its parent plant. It's an efficient way for a plant to distribute its offspring far and wide. It does mean, however, that we are in competition with birds for the berries we can eat.

Elder berries, for example, hang invitingly on red stalks and are consumed by blackcaps, whitethroats, and garden warblers, and a tree shaking as if in a storm is likely to be in the throes of an invasion by starlings. They strip the tree bare. The migrants among them are stocking up for their journey south, and it's a convenient fuel. The berries are small enough to be swallowed whole, have a relatively thin skin to digest, are rich in sugars, and the birds use very little energy to harvest them, unless of course they're competing with blackbirds, wood pigeons and those unruly gangs of starlings. Spotted flycatchers and redstarts might also join the fray, plucking off the insects that gather around the bruised and rotting berries. It's all a sweet and sticky farewell to summer.

Exploding plants

The pink orchid-like flowers of Indian balsam start to wither in the autumn. They have been a boon to the late nectar feeders, but this invasive species from Asia, with which we have an abiding love–hate relationship, is an explosive disperser. Its seedpods swell, and, as they dry, develop internal tensions. At the slightest touch they explode, scattering the seeds up to seven metres from the parent plant. Gorse, which flowers throughout the year, has a similar ballistic seed dispersing mechanism. Its hairy seedpods blacken and ripen in the sun, and on an especially hot, dry day they burst open with an audible crack. The diminutive hairy bittercress is another exploder. Standing little more than 30 cm tall, this little plant, with four-petal white flowers, grows on gravel, bare earth and even in the gaps between paving stones. Its seeds are contained in long, narrow, upright-pointing pod-like siliquae. When ripe the sides of the siliquae coil from the bottom to the top and, when touched, they burst, sending the seeds flying.

 # Bat swarms

Bats do something unusual this month. They swarm, behaviour shown by Daubenton's and Natterer's bats, as well as both species of pipistrelle. Natterer's bats, for example, swirl around together in large numbers outside the entrances to caves and other underground sites. It's thought that swarming is one way in which bats of the opposite sex from different summer colonies find each other. It's one way to freshen the gene pool and reduce the chance of inbreeding. The swarms consist mainly of males, with a ratio of about 4:1. Female bats might visit several different swarms in a night, although both sexes tend to attend the same sites year on year. The males also ensure they're ready for the action by roosting close to the swarming site, while the females tend to roost further away. The cave, whose entrance hosts the swarm, however, is not used for summer roosts, but it's likely to become the swarm's hibernation site during winter. It is thought the swarming behaviour has a secondary function. The bats possibly assess the site's potential as a winter home, and exchange information amongst themselves about the conditions in the cave, such as its microclimate, which will be important for their survival through winter.

Small is beautiful ... but metabolically expensive

Pygmy shrew populations peak in September. These tiny insectivorous creatures with tiny eyes, pointy face and a long nose, live life in the fast lane. They can be told apart from the other shrews by their longer tails, and they're much quieter when they go hunting. They feed almost all day and night on beetles, spiders and woodlice because they need to eat 125 per cent of their bodyweight each day to survive. One advantage of being small is that the shrew is less conspicuous to predators, but the price to be paid is that it has a large surface area compared to its volume, so it loses heat rapidly. It has to pile on the calories, but such frantic activity seems to limit how long it remains on this earth. Shrews live no longer than a year, so last year's babies will have raised this year's young, and they'll be pushing up the daisies by October. The pygmy shrew is one of our smallest mammals, a touch heavier than a pipistrelle bat, and it's found all over the country, although they're more common than common shrews on moors and boggy places, so these are the shrews you're likely to come across on, say, the North York Moors. They're absent from Shetland, the Scillies and Channel Islands, but are found on the Isle of Man and the islands of the Outer Hebrides.

Year of the Fox

Adolescent foxes are now almost indiscernible from adults in size and behaviour. Inevitably, foxes come from competitive families with skirmishes breaking out between parents and offspring as well as the usual sibling rivalries. Fights can be noisy and injuries to forepaws are common. As they hunt for the first time alone, young foxes still have the hedgerow harvest to sustain them.

 ## Tweet and greet

The sound of September is on heather moorlands. In the autumn, red grouse, a subspecies of the Eurasian willow grouse, begin to pair up. The male struts, puffs up its feathers and leaps into the air, calling with a distinctive series of guttural sounds that end with 'go-back, go-back, go-back'. Normally, its russet-coloured plumage offers good camouflage on the moor, so the birds are hard to spot, even though the male has bright red wattles above the eyes but, should you disturb them, you'll be confronted by frantic, whirring wing beats, and see the birds disappear rapidly over the brow of the hill. Heather moorlands and red grouse are to be found in upland areas throughout the British Isles, especially north and south west England, Wales, Scotland and Ireland. Look out also for birds of prey, families of stonechats and the bilberry bumblebee.

Highest and lowest hours of sunshine recorded for September since 1929

☼	Highest		Lowest	
England	191.6	1959	90.4	1945
Wales	197.3	1959	76.4	1956
Scotland	141.6	1959	67.9	1965
Northern Ireland	164.4	1991	72.5	1962

 ## When the tide goes out … and out

Around the time of the autumn equinox, low tides can be unusually low, exposing parts of the foreshore that are underwater for most of the rest of the year. It's a good time to go rockpooling, and hope for some exotic finds. A real treasure is the sea mouse. It gets its name from a similarity to a terrestrial mouse, except rather bedraggled and without a head! It's actually a polychaete or bristle worm that ploughs about in sandy mud. The sea mouse is about 15 cm long, with grey-brown bristles on its back and long iridescent hairs on its side that glisten red, blue, green and gold. They're a defence mechanism that gives a warning to potential predators. The underside resembles the sole of a shoe.

Look below flat stones at low water and underneath could be a squat lobster, but you have to be quick. One flick of its tail and it shoots backwards. If you have a net, place it behind the lobster and approach from the front. It'll dart right in.

We have more than 15 species of hermit crab, the most familiar being the common hermit crab, the largest species recognised by its size – up to 15 cm across the legs – and the large right claw. Adults often occupy the shells of common whelks, which they sometimes share with an intruding ragworm. The shells become covered in all sorts of creatures from barnacles and calcareous tubeworms to sea anemones. The stinging cells of the sea anemone protect the hermit crab from predators, and the anemone benefits from food thrown up by the crab, a relationship known as mutualism.

Rocks and seaweed are hiding places for the butterfish or rock gunnel. It's long, slender and eel-like, with rows of black or brown spots edged in white or yellow. It has a single dorsal fin running the length of its back. The butterfish gets its name from being extremely slippery and almost impossible to pick up on account of the mucus covering skin with no scales. If stranded, butterfish can breathe air and stay alive until the tide returns.

Several sea urchins might turn up in rockpools, the relatively small purple-tipped sea urchin being the most common, but amongst the kelp beds at very low water you just might come upon a whopper – the common sea urchin, whose hard shell or test is often sold in souvenir shops. Look closely and you'll see it is covered with short spines. Between the spines are tube feet, which are used for walking, and tiny pincer-like pedicellariae, which clean the urchin's shell, although you'll need a magnifying glass to see them.

To observe all these animals clearly and in their natural environment, one trick is to cut a large hole in the bottom of a plastic bucket and put transparent Perspex in its place. You'll have the shore walker's equivalent of a glass-bottomed boat, and you can watch shore life underwater without disturbing it.

 ## Coastwatch: whales and dolphins

From the path on top of a cliff, almost anywhere in the British Isles, you have the chance to spot sea mammals. A telescope or binoculars are useful, but many can still be seen with the naked eye. Simply find a headland, then sit, wait and watch, your chances of success greatly increased on a bright, calm day with a flat sea. Seals are common inshore, but just offshore are some of the largest animals that ever lived on Earth – not dinosaurs, but whales.

A surprising 29 species of whales and dolphins have been recorded around our shores throughout the year, and many come close to the shore when feeding or migrating. Watch out for seabirds feeding on the sea's surface, known as a 'hurry', as this is a likely spot for cetaceans also to be feeding down below, and check out moving boats for signs of dolphins riding their bow waves.

DOLPHINS

In Cardigan Bay, west Wales, and off the Scillies, Cornwall, large pods of common dolphins, some 500-strong, come inshore to feed. It is the species most likely to ride the pressure waves of boats, and is recognised by the yellow markings on either side of its body. They can be spotted on occasions almost anywhere along the south coast. In 2018, a couple of common dolphins made it as far as Hammersmith in the River Thames.

Other dolphin species include the white-beaked dolphin and Risso's dolphin, the latter recognised by its bulbous head with no beak and the white scars it carries on its head and back. Risso's have been recorded off north-west Scotland, Northern Ireland, west Wales and Cornwall, but by far the greatest numbers of sightings are of bottlenose dolphins, a large, grey-coloured dolphin with short beak and distinct melon on the forehead. A vantage point that regularly has bottlenose dolphins close to shore is Strumble Head, for bottlenose dolphins often appear in and around Cardigan Bay, west Wales. Two other hotspots are off Durlston Head, near Swanage, and in the Moray Firth on Scotland's east coast, but they can turn up almost anywhere around the British Isles. Along with harbour porpoises, they are probably the most commonly seen cetaceans in British waters.

PORPOISES

Almost anywhere around the British Isles, you can see harbour porpoises chasing shoals of herring into bays and estuaries. They're not particularly big, about two metres long, and are coloured dark grey on the back with lighter flanks. Unlike most of the dolphins, they have no beak, and a relatively low dorsal fin. You might even hear them, before you see them, for they make a loud spouting noise, while 'porpoising' in and out of the water, which, along with their slightly rotund shape, has led to the nickname 'puffing pigs'. In the Moray Firth, you might also witness bottlenose dolphins harassing and even killing porpoises; nobody knows why.

KILLER WHALES

Orcas or killer whales are more prevalent around Scottish coasts, particularly off Orkney and Shetland, although they have appeared off the Welsh coast, the Scillies and even in the English Channel, near Folkestone. Most pods are migratory, feeding either on fish or seals, depending on what is seasonally abundant, whilst one group living around the Hebrides, known as the 'west coast community', is resident and seems to prefer porpoises and minke whales to fish. One west coast individual named John Coe, recognised by a large notch in his tall, sword-like dorsal fin, has turned up off north east Ireland and Pembrokeshire and, in 2015, a lone unnamed male orca was seen devouring a seal pup off Strumble Head.

Other toothed whales include northern bottlenose whales, which have been seen around Skye, and long-finned pilot whales that occasionally visit Orkney and Shetland and have even been spotted off Northumberland.

MINKE WHALES

August is a good time to see minke whales on north-west coasts, especially in the Minches between the Scottish mainland and Tiree,

Orca

Minke

Humpback

Coll and Mull. Another hotspot is the Gulf of Corryvechan, between Jura and Scarba, where the whales feed in the third largest whirlpool in the world. On the east coast they have been seen as far south as Yorkshire, and on the west coast off Cornwall. At up to 11 m long, the minke is one of the smaller baleen whales. Look for the tall sickle-shaped dorsal fin, and, if you should be lucky to see one breach or spyhop, you'll see that the head and snout is a slender, pointed triangle, and the flippers have a distinct white band. The blow is not often visible, but they have a regular breathing pattern of 5–8 blows, each separated by about a minute, followed by a dive that can last up to 12 minutes.

GIANT WHALES

Humpback whales have also been seen off Scotland, especially Shetland, as well as off west Wales, and in parts of the south coast of England. One was just 100 m from the shore at Yyns Lochtyn, Ceredigion, another just ten metres from the beach at Slapton Sands, South Devon, and a third was seen from the Lands End Hotel near Sennen Cove, Cornwall. Humpbacks are instantly recognised by the 'hump' in front of the small dorsal fin. If lucky enough to see one breaching, you'll notice it has extremely long pectoral fins, and when it dives deep it raises its tail fluke to reveal a black-and-white pattern that is unique to each whale. Fin whales, the world's second largest living animal, are sometimes seen along the west coast of the British Isles, and 'lost' sperm whales have pitched up along the east coast, as did a sei whale (the third largest baleen whale), which appeared off Whitby in 2017.

These encounters with the giant whales are generally few and far between. For a better chance to see them, you need to visit the west coast of Ireland, where fin whales have been spotted from Cape Clear and Galley Head, in Cork, or take a specialised boat trip, like those from the Pembrokeshire coast that visit waters at the edge of the Celtic Deep. Here, the smaller whales and dolphins are common and fin whales are known visitors, and you just might bump into the largest animal that has ever lived – the blue whale … but that would need something vital to any whale-watching endeavour – oodles of good luck!

Sand castles and paddling pools

At first sight, the inter-tidal zone of a sandy beach might seem a barren place for wildlife. Waves are either eroding or depositing material on the shore so the sand is constantly shifting, and during autumn and winter storms anything living is pulverised by the surf. Yet, there is life here, and plenty of it, but you can't readily see it: it's buried beneath the sand. All it takes is to look for the right signs, and to do a little digging.

At very low water, around about the time of the autumn equinox, look for little dimples or holes in the wet sand close to the water's edge. They're signs that something is living there, and it could be one of three creatures – a crustacean, an echinoderm or a mollusc. If you dig and locate something immediately, it'll be one of the first two, and, if it disappears without trace it'll be the last one.

The crustacean is the masked crab. It is shaped more like a lobster, and both sexes have a pair of long claws, although the male's are exceptionally long, even longer than its body. It gets its name from the pattern on its back, which looks like a human face. The crab burrows backwards into the sand and breathes using its antennae. It fuses together the bristles on its second pair of antennae to form a tube through which it draws down oxygenated water. When the tide goes out, the tiny hole in the sand is where its breathing tube sticks up.

The echinoderm is the heart urchin or sea potato. It is heart-shaped rather than spherical like most other sea urchins, and covered by a dense mat of short, flattened spines. It burrows down to about five centimetres below the surface, and, like the crab, the hole in the sand marks the entrance to its narrow respiratory funnel, which it keeps open with its long tube feet. Occasionally, you might find urchins with tiny bivalve molluscs or amphipod crustaceans living in their burrows. Up to 14 molluscs have been found alongside a single urchin.

The third burrower is the razorshell or razorclam. It is a bivalve mollusc with long, narrow valves that are parallel-sided and slightly curved. When the tide is in it lives just below the surface of the sand, with two short siphons. It draws in water through one and expels it from the other, leaving a keyhole-shaped depression in the sand. However, if you try to dig this character out of the sand you'll have your work cut out. Using its long and muscular foot it can descend rapidly to a metre below the surface, well out of digging range. The clam, however, is ultrasensitive to salinity; so one way to catch one is to drop some table salt down the hole. The clam immediately shoots up to the surface!

Some creatures leave more obvious signs of life. The lugworm has two holes: a funnel-shaped entrance, down which water and food is drawn, linked by a U-shaped burrow to an exit marked by a little, but very obvious, pile of sand. The peppery furrow shell is a bivalve mollusc with two siphons, which burrows down to 20 cm deep. Its inhalant siphon is especially mobile and leaves star-shaped markings on the sand where the animal has been feeding.

Less obvious creatures can be found in pools of water left behind by the receding tide. Here the Perspex-bottomed bucket is useful (see page 256) or, failing that, replace the bottom of an ice cream or margarine tub with cling film and place it on the water. Brown shrimps try to hide by sweeping sand over themselves using their long antennae. Ghost shrimps, which are mycids rather than true shrimps, are invisible apart from their black eyes, the only part of them that has any pigments. And there might be fish trapped too, such as sand eels, dragonets and young plaice, topknots and flounders, but there is one fish that you will want to avoid – the lesser weaver.

The lesser weaver lies buried in the sand with just the first spines of its dorsal fin showing. Should you stand on a weaver, the spines stick into the foot and inject venom. The sting is very painful, but the toxins are denatured easily with very hot water, as hot as you can stand. Lifeguards on beaches in Devon and Cornwall will already have the kettle on by the time you reach them. As soon as they see somebody hobbling up the beach, they know it's a weaver!

 ## All washed up

While the strandline in winter is littered with mainly wood, plastic, shells and seaweed, later in the year jellyfish and their relatives arrive. The jellies come into shallow water, sometimes gathering in great numbers to breed. All it takes is a rough sea and an onshore wind, and they become stranded.

The most common jelly is the moon jellyfish. In the sea it resembles an upside-down saucer, with four distinct dark purple circles (reproductive organs), but on the beach it becomes a flat blob, coloured blue, with no long tentacles visible. It's harmless, so you can touch it without the fear of being stung. It's found almost anywhere around the British Isles.

An orange-brown blob with long tentacles is likely to be our largest jelly, the lion's mane jellyfish. It can be up to a metre across, with very thin tentacles that can be more than 20 m long, although by the time it is washed up, most of the tentacles will have broken off. However, don't touch them as they do sting. They have become common on Scotland's north-east coast.

The compass jellyfish is another common jelly. Its orange-brown bell has a pattern reminiscent of a compass face with 16 dark-brown V-shaped lines radiating from the centre. The pattern is evident even when the jellyfish is stranded. This one gives a painful sting so beware. Similarly, the mauve stinger jellyfish has a sting likened to an 'electric shock', and bluefire jellyfish stings are like a bee sting. Bluefires are common in Scotland, but are seen as far south as Lundy.

In recent years, the barrel jellyfish has been seen more frequently than it used to be. In the sea, the bell is up to 90 cm across and tan-coloured. On the beach it loses its colour, to become a large grey hemisphere of jelly, but its arms are very distinctive. Underneath it has eight thick arms, which have cauliflower-shaped tissues close to the bell and end with translucent paddles. As a plankton eater, its sting cells are harmless to humans. They are common on western coasts and in the English Channel.

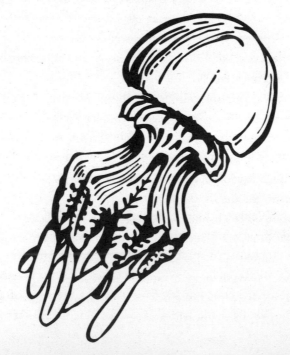

The Portuguese man o' war, on the other hand, has powerful stinging cells, capable of causing great pain, and, in at least two cases in the UK, it has caused deaths. Unlike the others, it is not a jellyfish, but a siphonophore. It is a colony of tiny animals, each specialised to do a specific job. When stranded, the purple balloon-like float is often still inflated, but do not touch the long, thin tentacles, even if the animal appears to be dead.

The stinging cells of both jellyfish and siphonophores can fire as long as the tentacles are wet, even though the rest of the jelly is dead. If you are stung, remove any jellyfish tentacles and scrape the area with a credit card to scrape away any sting cells left behind. It is said vinegar neutralises the poison, but who carries that to the beach? More practical is to apply a heat pack or immerse in hot water to relieve the pain and any swelling when you get home. Pain-killers also help, but if symptoms become more severe seek medical help immediately.

 ## Best bitter

The wild hop is a native British plant to be found mainly in the hedgerows and woodlands of the southern half of Britain. It often smothers other vegetation, coiling itself clockwise around other plants and anchoring its red-ridged stems with stiff, backward-pointing spines. It's a form of climbing that is described as a 'bine', contrasting with a plant with tendrils, which is called a 'vine'; so, hops should rightly be called hop bines rather than hop vines.

Male and female flowers grow separately, and the real ale enthusiasts amongst us would only be interested in the female flowers, for, when the cone-like fruits mature and turn a golden brown during September, they contain the vital ingredients that make beer taste bitter. These seed-cones or strobiles hang like bunches of grapes, and if you peel back the layers of overlapping, paper-thin bracts, you'll find yellowish-coloured granules scattered about the cone. They look like pollen but they're not. They contain a waxy blend of aromatic oils and resins, and it is these that flavour beer. They are also used as herbal medicine, good for inducing sleep, it is said. Pillows stuffed with hops apparently calmed down George III and helped him beat his insomnia.

Before the 15th century, beer was flavoured with all manner of plants, such as bog myrtle, ground ivy, dandelion, burdock root, marigold, heather, stinging nettle, spruce, and wormwood, but brewers found that beer keeps better if they use hops. Hops won out and the bines were eventually cultivated commercially, especially in Kent, for which the hop is the county flower.

 ## Arrivals and departures

The British Isles is a crossroads for bird migrants. Some are arriving for winter, others departing for warmer climes. There are also those that are just passing through, and an unlucky few that have been blown off course. They are all escaping something.

Throughout the month, many bird migrants are heading our way to avoid the extreme temperatures of the continental climate of mainland Europe. They come from the north east, to escape the freezing conditions of the Arctic, and from the south east to take advantage of the normally mild but wet maritime climate of the British Isles in winter. In recent years, things have been turned topsy-turvy. The position of the jet stream across the northern hemisphere has resulted in exceptionally cold, snowy weather across our islands, but most of the migrants have yet to change their annual cycle. It's business as usual for the estimated 17 000,000 birds that use the British Isles for migration.

The autumn migration is less frenetic than the spring. The urgency to reproduce has gone. Parent birds have done what they have to do, and now they have time to prepare their bodies for the long journey ahead. Across the country there are regular flyways and refuelling stops, and so headlands, bills, peninsulas, mulls and islands become key bird-watching sites. The inter-tidal zone on coasts in and around estuaries are where you can see migrating birds feeding or resting. Even your local supermarket car park, with its sugar-rich, berry-laden bushes between parking spaces, can be a migrant hotspot.

On the border between Scotland and England, the Tweed Estuary is a well-known gathering place for mute swans. In the autumn, swans from elsewhere join the 200 permanent residents, swelling the population to 800 birds at peak times. Some come as it's a safe place to moult, and then head back to their home waters, while others spend the entire winter here, along with other exciting birds, such as red-throated divers.

Flamborough Head in Yorkshire and Spurn Head at the mouth of the Humber project into the North Sea and are probably two of the best places in England to see bird migrants, which include young terns – Arctic, common and sandwich – which shadow their parents, learning about their home environment, before heading south. Divers, gannets, shearwaters, numerous species of waders join the throng, and even songbirds can be seen resting before they push on south. And, if you're really lucky, you might see a short-eared owl, recently arrived from the continent, out hunting during the day. It's a busy junction. Up to 15,000 birds have been seen to pass through Spurn on a single busy autumn day.

Close to Snettisham on the Wash and Cley on the north Norfolk coast, birds arrive from northern Europe in huge numbers, such as bar-tailed godwits and dunlin. Listen out for the loud honking of pink-footed geese, one of the first species of migrant geese to reach our shores from their breeding sites in Greenland, Iceland and Svalbard. 'Whistling' whimbrels are here too, passing through on their way to North Africa from breeding sites in the Western Isles and on Shetland. The Firth of Forth is another hotspot for them.

On the south coast, the cliffs of Beachy Head and the Seven Sisters are the places to see the last of the swallows and martins, and maybe even a young cuckoo or hobby. Portland Bill is the perfect place for migrants to pause before they tackle the English Channel. Great skuas, shearwaters, spoonbills, sanderlings, wheatears and ortolan buntings have been 'ticked' here, and there's a good chance to spot insect migrants like the painted lady butterfly and the silver-striped hawk-moth. In Poole Harbour, ospreys are sometimes seen fishing near the reed beds at Arne, before heading for Africa. Brent geese fly in from Russia, avocets arrive from Canada and Greenland, and even rare black-tailed godwits drop in. In winter, it can be home to 30,000 birds from north of the Arctic Circle and Europe.

During the autumn, the food-rich muds in Northern Ireland's Strangford Lough are a refuelling stop for passage migrants, and over winter the lough and other estuaries on the north coast play host to almost the entire world population of 30,000 light-bellied brent geese. They're joined by knot and bar-tailed godwit. In late September, Lough Beg might see the first of the whooper swans from Iceland, the rest following during October. Greylag geese, white-fronted geese, greenshank and wigeon are here too.

Around the Isle of Skye, on the Scottish west coast, large flocks of guillemots, razorbills and Manx shearwaters gather before heading south; great northern divers and Salvanic grebes overwinter offshore; and there's always the added bonus of spotting a golden eagle or the massive white-tailed eagle, both Scottish residents.

Holyhead in north Wales fills with continental birds heading east towards Ireland for the winter, and Bardsey Island and the Lleyn Peninsula will see many different songbirds passing through, with especially large numbers of willow warblers, chiffchaffs and goldcrests each autumn. Seabirds are a feature of St David's Head and Strumble Head, on the westernmost tip of south Wales, and rare transatlantic vagrants, blown way off course, drop in on the Scilly Isles – a twitcher's paradise.

 Sunrise and sunset times for Britain's capital cities

30th September	⌃ Sunrise	⌄ Sunset
Belfast	07.25	19.02
London	07.00	18.40
Cardiff	07.12	18.52
Edinburgh	07.14	18.50

OCTOBER

The night temperature drops markedly, a sure sign that the seasons are changing. By dawn, the grass is covered with dew but the sun is becoming so low that it might linger until late morning. The first frosts cause insect numbers to plummet and they trigger a renewed sense of urgency as hibernators stock up on food and look for safe places to spend the winter.

Millions of visitors are piling in from all points of the compass to spend the winter with us, the last of the leavers are on their way out, and our largest mammals are fighting it out for the right to father the next generation. On the farm, fields are ploughed and sown, and the rural landscape has become a blend of browns, reds and golden yellows as the leaves change colour and fall. Periods of quite mild weather can be shattered by storms that strip branches bare, burying the woodland floor in a thick carpet of leaves to be infiltrated by threads of fungal hyphae that break it all down, extract the nutrients and recycle them for the next growing year.

Sunrise and sunset times for Britain's capital cities

1st October	Sunrise	Sunset
Belfast	07.26	18.59
London	07.01	18.38
Cardiff	07.14	18.50
Edinburgh	07.16	18.47

 ## Hallowe'en

On the Scottish Island of Lewis an important annual ritual used to be performed on 31st October. That night, a farmer would wade into the sea, chanting as he went, to stir the sea-god Shony. He carried a cup of ale, specially brewed by the good folk of Bragar, and poured it into the sea, an offering that would encourage Shony to guarantee a good crop of seaweed to fertilise the fields during the coming year. After the ceremony, the people went to the church, blew out the altar candle, and repaired to the fields, where they drank ale, sang and danced the whole night through. The seaweed, though, had a sinister origin. Shony once caught a young girl in a net, but when she would not give him her love he anchored her to a rock and, even today, her long brown hair can be seen waving in the shallows at low water.

The redbreast's note is very sweet and pleasing; did it not carry with it ugly association of ideas and put us in mind of the approach of winter.

Gilbert White, 16th October 1776

 ## Flower of the Month

October might be the tenth month in our modern calendar, but the traditional month of Gort, from 30th September to 27th October, is the eleventh month in the Celtic Year, known as the Ivy Moon. It is the pagan month of the ivy flower, for this ubiquitous plant moves centre stage, one of the last wild flower spectacles of the year. Across the British Isles it is completely out of step with most other flowering plants, but, in one way or another, it has benefitted wildlife throughout the year, and is now a vital food source at a time when any surviving insects are faced with a dwindling supply.

It is often said that ivy strangles and sucks trees dead, but the reality is that it simply uses the tree for support, latching on with

specialised hairs. It's not a parasite. The evergreen leaves are 3–5 lobed in young plants and oval in mature ones, and the dark green foliage has been a nesting site for small birds, such as the diminutive wren, a summer roosting site for small bats, a hiding place for small mammals, and it will offer a dry hibernation site for insects during the coming winter. The flower buds, which only appear on mature plants, are food for the caterpillars of the holly blue butterfly. At dawn, the pompom-like umbels of yellow-green flowers secrete drops of nectar, a godsend for late flying insects, such as queen wasps, flies, moths and butterflies, which are drawn to the musty-scented flowers.

In southern parts of Britain and the Channel Islands, you might spot ivy's very own bee – the aptly named ivy bee, first recorded on the UK mainland in 2001. It's a touch smaller than a honeybee and can be recognised by a hairy orange-brown thorax and the bold black and yellow stripes on its abdomen. It is one of the last solitary bees to emerge, so it is relatively easy to identify. The female burrows into loose earth or sand creating underground chambers that she stocks with ivy pollen for her hatching larvae. Many females might nest close together in sand banks.

An even rarer visitor is the golden hoverfly, which has only been spotted in four places in south-east England. The fly is large and furry, with distinctive black antennae with white tips, golden bands of hairs across its abdomen, and just one pair of wings. The female lays her eggs in holes in rotting wood, where her larvae can feed on bacteria and fungi through the winter and spring, until they pupate and change into adults in late summer the following year. Should their nursery holes flood after an autumn or winter deluge, they have tail-like breathing tubes to help them survive.

The crown of Dionysus

In folklore, ivy has always been seen as a magical plant that will keep evil spirits at bay. The Romans crowned winners of poetry contests with ivy, and the ancient Greeks awarded the winners of athletic events with ivy wreaths. A wreath worn on the head was also a sure way to prevent you from getting drunk, and it is often depicted on the head of Dionysus, the god of wine and winemaking. In the British Isles it was also considered a symbol of faithfulness, so a newly married couple were given a sprig of ivy, a custom still maintained today by including ivy in a bride's bouquet. In the country, the last sheaf of the harvest was bound with ivy, the so-called harvest bride or ivy girl. It was given to the farmer who was last to bring in his harvest, a symbol of bad luck rather than good, and a penalty until harvest time the following year.

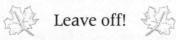 Leave off!

The changing colour of autumn leaves is one of the great wildlife spectacles of the month, and it's all down to some fancy chemistry. The trigger for this is not temperature, humidity or rainfall, but the hours of darkness and light, although those other factors can have an influence on the speed of the process. As the nights lengthen and the days shorten, there comes a critical time when the tree begins to produce a hormone that is sent to every leaf on the tree. The result is the production of a corky layer of cells that slowly cuts off the leaf from the rest of the tree and forms a protective seal. Eventually, all that holds the leaf to the tree are the vascular tissues – the xylem and phloem – and these break or are torn by the wind, and the leaf falls. Before the leaf is sealed off, however, it needs to retain as many of its nutrients as it can, so it's a race against time.

The first stage is to break down and reabsorb all the chlorophyll. This is the green pigment in leaves that is the key ingredient in photosynthesis. It's broken down and replaced throughout the summer, but in the autumn that process stops. It's expensive to produce chlorophyll and the other chemicals in leaves, so, when the tree discards its leaves, it doesn't want to throw them away. It breaks them down and stores the constituent parts for use again next spring. Leaves, however, are not only filled with chlorophyll. There are other pigments present too.

During the spring and summer, chlorophyll masks the yellow colour of xanthophylls and the red and orange colours of carotenoids. With the chlorophyll gone, these colours shine through, presenting us with such a dramatic autumnal display. It is short lived, however, for they are also degraded and reabsorbed. Only waste products, such as tannins, are left behind, giving the leaf its final brown colour.

So, why does a tree do this? Basically, leaf fall is a form of self-protection. Leaf surfaces lose water during the natural process of transpiration, so when the temperature drops in winter and frosts are on the ground, less water is available to be absorbed by the roots. The tree experiences what amounts to a drought, so keeping its leaves would hasten the process of dehydration. The leaves of deciduous trees are also relatively delicate and would easily rupture because of the ice that would form inside their cells, and, in high winds, a deciduous tree in full leaf would be highly vulnerable to be blown over.

In Britain, the first trees to change the colour of their leaves are usually horse chestnut, elder and beech, the beech having stunning russet-brown leaves that generally remain on the tree through winter, as do the leaves of the oak. The leaves of wild service trees resemble maple leaves and turn a vivid coppery-red in October, a sure sign of ancient woodland, and the yellow leaves of aspen – one of the first trees to colonise Britain after the last Ice Age – shimmer in the breeze.

As gardeners, we tend to clear all the leaves from lawns and flowerbeds, but it's not a bad idea to leave a few. Earthworms pull them down into the soil and help enrich it; in fact, if you have a look at night, you might catch a worm doing just that.

 ## Highest and lowest rainfall in millimetres recorded for October since 1910

	Highest		Lowest	
England	164.8	2000	15.9	1969
Wales	303.5	1967	30.8	1947
Scotland	258.1	1935	19.4	1946
Northern Ireland	210.7	2011	34.2	1951

 ## The gall of it!

With the leaves gone, many plants can be seen to sport galls. Minute wasps cause them to form by tricking the plant into producing an ideal home for their offspring. The female deposits her eggs in the plant's tissues, and the tiny hatching grubs irritate their host so much that it produces extra tissue to isolate them. The grubs live inside the gall, safe from the vagaries of the weather and with food on tap to fuel their development.

The most obvious galls are the smooth, round, marble-sized galls on common and sessile oak trees, so-called 'oak nuts' or oak marble galls. They are to be found on oak buds, where they are coloured green at first, turning to brown as the seasons pass. Each has a single wasp larva developing inside, and by autumn it will have a tiny hole in the side, like a woodworm hole, indicating that the occupant has already grown up and fled; no hole, and it's still inside. The emerging adult female is asexual but it lays eggs in the buds of turkey oaks, where they continue to develop until spring, when the next generation of sexual adults emerges, mates and lays eggs in an oak tree once again to form next year's galls. Lesser-spotted wood-peckers, bank voles and yellow-necked mice are known to break open galls in order to feed on the larvae inside, and blue tits peck holes in the woody gall to reach them.

The wasp itself is not a native species. It was introduced to south west England by accident. Ink makers imported marble galls from the eastern Mediterranean. The tannic acid they contained made excellent ink. The wasp, of course, came with them, and it soon spread throughout the British Isles.

Titmice and finches search in the leaf litter below oak trees for another type of gall – the spangled gall. It forms as a tiny yellow or ginger-brown dimpled disc on the underside of oak leaves, each with an even tinier inmate. In the autumn the galls drop to the woodland floor or they fall with the leaves, where they spend the winter. Female wasps emerge in spring and lay their eggs in the oak's male catkins, causing round, yellowish-green fleshy galls to form, called currant galls.

A fourth type of gall on the oak is the oak apple. At up to four centimetres across, it is much larger than the marble gall, and is a flat-tened sphere. While the marble gall is woody, the oak apple is spongy in texture and coloured brown and white with a touch of pink. It too is caused by a gall wasp, and inside are up to 150 wasp larvae each with their own chamber. When the adult wasps emerge the gall is riddled with holes, and they are the sexual generation of this species. Their eggs are laid on the roots of the oak, where they cause marble-like galls to form. The asexual female worms its way out and lays its eggs in a leaf bud, where the oak apple is formed. And, if that's not all, there are silk button galls, oak cherry galls, acorn or knopper galls, and oak artichoke galls that form on the oak's male catkins. They're just a few of the 30 or so types of gall that can form on an oak tree.

Many plants have their fair share of galls too. Of the most common: robin's pin cushion is a red, feathery structure on wild roses; tassel galls, caused by the jumping plant louse, are found on the flower heads of rushes; reed cigar gall is, as its name suggests, cigar shaped and forms on reed stems; the prickly witch's broom is caused by a fungus and is found in birch and cherry trees; the red inverted comma shape of the nail gall is found on the underside of lime leaves; the spruce pineapple gall is caused by aphids; and the fern gall is made by a fly that causes the tips of fern leaves to curl and deform. They are just a few of the more than 1,000 types of galls that we can find here in the British Isles.

 Fungus foray

October is still very much mushroom and toadstool season. The fruiting bodies of the shaggy ink cap appear on lawns, grass verges on roadsides, and just about anywhere the soil has been disturbed. At first it forms an elegant conical shape cap with flaking scales, reminiscent of a lawyer's wig, its alternative common name, but when most of its spores have been released, it degenerates into an inky black mess from which any spores left behind are carried away by flies. There are several species, some growing on cow or horse dung. They can be found throughout the British Isles, but are only edible when young and fresh.

Among the most intriguing shapes at this time of the year are the earthstars. Starting out like puffballs, they split, with the star-shaped flaps lying flat to the ground, surrounding a ball-shaped spore sac, stalked in some species and unstalked in others. The most widespread species is the collared earthstar, without a stalk. If you gently poke the onion-shaped sac, the spores squirt out. Normally raindrops would do the same job.

For startling colour, the waxcaps cannot be beaten. They grow on grasslands, and stand out because of their vivid colours – red, yellow, orange, apricot, pink, blue-green, lilac and green, but the brightest must be the scarlet waxcap, which almost glows against the green background of grass. The group gets its name for the cap, which is typically waxy, slimy or greasy.

For geometric precision, the red-cage fungus is a winner. It's a relative of the stinkhorn and just as smelly, starting out as an egg-shaped ball in the same way, but when the outer layer of the egg bursts, it expands to form a vermillion, basket-like lattice, up to 15 cm across. Insects, attracted to the smell, spread the spores, which are in a layer of green goo inside the basket. It is common in the Channel Islands, but rare in mainland Britain.

Most of these extraordinary fruiting bodies grow, erupt and collapse within 24 hours, or, at best, a few days, but during that short time they become the elevated launch pads for fungal spores. They are blown by the wind and, in *Autumnwatch* 2017, Gillian Burke shows just how important they are.

'When the spores land,' she explains, 'they send out feeding tubes, known as hyphae. They ooze a cocktail of enzymes that rot and digest putrefying organic matter, absorbing the nutrients that are released. They grow and divide, creating a web of hungry fingers probing for sustenance – a living, creeping recycling machine.'

It means the intricate tangle of thin, thread-like filaments hidden below our feet, rather than the showy mushrooms, are the engine room of the fungus, the whole caboodle known as the 'mycelium'. In some species the mycelium wraps itself around plant roots, leaching out precious sugars but, in return, it helps feed the plant with nitrogen and phosphorus.

'This unlikely alliance is so important,' Gillian points out, 'that 90 per cent of our plants are utterly reliant on fungi for survival. By breaking down dead wood, cleaning the soil, and recycling nutrients by the most intimate relationship with living plants, fungi are vital to life on Earth.'

Curiously, despite being very familiar living things, scientists down the centuries have had difficulty in classifying fungi. Their fruiting bodies look like plants, but fungi are more closely related to animals. Like animals, they cannot make their own food, and they have been on this planet for an awfully long time – about 1.5 billion years!

 ## Sugar spree

Wasps can be a problem in the autumn. Starting in September and continuing into October, worker wasps have completed their brood-rearing duties. Their old queen has lost her influence over them, and so they fly about drowsily. They have nothing to do until they die during the first frosts, although a few will survive into November.

Throughout the summer they hunted for insects to feed the new generation of wasp larvae, and in return the grubs rewarded them with a sugary secretion. With their sugar source gone, they have to find other ways to get a sugar rush, so they are attracted to sweet things, such as rotting berries and windfall fruits, as well as jam sandwiches at picnics on fine autumn days. The queens, however, are very busy.

During September they will have embarked on a nuptial flight to mate with the males, sometimes ending with a rough-and-tumble session on the ground, but now they search for their winter hideaway. The queens generally spend the winter behind loose tree bark, under eaves, and the tin roofs of garden sheds. They seem almost to shut down, their wings flat against the body, legs folded in and their jaws gripping firmly the surface underneath – the 'hibernation pose'.

The old nest is never re-used so if you come upon one, say, in an outhouse, you can safely dissect it. It is usually about the size of a soccer ball and made of paper. The wasps might well have scraped off wood from your garden furniture to make it. They chew the wood and mix it with saliva; not very different to the way we make paper. If you gently tear it apart you'll see that it consists of up to 12,000 hexagonal cells. These are the brood cells in which the larvae fattened and developed. What you won't see is that in the ceiling and walls of each cell there are particles of a weakly magnetic mineral called ilmenite, an ore of titanium, which serves as a kind of reference point for ensuring the symmetry of the cells and the orientation of the nest during its construction in the dark, much like the keystone in a building. In the spring the new queens will emerge from their hibernation sites to start the precision building process all over again.

 # Highest and lowest average temperatures (°C) recorded for October since 1910

	Highest		Lowest	
England	17.3	1921	2.8	1919
Wales	16.3	1921	3.9	1912
Scotland	13.6	1959	1.9	1981
Northern Ireland	15.1	1969	3.1	1917

 Going nuts!

Oaks are shedding their acorns this month. They drop to the woodland floor, where an insulating layer of fallen leaves is waiting to protect the developing seeds from frost. Even so, many will be eaten or stored by jays, wood pigeons, mice and squirrels. The wood pigeons are binge eaters. They consume them greedily, keeping as many as 12 at a time in their crop, with no interest in stashing food away to be consumed later when times are hard. Jays, on the other hand, plan ahead. They cache them for the winter, up to 3,000 in a single month, but their initial zeal is tempered by their unfortunate knack of forgetting where they buried most of them, so germinating seeds are spread far and wide. Nuthatches jam them into crevices in bark and hammer at them noisily until they gain access to the protein-rich seed inside. They collect hazelnuts too. They're unusual birds in that they can clamber down a tree trunk headfirst, sometimes meeting tree creepers climbing up.

Grey squirrels tend to pick hazelnuts while they're green, so native animals, which prefer the ripe nuts, are deprived of them. However, their digestive system can't cope with too many at a time, so they are buried for later consumption. Like the jays, they forget where they've hidden their nuts, so the hazel saplings get a chance to grow.

Red squirrels, which are making a comeback in some parts of the country, are out collecting fruit and nuts, like the other hoarders. When they come to bury them, they first pretend to do it several times, in case an interloper intent on filching their cache is watching. The squirrels are beginning to look their best at this time of year. During the summer, the tufts of hair on their ears were missing but, in the autumn, they grow back, so it's a good time to look for and admire them. They're solitary now that the breeding season is over, but it's the time when you're more likely to see them, especially at dawn and dusk, because there are many youngsters out searching for their own territories. Loud 'chuck-chuck-chuck' calls and a frantic waving of tails accompany any of their highly charged confrontations.

 ## Where to see red squirrels

Brownsea Island in Poole Harbour; Borthwood Copse and Bouldnor Forest on the Isle of Wight; Castle Eden Dene in County Durham; Snaizeholme Red Squrrel Trail in Yorkshire; Throckley Pond near Newcastle; Kielder Water and Forest Park, Allen Banks,

Staward Gorge, Wallington, East Cramlington Pond, Holystone North Wood, Holystone Burn, Tony's Patch in Northumberland; Whinfell Forest, Whinlatter Forest Park, Aira Force, Miterdale, Grizedale Forest, Smardale Gill and Wreay Wood in Cumbria (whose reds tend to have blonde tails); Sefton Coast, Freshfield Dune Heath in Lancashire; Formby near Liverpool; Dalbeattie Forest in Dumfries and Galloway; Loch of the Lowes in Perthshire; Glenmore Forest Park in the Cairngorms; Belvoir Forest Park and Lagan Valley Regional Park near Belfast; Mount Stewart in County Down; Clocaennog Forest in North Wales; and Plas Newydd, Myndd Llwydiarth and Newborough on Anglesey.

 ## Incy Wincy spider

With the morning mist comes gossamer. Young spider and adult money spider numbers peak at this time of year, and their silken threads crisscross the meadow. Tiny droplets of water from the atmosphere condense on the strands to create a silvery 'gossamer day'. As the threads dry and the morning breeze picks up, the spiders are hoisted into the air in a behaviour known as ballooning. Generally they find a high point from which to launch themselves into the air, produce several strands of silk that wave in the wind, like a parachute, then they let go and off they fly. It's the way young spiders travel on the mild mornings of an Indian summer.

Their bigger relatives are also more obvious this month. The female garden orb-web spider, the one with the cross on her abdomen, can often be seen in the centre of her orb web, her body swollen with up to 900 eggs. When ready, she'll spin a silken sheet for the newborn and stand guard until the spiderlings disperse, no doubt on their silken parachutes.

Even more spectacular is the female wasp spider. She too is reaching full-size, her body about 1.5 centimetres long, but it is the colour that is striking – wide yellow stripes alternating with narrow black stripes. Her web is usually slung low down, in order to catch grasshoppers and crickets, and has a conspicuous zigzag pattern of white silk, known as a stabilimentum, which reflects ultraviolet light. Scientists are unsure what its function may be. Some say it could entice in more prey, because ultraviolet light is visible and attractive to insects. Others suggest it warns large animals not to run or fly into it and damage the web.

The wasp spider is a European beauty that arrived here in the 1940s and is now widespread along the south coast, as far west as Cornwall. It has been spotted in recent years around London, and one place to see it is the uncut meadows in Bushy Park.

 Year of the Fox

It's the month most young male foxes come of age. The fox family disperses, with young adults being the first to leave. It's a treacherous time. If the young dog fox crosses into an occupied territory he will be seen off in no uncertain terms. However, he is most at risk from traffic as he strikes out into unfamiliar terrain, searching for a vacant patch of land. His diet contains less fruit and more earthworms at this time of year.

 Stag party

Our largest native mammal is in a feisty mood this month. It's the rut. Red deer stags are competing for the right to mate, and they don't care who's in the way, so watch out. However, they do … at least to our eyes … the most absurd things.

First they bellow loudly with deep guttural belches, trying to match or beat opponents roar for roar, and, if that doesn't impress, they thrash the undergrowth with their antlers to such an extent that they end up wearing a ragged and (frankly rather silly) 'hat' of dangling vegetation. Their coats are often darkened because they roll in their own urine. If a challenger is unimpressed, then things get serious. It's time for a bit of parallel walking, and, when this happens, trouble is not far away.

The stags size up one another, walking first one way and then the other. They will have put on a lot of muscle around the neck, so they hold their heads high, their fully grown antlers with up to 16 points on mature stags, ready to do battle. If they are about equal in stature and the confrontation has gotten this far, it's unlikely one will back down. At some unknown signal, they clash antlers. One aim is to dominate the higher ground, and they push for all they are worth to stop their opponent from moving them backwards. If one loses ground, it is eventually the loser, but if the two are equally matched the fighting can result in the death of one of the contestants.

Fallow and sika deer rut at this time too. Fallow deer are not as noisy or violent as their larger relatives. Bucks have more flattened antlers, similar to the extinct giant Irish elk to which it is related, but they use them in the same way as red deer when bucks come to blows. Strategies can vary. Some bucks have a rutting stand, often below an oak tree, and does come to check them out. There can also be several bucks and few does, like a lek, in which the does again do the choosing, or a buck, with a harem of many does, is challenged by another buck who fancies his chances. Sika stags defend territories, which usually includes a wallowing hollow, and/or a bevy of hinds. Unattached males probe these areas, seeking out a stag to challenge. Their calls vary from burps to screams and even loud whistles.

 ## Where to watch deer

- Exmoor National Park: private companies organise red deer safaris.
- New Forest, Hampshire: all six deer species are present.
- Richmond Park, Surrey: red and fallow deer in the city park.
- Woburn Abbey Deer Park, Bedfordshire: red and fallow deer, Père David's deer, sika, axis, rusa deer, barrasingha, Chinese water deer and muntjac.
- Minsmere, Suffolk: England's largest red deer herd; RSPB has 4WD excursions.
- Cannock Chase, Staffordshire: five species – red, fallow, roe, sika and muntjac.
- Fountains Abbey and Studley Royal Park, North Yorkshire: 500 red deer.
- Lyme Park, Cheshire: red and fallow deer in an ancient hunting estate.
- Levens Hall Deer Park, Cumbria: black-coated herd of fallow deer.
- Aviemore, Inverness-shire: red and roe in Caledonian pine forest in Ryvoan Pass.
- Isle of Jura, Inner Hebrides: Jura is Norse for 'deer island'.
- Isle of Rum: site of a long-term red deer study.

Highest and lowest hours of sunshine recorded for October since 1929

☀	Highest		Lowest	
England	138.4	1959	60.5	1968
Wales	119.5	2010	49.6	1968
Scotland	106.4	2003	49.1	1935
Northern Ireland	114.7	1939	53.4	2011

 ## UK's newest damsel

Richmond Park is not only the place to see rutting deer, it is also the adopted home of a new arrival on these shores – the willow emerald damselfly. This flying jewel was first recorded in any numbers in Suffolk in 2009, and with our warming climate it is spreading, as far north as Gibraltar Point in Lincolnshire, south to the Channel coast of Kent and as far west as Tattenhoe Park in Milton Keyes, Buckinghamshire. It is one of four species of emerald dragonflies living in this country; a group known for its habit of resting with the wings partly open, rather than closed as with other damselflies.

The willow damselfly is also unique in that it deposits its eggs not on aquatic plants, but on the branches of willow or alder trees overhanging the water. The female stabs the bark and lays two eggs in each star-shaped hole. Here, they overwinter, hatching out in spring. The nymphs drop directly into the water and develop in the usual way but, for now, the aerial displays of courting males and females are a brand-new autumn spectacle.

 ## Big-eyed seal pups – seriously cute!

About 50 per cent of the world's population of grey seals breeds on British coasts, and they drop their pups later in the year than do common seals. Late October is a good time to see the first arrivals. A pup is born with a white coat, which is warm but not waterproof, and it is left on the beach while its mother continues to search for food at sea. She returns frequently to feed milk to her offspring, and it is so rich in fats – about 60 per cent, that it gains weight by about 2 kilograms a day. After just three weeks, it is abandoned and must fend for itself. By this time it has grown its waterproof juvenile coat and insulating blubber jacket, and, after the moult is complete, it goes to sea. The mother, meanwhile, mates almost immediately but development of the fertilised egg is delayed, so the next pup will be born at the same time next year.

 ## Where to watch grey seals

About 25,000 grey seals are to be found around the Orkney Islands, a tranquil spot to watch them being the Brough of Birsay. They start pupping in October. The low-lying, uninhabited Monarch Islands of the Outer Hebrides are an undisturbed refuge for a large number of grey seals. It's an excursion by boat on calm days, for the sea can be pretty wild when the wind gets up.

Skomer Island, off the south-west tip of Pembrokeshire, has about 160 births a year, and they also start to pup in October. At low tide at Mutton Cove, in west Cornwall, grey seals can be seen from the cliff top at Godrevy Point, which overlooks the cove, and in nearby Falmouth Bay, seals can be observed at Pendennis Point.

There are key grey seal rookeries at Blakeney Point and Horsey Beach in Norfolk, although you might encounter them almost anywhere around the Norfolk coast, basking on sandbanks. Pupping here starts a little later in November. Viewing areas at the foot of the sand dunes at Donna Nook, in Lincolnshire, make this an accessible place to watch them without disturbing the mothers.

One of the largest grey seal rookeries on the east side of the country is on the Farne Islands, off the Northumberland coast, where up to a thousand pups are born each year. Inquisitive mothers will often approach and swim alongside organised boat trips. Chanonry Point, Portgordon and Findhorn on the shores of the Moray Firth are also grey seal spots, the Moray Firth being the breeding area for about 90 per cent of British grey seals.

Wherever you are, be sure not to disturb the mother grey seals. Don't go too close. They are easily spooked and might abandon their pups. If watching from the land, keep dogs under strict control, or, even better, leave them at home. Don't approach a seal that appears to be dead; it may only be sleeping. Seals bite! Seal bites often become infected and are slow to heal.

 ## Seasonal spectacle

If it's October, the RSPB Snettisham Nature Reserve on the Wash, in north-west Norfolk, is a must. Each year at this time more than 40,000 waders gather here to roost; the majority are knots, dumpy wading birds with relatively long wings. Knot watchers say it's one of the most dependable wildlife spectacles in the country, but you have to be up before dawn to see it.

The birds feed on mudflats and in saltmarshes, but they are submerged during high tides, especially spring tides, so the knots have to move up the shore. As the water creeps higher, they are packed ever tighter together, until the entire foreshore becomes a living, moving grey carpet. When they take to the air en masse, the aerial ballet is breathtaking. The birds wheel back and forth like a giant, dark amoeba, with rippling streaks of silver from the underside of their wings spreading through the dense flock. Bird watchers say that you can feel the rush of air from their wings as they swoop low overhead. They head for their high tide roost, until the tide turns, and a trickle of smaller batches of birds return once more to feed.

The knot spectacle is not confined to Snettisham. These birds can be seen in large numbers at the following muddy estuaries: Ribble Estuary and Morecambe Bay, Lancashire; Dee Estuary, Cheshire; Humber Estuary; Thames Estuary; Solway Firth; Firth of Forth; and Montrose Basin.

 ## Coastwatch: strandlines

Autumn storms throw up all kinds of interesting flotsam and jetsam onto the country's beaches.

The steeper the beach the more obvious the strandline, and one of the most common pieces of natural flotsam is a clump of papery, polystyrene-like egg cases of the common whelk, and they are not the only leftovers from the spring and summer breeding seasons. The predatory sting winkle's egg cases resemble a partly eaten corn-on-the-cob, with tiny upside-down, heart-shaped chambers. The necklace shell or moon snail produces a collar-shaped skirt around its shell to protect its eggs, and this falls away after the eggs have hatched.

Squid eggs look like the head of a mop. The mother usually deposits them in safe places, but the sea is fickle and occasionally they are ripped from the nest site and end up on the beach. Camber Sands in East Sussex is one beach where they sometimes wash ashore. The lumpfish is a small, dumpy fish of rocky coasts, whose pectoral fins are modified like suckers. Its eggs or roe are a culinary treat of local caviar, but, when washed ashore after the breeding season is over, they look like a dried mass of tapioca pudding.

The brittle 'bone' of the cuttlefish, so loved by pet budgerigars, is all that's left of the dead cephalopod. In life, the cuttlebone is an internal shell that supports the animal's body, a bit like a backbone, and it is chambered and filled with gas so functions also as a buoyancy aid. Shells of gastropod molluscs, of course, are carried on the outside of the body, and those of mussels, cockles, razorshells and the occasional oyster can usually be found on the strandline.

Goose barnacles look like molluscs, but they are crustaceans. They are the stalked open ocean relatives of the acorn barnacles of rocky shores, and they resemble young barnacle geese, hence the common English name. After a storm, they might well be washed ashore attached to driftwood. The wood itself might be riddled with wood-boring animals, such as the shipworm – not a worm, but a wood-eating mollusc, and the clam-shaped common piddock, which can even burrow into rock. Many small holes in driftwood could be the work of the gribble, a tiny isopod crustacean that can occur in such numbers that it can make light work of a wooden wharf, which might well break up and fall into the sea during the next autumn or winter storm.

A rare arrival is the by-the-wind sailor, and it usually turns up in huge numbers, littering entire beaches. These non-stinging cousins of the Portuguese man o' war have a prominent sail on top of their disc-shaped bodies, coloured a deep blue. Normally they float offshore on the sea's surface, the wind filling their sails to propel them downwind or at a slight angle to the wind to who knows where. During a storm things may not go to plan and they are washed ashore, where they bleach to a ghostly white. Interestingly, some have a sail that is set like a backslash (left-handed) and others a forward slash (right-handed). This could reflect a preference for sailing direction in the northern and southern hemispheres, or it could have something to do with reducing the chance of pitching up on eastern or western shores at the edge of the ocean. Nobody knows which is true.

 ## Arrivals and departures

This month the travellers are fish – Atlantic salmon, sea trout and European eels. The salmon and trout are arriving and the eels leaving, both having embarked on extensive journeys that take them in and out of saltwater and fresh in order to breed.

In the autumn, an adult salmon arrives at the same river it left as a smolt, a couple of years previously. It has been out in the North Atlantic and Norwegian Sea feeding and rapidly fattening up and when it returns, navigating most of the way probably by the Earth's geomagnetic field, it recognises the 'smell' of its home river. After a period of autumn rains, when the river is in full spate, the salmon heads upstream. Salmon usually go by day and sea trout make the journey at night. They leap over barriers, such as small waterfalls, rapids and weirs, sometimes taking ten or twenty attempts before success. Bigger obstructions, such as dams, often have fish ladders with observation windows in the side, such as the fish ladder at Pitlochry, where you can see salmon or trout swimming past. They continue up the river to their headwaters until they reach gravel beds suitable for spawning. These are the salmon redds, where a female uses her tail to excavate a shallow depression in which to deposit her eggs, and a male moves alongside to deliver his milt. Many fish die immediately afterwards. Only a few, now called 'kelts', make it back to the sea. One individual in an Irish River returned three times to spawn.

The adult eel travels the opposite way. On moonless autumn nights eels squirm over wet grass, taking shortcuts from one stream to another, in order to find the river that will take them quickly to the sea. They will have been in freshwater for the best part of a decade, growing, developing and fattening up for the moment – and nobody knows what the trigger is – that they are ready to start out on an extraordinary journey to breed.

They develop large eyes, silver flanks and white bellies, like an open ocean fish which is darker on the back than the belly, a pattern known as countershading. The dark colour blends in with the ocean depths, hiding them from predators above, while the white belly blends in with the sunlight coming from the surface, camouflage against predators below.

The destination of these silver eels, which can be up to a metre long, is the Sargasso Sea, in the North Atlantic about 5,000 kilometres away, and they have to get there by April to have a chance to spawn successfully. Left to themselves they wouldn't make it, so, instead of swimming as the crow flies, the eels get a helping hand by following the currents of the North Atlantic Subtropical Gyre, first towards the Azores and then around towards the Caribbean and into the Sargasso. At night they swim close to the surface, but during the day they dive down to as much as 1,000 metres. They do not feed en route, so it might be a way to avoid predators. It might also be a way to arrive on time and ready to breed. The warmer waters during the night ensure that the metabolism of this cold-blooded fish is at an optimum to speed it along, while the cooler waters by day slow their sexual development so they maintain their streamlined shape. Ironically, although marine biologists know that spawning takes place in the Sargasso, they have yet to actually find an eel there. The story of our common eel continues.

Sunrise and sunset times for Britain's capital cities

31st October	Sunrise	Sunset
Belfast	07.25	16.49
London	06.53	16.35
Cardiff	07.05	16.47
Edinburgh	07.18	16.34

NOVEMBER

November marks the return of winter, a time of short days, cold winds and the first hard frosts. It's dark and can be damp, and the leafless landscape is stark against the grey background of cloudy skies, but, with the vegetation gone, birds' nests are clearly visible and animal runways easier to spot. And, compared to the icy Arctic and mainland Europe's continental climate of extremes, our maritime climate is still relatively mild, so the British Isles is a favoured place for many birds to spend the winter.

 ## Sunrise and sunset times for Britain's capital cities

1st November	↑ Sunrise	↓ Sunset
Belfast	07.27	16.47
London	06.54	16.33
Cardiff	07.07	16.45
Edinburgh	07.20	16.31

 ## Beechnuts, ducks and squirrels

The first of the month is All Saints' Day. It is said that if a beechnut is wet on this day, it will be a wet and windy winter, but if it is dry, it will be a hard one. Similarly, on the 11th, which is St Martin's Day or Martinmas, the behaviour of ducks provides us with a weather sore:

If ducks do slide at Martinmas
At Christmas they will swim.
If ducks do swim at Martinmas
At Christmas they will slide.

St Andrew's Day on the 30th was the traditional day for hunting squirrels, but with so much ale drunk by the would-be hunters, together with much merriment, mischief-making and bad behaviour, most squirrels had an evens chance of surviving till nightfall.

> Leaves fall very fast. My hedges show beautiful light & shades: the yellow of the tall maples makes a fine contrast against the green hazels.
>
> Gilbert White, 2nd November 1780

Flowers of the Month

There are only a few plants flowering this month. Most are small and lodged in places with favourable microclimates. The white flowers with deeply lobed petals of common chickweed are common on roadside verges and waste ground. The whorls of purple flowers of red dead-nettle occur in the stubble fields of arable farmland. There are clusters of small white flowers, like flat umbrellas, of yarrow, and the dandelion-like flowers of autumn hawkbit. The bright blue flowers of common field speedwell are found growing on farmland and in gardens.

Groundsel flowers all year round, and white dead-nettle flowers in November despite having clusters of white-green flowers, resembling an Elizabethan neck ruff, that should be pollinated by bees. Most bees, of course, will have disappeared after the first frosts, but a few bumblebees, such as white-tailed and buff-tailed bumblebees, are still flying in parts of the far south west of England, and continue to do so throughout the winter.

One unusual 'flower' is the carline thistle. Although the flowers have been dead since the autumn, they open again on sunny days.

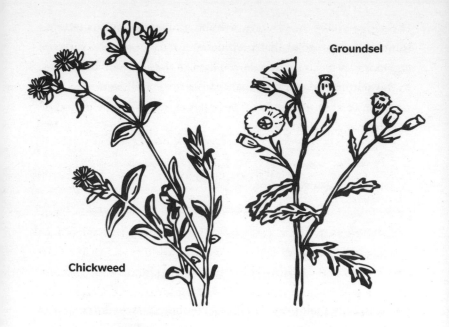

Groundsel

Chickweed

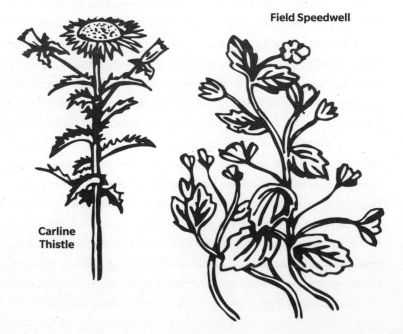

Field Speedwell

Carline Thistle

Papery, petal-like, star-coloured bracts, which respond to changes in humidity, surround the dead blooms. They open when it's dry and close up when it's wet, somewhat like the scales of pinecones. In this way, the flowers seemingly last for ever. The thistle was once used for weather forecasting. The bracts close during the period of high humidity preceding rain.

 ## Fungus foray

Some fungi do not grow up from the ground, but from the sides of trees. These are the bracket fungi. The aptly named beefsteak fungus is one of the most striking. It is dark red on top and pale yellow underneath, and grows on the trunks of oak and sweet chestnut trees. If you cut into it, a blood-like fluid oozes out. Chicken-of-the-woods is a sulphur-yellow bracket fungus, usually found on oak, beech, chestnut and cherry. It gets its name from the texture of its flesh, said to be like cooked chicken. Both are edible.

King Alfred's cakes are bracket fungi that look remarkably like some burnt-to-a-cinder scones, and tinder or hoof fungus is shaped like a horse's hoof. It gets its 'tinder' name from the way you can hammer the fungus flat and, if you light it, it will smoulder for a long time. It grows on birch trees in the north of England.

The aptly named turkeytail bracket fungus resembles the tail feathers of a North American turkey. It encrusts rotting tree trunks. The oak bracket fungus looks like bread dough pushing out of the trunk, and, if the lacquered bracket fungus is damaged, it oozes a thick yellow resin that dries to a hard, shiny surface, hence the name.

All these bracket fungi differ from most other fungal fruiting bodies by being long lived, some many years old. Some grow on rotting wood, but several grow on living wood and are responsible for weakening boughs, causing them to break during storms.

Travelling slime

The fruiting bodies of some very unusual living organisms can be seen in wet grass or on tree bark at this time of year. Some are yellow and white and look like scrambled eggs, others like macaroni cheese, and then there are chocolate stalks, rows of pink ice lollies, rotting half tennis balls and one species that looks like a cross between fish eggs and dog's sick. They belong to slime moulds, a curious collection of living things that, down the centuries, have defied classification. They resemble fungi, but behave like animals.

They start out as 'blobs', like the single-celled amoeba found in most biology textbooks. They move like it too, engulfing the bacteria and fungal spores on which they feed, but there the similarity ends. The slime mould grows, sliding over the bark of a tree, over leaf litter or across your lawn like some science fiction slime monster, engulfing more and more bacteria. It expands to become a gigantic single sac with many nuclei that can be enormous. One of the biggest species is the tapioca slime mould. A 40-cm-long specimen was found on a tree in a coastal valley near Durham. It looked like 'lumpy porridge or semolina poured over the trunk' according to Hewitt Ellis, its discoverer. A larger one from north Wales was over a square metre, weighed over 20 kg, and covered whole tree stumps. The even scarier thing is that slime moulds appear to be surprisingly bright.

Despite lacking a nervous system, let alone a brain, a slime mould can negotiate mazes in the laboratory. It sends out tendrils of cytoplasm that 'explore' the labyrinth, until food is located. Then it draws in the unsuccessful branches and puts all its energy into the successful one. A single thick tube of slime slithers along the shortest route to the food source. And, if it is given a choice of several foods, each with a different nutritional content, it will eat them proportionately so it receives a balanced diet. 'Slime moulds,' according to one scientist who studies them, 'are redefining what you need to have to qualify as intelligent.' Now that really is scary!

Highest and lowest rainfall in millimetres recorded for November since 1910

	Highest		Lowest	
England	174.5	1929	17.0	1945
Wales	336.9	1929	23.1	1945
Scotland	262.0	2009	28.8	1945
Northern Ireland	220.0	2009	29.4	1942

 Just hanging around

With most flowering plants shutting down for winter, it allows other types of plants to have a moment in the limelight. Ferns that would be more at home on rocky cliff sides are quite at home on crumbling masonry. While most ferns die back in the colder half of the year, those in the spleenwort family are evergreen, so they continue to grow even in winter. Wall rue has leathery fronds with triangular pinnules and grows out of the mortar in old walls, such as those in old railway stations, where you might also find the Hart's tongue fern, named for the shape of its fronds – like a deer's tongue.

The rusty-back fern has orange-brown scales covering its buds on the underside of its fronds, and is frequently seen growing on brick railway arches, where it survives extreme drought and exposure to the sun. The delicate maidenhair spleenwort resembles the maidenhair fern, and you can tell it from the green spleenwort by its black instead of green stems. The name 'spleenwort' comes partly from the old English name 'wyrt' meaning plant, herb, or vegetable, and partly from its use in days gone by as a medicine to treat disorders of the liver and spleen.

 ## Living carpet

On the woodland floor, mosses produce new winter growth, light green at first and dark green as the plant matures. They prefer damp, shady places, because they need water for the moss's male cells, or antherozoids, to swim to the female egg cells of a neighbouring plant. The fertilised female cell grows into an embryo that sends up a spore capsule. Mosses produce spores, rather than seeds, for dispersal. The velvety carpet moss is recognised by its pendulous spore capsules on long stems. Like all mosses, it has no roots. Root-like rhizoids anchor it, and it's most usually found on muddy streambeds and the base of tree trunks, where it forms dense green mats.

The spore capsules of feather moss resemble red birthday cake candles. Its leaves are distinctive in that they have different shapes on different parts of the plants. From the main stem they are heart-shaped with an elongated tip, at the shoot tips they compact together to form a star shape when viewed from above, and branch leaves are egg-shaped with short tips. Feather moss is one of the most common types to be found in the British Isles, appearing on lawns, banks and woodlands, where it might grow up trunks and branches of trees.

The common smoothcap has reed mace-like spore capsules on long stems. If you gently pull away the long narrow tip or 'beak' of the capsule you'll find a pepper pot mechanism underneath, similar to a poppy seed capsule, from which the spores are shaken into the air. The species is also known as Catherine's moss, on account of its previous genus name *Catherinea*. The Catherine in question was none other than Catherine the Great of Russia.

Stream banks are home to the shining hookeria, a moss with broad, flat, overlapping, almost translucent leaves that glisten when wet; and if you take a close look you can actually see the unusually large hexagonal leaf cells. Hart's-tongue thyme-moss is found on damp soil in woodlands, under trees or in clearings. It is unusually large, up to 15 cm tall and branched like a miniature tree, and its leaves are tongue-shaped and a translucent light green.

The spore capsules aside, moss is more easily identified by the shape and configuration of its leaves, and you'll need a hand lens and a good field guide to tell one from another.

 Highest and lowest average temperatures (°C) recorded for November since 1910

	Highest		Lowest	
England	12.3	2011	-0.5	1915
Wales	12.0	2011	-0.8	1915
Scotland	10.6	2011	-1.6	1919
Northern Ireland	11.7	2011	-0.6	1919

 Seasonal spectacle:
Starling roosts

One of the year's great birding spectacles must be starlings gathering together in great flocks, known as 'murmurations', just before the birds settle in their night-time roost. The event is all the more impressive this month, because visiting starlings escaping the icy clutches of Eastern Europe and Russia swell the British population. The great swirling flocks, constantly changing shapes like giant amoebae in the sky, almost defy description, but this didn't stop

English poet and Jesuit priest Gerard Manley Hopkins having a try. In his journal for 1874, he wrote:

Nov. 8 – Walking with William Splaine [described in footnotes as a steady worker], we saw a vast multitude of starlings making an unspeakable jangle. They would settle in a row of trees; then, one tree after another, rising at a signal, they looked like a cloud of specks of black snuff or powder struck from a brush or broom or shaken from a wig; then they would sweep round in whirlwinds.

Such a scene is best witnessed on a cool, clear evening, when the wind has dropped. Starlings will have started to gather from late afternoon, and may fly in from up to 50 km away. Just before sunset, they settle temporarily on wires, aerials and trees, the smaller flocks slowly amalgamating into bigger ones, and that's when the show begins. The sky fills with shape-shifting clouds as thousands fly together in intricately coordinated patterns. It's hard not to wonder how these little birds, packed so tightly together, don't bump into each other and fall out of the sky. The secret is that they are not as tightly packed as you might think. They seek an optimum density from which they can still gather information about their surroundings.

The birds gather in such dense flocks because there is safety in numbers, although peregrines, harriers and sparrowhawks target flocks, causing the birds to perform dramatic aerial manoeuvres to escape. One would think that the ideal flock, then, would be wall-to-wall birds, but this isn't so. Scientists at the University of Warwick have analysed flock density and found that there are always gaps where you can see the sky, and those are key to flock movement. Each starling monitors constantly the flight path and movements of six or seven of its nearest neighbours, while also checking out the light areas of sky between them. So, one bird is watching seven other birds and the light and dark patterns within the flock, and those seven are watching another seven each, and so on through the flock. It means one part of the flock can be moving one way, say, to avoid a peregrine, while the other part is moving in another direction, and the birds appear to do this without thinking – it's instinctive.

Peak murmurations occur during cold spells, and, when the aerial show is over, they drop down like streaks of lightning into the roost site below. Here, they squabble – shouting, posturing and jabbing at each other with their sharp bills during vicious fights for the best roosting spots. Eventually, they settle and then they all preen. They also chatter constantly, with the full range of starling calls – squawks, whistles, rattles and warbles – leading some observers to wonder whether they might be exchanging news about good places to feed, although it would be hard to prove.

Roost sites vary. Reeds growing in water are safe from terrestrial predators, such as foxes, but there are good roosting sites in dense conifer woodlands, the superstructure and ledges of bridges, seaside piers, railway stations and other city buildings.

In 2010, *Autumnwatch* visited Aberystwyth pier in the company of starling expert Chris Feare. The team's remote thermal cameras were set up underneath the pier to record the night's events, and they revealed that roosting sites were subject to a hard-fought pecking order. Mini-alcoves immediately below the pier's floorboards were the prime spots. Two or three adults occupied each niche. Below them, on beams more exposed to the wind, were youngsters experiencing their first winter, and on the lowest beams were young females.

At first, the young birds bickered and fought for the best sites, just like the adults, but eventually the cold forced the fighting to stop and they huddled closer together for warmth. Microphones picked up snatches of blackbird song, moorhen and curlew calls, and tawny owl hoots, indicating they were using their great capacity for mimicry, which male starlings use to defend nesting territories in spring, in the winter roosts as well.

Come the morning the birds did not leave en masse, but in well-organised smaller groups. One interesting thing that Chris revealed was that although the birds tend not to collide when dropping down in the evening, the sleepy-heads do bump into each other when leaving in the morning!

Where to see murmurations of starlings

Roost sites change from month to month and from year to year, but the following are likely spots:

- RSPB Ham Wall, Westhay Moor and Shapwick Heath NR, Somerset
- Slapton Ley, Devon
- RSPB Newport Wetlands, South Wales
- RSPB Fen Drayton Lakes, Cambridgeshire
- Royal Pier, Aberystwyth, West Wales
- West Pier, Brighton
- RSPB Leighton Moss, Lancashire
- RSPB Saltholme, near Middlesbrough
- Gretna Green and Rigg, Dumfries and Galloway
- Forth Bridge, near Edinburgh
- Albert Bridge, River Lagan, Belfast
- Runcorn Bridge, Cheshire
- Snape Maltings, Suffolk

Traditional collective nouns
for British wildlife

- A murmuration of starlings
- A cete of badgers
- A sedge or sege of bitterns, cranes or herons
- A wake of buzzards
- A murder of crows or magpies
- A bellowing of bullfinches
- A tok of capercaillies
- A chattering of choughs
- A gulp of cormorants
- A covert of coots
- A parcel of deer
- A trip of dotterels
- A badling of ducks
- A fling of dunlins
- A convocation of eagles
- A charm of finches
- A leash or skulk of foxes
- A gaggle of geese (on land)
- A skein of geese (flying)
- A covey of grouse, partridges, quail or ptarmigans
- A clattering of jackdaws
- A party or scold of jays
- A deceit of lapwings
- An exultation of larks
- A sord or sute of mallards
- A labour of moles
- A watch of nightingales
- A parliament of owls
- A mischief of rats

- An unkindness of ravens
- A walk or wisp of snipe
- A host of sparrows
- A caravan of stoats
- A scream of swifts
- A spring of teal
- A fall of woodcocks
- A descent of woodpeckers

 ## City birds

Starling roosts in city centres have declined in recent years. The damage caused by their droppings has meant that birds have had to be moved on. Bristol Temple Meads railway station once had a wonderful roost that commuters could watch leaving early in the morning. It probably did more good for wildlife than many a conservation initiative because it was right there in front of people – the exodus every morning and the swirling murmurations in the evening. Most people were simply in awe of the spectacle unfolding before their eyes.

Pied wagtails like cities too. City centres are a touch warmer than the surrounding countryside. With the UK's population increased by the arrival of migrants from the continent, November is a good time to see them. They're more scattered during the day, feeding wherever they can find something to eat, and in the evening they flock to a single tree or rooftop, where, like a scene from Hitchcock's *The Birds*, they line up to roost at night. However, whatever you do, don't park your car underneath. Naturalist Nick Baker tells of a time he arrived at the railway station and couldn't understand why nobody had bagged a particularly convenient parking space. When he returned, he realised why: he'd parked under a pied wagtail roost and his car was covered in hundreds of white spots of wagtail guano!

Bullfinch

Greenfinch

Pied Wagtail

Starling

Car parks are also an unlikely place to find greenfinches. The trend to plant the easy-maintenance Japanese rose between parking spaces has drawn the birds in. They feed on the giant rose hips, especially after they have been softened by frost. Any place where maintenance is lax might have dock weeds growing, and their seeds attract bullfinches. If you spot the male with his crimson-red chest, then his slightly less flamboyant partner is probably nearby. Other amenity plants, such as cotoneasters, holly and rowan or mountain ash are like a magnet for redwings and fieldfares that have arrived from Scandinavia, and maybe even waxwings.

All these birds, of course, have to watch their backs for their roosts and feeding sites are often stalked by sparrowhawks. These birds rely on surprise. They appear suddenly from behind hedges like stealth fighters, following every twist and turn of their target. Then they glide in low for the snatch. A yellow undercarriage armed with fierce talons completes the job; and, if the prey escapes, they might well hang around, waiting for it to break cover. They'll also scan and hunt from a perch, soar and stoop, quarter, and hunt on foot. In winter, they specialise in taking small birds from bird tables, but their success rate is not that amazing. They fail in nine out of ten attacks.

Sparrowhawks were formerly woodland predators, small birds of prey adapted to hunt in dense forests, so gardens are perfect for them; in fact, they are the most likely birds of prey you'll see in your garden. Prey size depends on whether the hunter is male or female. The smaller males take birds up to the size of thrushes, while the noticeably larger females – twice the weight of males – can easily tackle a wood pigeon. They'll eat other food, such as small mammals, insects and earthworms, and some are able to snatch bats from midair. And, despite their failure rate, their annual catch is impressive. During the course of a year, a pair of sparrowhawks might catch the equivalent of 2,200 house sparrows, and

600 blackbirds or 110 wood pigeons. It's one reason bird table bird watchers dislike the bird. However, long-term studies of songbirds and sparrowhawks have revealed that they are not responsible for diminishing songbird populations. The argument goes like this:

If an entire blue tit family survives until winter, then food becomes scarce and competition for it is fierce. When the temperature drops in November, for example, about a third of the season's new blue tits die of starvation or perish from the cold. So, even without predation, the number of fledging songbirds remains constant because of a finite amount of food. Interestingly, sparrowhawks need to catch about a third of songbirds to survive themselves. The figures match. It means sparrowhawks are taking the surplus of songbirds that are destined to die during their first winter anyway, with or without predation.

You can see sparrowhawks in almost any part of the country, but blink and you'll miss them.

 ## Asian interlopers

Chinese water deer are not native British mammals, but they have established themselves in parts of Bedfordshire, the Cambridgeshire Fens and Norfolk Broads. In their native homeland in China and Korea their numbers have dropped to such an extent that now 10 per cent of the world's population is living in this country. They arrived first in the 19th century, when they were released into deer parks. Some escaped and became feral, living in reedbeds, alder carrs (waterlogged wooded terrain) and rough grasslands that stand in for their native river valleys. Bucks can be recognised by the large canine teeth that extend down from the upper jaw as small tusks. Unlike all other British deer, they do not carry antlers.

November is the start of the rut. These animals are solitary for most of the year, but now a buck and a doe defend a territory, the pair remaining together throughout winter and spring, until April. They scent mark trees and bushes using scent from the preorbital glands below the eyes, and create dung piles as territorial markers. The bucks are very aggressive to any other bucks trying to muscle in on their patch. They parallel walk, like other deer, to size up the opposition, but without antlers any fisticuffs are rather muted. Even so, they can and do injure one another.

They have several calls. When alarmed they bark. Bucks chasing bucks make a rapid 'whickering' sound and, during courtship, bucks emit whistles and squeaks. If chased, both sexes scream.

With all this activity, dusk in early winter is a good time to see them, and one known hotspot is the Norfolk Wildlife Trust's Hickling Broad nature reserve, where there are also large numbers of hen harriers roosting in the reed beds near Stubbs Mill during winter.

Coastwatch: Stuck fast

Storms and surf dominate the shoreline this month. Larger species of crabs and many of the fish of the rocky shore move into deep water, leaving juvenile fish, such as young rocklings and shannies, in rockpools. The churning action of the waves, however, and a drop in the water temperature to a critical 11°C, stimulates limpets to spawn.

Limpets are the conical-shaped shellfish that are commonly seen on rocky shores. A muscular foot and a chemical secretion enable the limpet to form such a tight bond with the rock that the animal is very difficult to remove, and the shape of its shell gives it a profile that protects it from crashing waves and strong currents. When the tide goes out, the tight seal also ensures it does not dry out, and the tough shell can resist the predatory attention of most seabirds.

Limpets are herbivores, scraping algae from the rocks using a 'toothed tongue' or radula. They move to feed over a large area at high tide, but tend to return to the same spot before low water. During spawning, many limpets in a particular area spawn at the same time, a behaviour known as broadcast spawning. Temperature is thought to be the main trigger. It increases the likelihood of eggs being fertilised, and reduces the chances of all the fertilised eggs being eaten by near-shore egg predators. At least some escape. Whether a limpet releases pale green eggs or white sperm into the water depends on their age. Younger limpets are male, but many change into females at about four years old.

 All washed up

Winter storms cast up all kinds of exotics. Aside from leatherback turtles, which come here quite naturally (see page 238), several species of sea turtles have found themselves hundreds of kilometres off course and have been washed ashore on beaches from the island of Guernsey in the south to the coast of Ayrshire in the north in recent years.

In 2017, for example, a young Kemp's ridley was found stranded but alive on the shore of Holywell Bay, near Newquay, in Cornwall. In 2015, one pitched up at Poppit Beach, in Pembrokeshire, and another at Chesil Beach in Dorset. In 2014, two Kemp's ridley turtles were washed ashore further north, one on Sefton Beach, near Formby on Merseyside, and another at Cumbria's Welney Island. Another had been found previously at Green Cliff Beach in North Devon, and one even made it to Saltdean Beach, near Brighton.

In November 2016, a closely related species, an olive ridley sea turtle, arrived moribund but alive on a sandy shore in the Menai Strait and, in 2015, a green sea turtle was found on a beach near Porthmadog in North Wales. Loggerheads have appeared in Guernsey, Jersey, Chesil Beach, Pembrokeshire, Anglesey, Ayrshire and off County Donegal.

All these turtles are tropical or subtropical species and by rights should not be in our waters. It's thought a sudden drop in sea temperatures off the east coast of the USA would have caused the beasts to become 'cold-stunned'. This left them lethargic, unable to feed, and at the mercy of the ocean currents that carried them across the North Atlantic Ocean and dumped them on our west coast.

Kemp's ridley sea turtle is considered to be the rarest species of sea turtle, and classified as 'critically endangered' by IUCN, which means that the species 'faces an extremely high risk of extinction in the immediate future', so conservationists have been very concerned about the way extreme weather changes have been having an impact. Those found on our beaches are probably just a small fraction of the number of turtles that have been swept off course. It's a species that can't afford to get lost.

Cuddy's duck

Eider ducks are noticeable this month and throughout the winter. After breeding, the males will have had their familiar black-and-white eclipse plumage for most of the summer, but as winter approaches they once more moult into their breeding finery. Their white chest feathers have a pink hue, and those on the back of the neck are coloured apple green. They gather in large rafts close to shore, the males very obvious, but the mottled brown females are almost invisible. While they are more likely to be seen on coasts to the north of Northumberland during the spring and summer, many can be found just offshore in the southern half of the country in winter.

The birds dive down and use their wedge-shaped bills to feed on crustaceans and molluscs off rocky shores, and they're no slouches in the air. Peregrines have been clocked at 200 mph in a stoop, but that's more or less a gravity-assisted, controlled fall. Swifts notch up 69.3 mph in display flights, but more usually pootle along, when on migration, at about 26 mph. Eiders, though, skim the waves at a staggering 47.2 mph in level flight, making it one of the world's fastest birds.

In Northumberland, they're known as 'Cuddy's ducks', named after St Cuthbert, a local saint who established one of the first bird conservation laws in 676 CE to protect them. The bird's other claim to fame is that female ducks line their nests with soft down feathers, and these have been collected traditionally to stuff pillows and bedcovers, hence the familiar 'eiderdown'.

 ## Eider hotspots

- Shetland
- Seahouses Harbour, Bamburgh, Farne Islands, and Lindisfarne in Northumberland

- RSPB Titchwell Marsh, Norfolk
- Belfast Lough, Northern Ireland
- WWT Martin Mere, Cheshire
- Scottish Seabird Centre, North Berwick, Scotland
- Firth of Tay, Scotland
- Montrose Basin, Angus, Scotland
- RSPB Mull of Galloway, Dumfries and Galloway

Party time ... but watch out for Mrs Tiggy-Winkle

This month, hedgehogs are beginning to settle down for they are one of the few British mammals that truly hibernate. They've fattened up on slugs, snails, beetles, worms, caterpillars, seeds and fruit as best they can since September, so they have a readily available, built-in food store for the long winter. They need to weigh at least 400 g to have a chance of surviving, preferably 500–700 g to be sure.

When the time comes, the hedgehog's body begins to change: its breathing rate slows; heart rate drops from 190 to 20 beats per minute; body temperature plummets; blood is diverted to the centre of the body and away from the peripherals; and its brain goes into a trance-like state. If disturbed it can still raise its spines in defence, and, if the weather is warm, it might wake up a few times and wander about looking for food to top up its store of fat and go to the loo. It might also change hibernation dens.

Hedgehogs select comfortable dens, safe from predators and sheltered from the weather, a place where the temperature does not drop below 5°C. Favoured spots are under piles of wood and leaves, but those are just the places where hedgehogs have to contend with our eccentric bonfire season, especially at the beginning of November. It's a risky time.

So, do check. If you have a pile of leaves or wood that you're about to burn, lift and move it. There might be a hedgehog underneath. In fact, to be safe, build your bonfire just before you set light to it, then 5th November can be a happy time rather than a nightmare.

While most hedgehogs have retreated from the world between mid-October and mid-November, there are a few that remain active until Christmas. If so, do put out food for them – not milk, it gives them indigestion. Meat-based dog or cat food is good (not fish-based), dried mealworms are welcome and there are commercially available hedgehog foods nowadays. They also need a fresh bowl of water. By the end of the year, they will all be hibernating to avoid the worst of the weather, emerging again in March or April depending on the location.

 ## After the flames

They say 'nature abhors a vacuum', and it's often evident after a fire, even something as small as a bonfire. By late spring, common cord moss colonises burnt ground, as does rosebay willowherb, an alien species known appropriately as 'fireweed' in North America. Redshank moss, a common British moss species, moves into burnt areas, its mass of golden leaves giving rise to green spore capsules on red stalks. Charred conifer wood sprouts the chestnut-brown to maroon-coloured pine fire fungus, and the great mullein, a flowering plant, might grow on last year's bonfire site. Known also as Aaron's rod, the two-metre-tall erect plant, covered by a grey or whitish down, produces a spike of yellow flowers. The caterpillars of the mullein moth sometimes devour it, and you can spot them by their costume of black and yellow dots. However, the 5th of November aside, it makes more ecological sense to compost your leaves than burn them.

Highest and lowest hours of sunshine recorded for November since 1929

☀	Highest		Lowest	
England	95.1	2006	37.0	2015
Wales	80.7	2006	31.5	2015
Scotland	64.0	2016	28.8	1997
Northern Ireland	80.2	1950	31.1	1962

 # Badgers and bloodsuckers

Badgers love their beds. It's an animal that spends all day snoozing underground, so plenty of effort goes into collecting bedding that's going to be cosy and comfortable. Their beds can be fashioned from hay, straw, moss, dead leaves and bracken, but before long, the resident badgers will find they are sharing their bed with an unwanted blood-sucking squatter. It's now known that badgers have resorted to some Gothic measures to end infestations.

The badger flea is, like all its brethren, a prolific breeder and an itchy pest. Fleas feed from a badger, glugging blood when they are hungry. However, they subsequently lay their eggs in the bedding, where before long the larvae will hatch, then pupate. The resulting adult will soon be tucking into badger skin and laying eggs of its own.

For their part, badgers are notoriously fastidious creatures, grooming themselves and each other for sustained periods to help counter flea infestation.

They also switch beds – and setts – on a regular basis. When they do they drag old bedding outside for an airing. Spread thinly on the ground, sunshine will kill the larvae in the bedding, which is later retrieved.

Bed-hopping like this is particularly effective against lice, which can't survive for long without a badger to nibble on. However, few badgers have access to enough setts to counteract the flea menace. Research has found that half of badger fleas will survive for seven weeks without a badger in sight. It takes about three months for fleas to die of starvation in a sett.

Perhaps that's why badgers seem to rely on an age-old method to keep the population of its high-jumping vampire-like parasite at bay. Like Dracula, fleas may well be deterred at the smell of garlic. A recently observed badger habit of lining a nest with wild garlic leaves and stalks helps deter the flea population.

 ## Year of the Fox

The family break-up continues, with some female cubs now electing to depart. At this time, fertile females are already casting an eye over the neighbourhood for potential dens to house their next litter. Spats over food and hunting rights are sometimes audible in the dark nights.

 ## Smart foxes ... or not so smart?

It has often been claimed that urban foxes are smarter than their rural cousins; after all, they have to survive in an urban jungle with so many dangers, like cars and people, and with rubbish bins now made to be fox and domestic cat proof, food is less easy to find than it once was. To live in towns and cities, surely the urban fox must be cleverer, but is it? In 2017, *Autumnwatch* tried to find out.

Gillian Burke went to a suburban garden on the outskirts of Bournemouth, and, with the help of Dr Dawn Scott, from the University of Brighton, set up a series of tests. The test rig consisted of a clear Perspex box with holes in it, so the foxes could see and smell any baits inside. A piece of chicken was used as bait and it was placed on a small disc-shaped bait tray, which was linked to the outside by a length of string. The idea was that, in order to gain the reward, the fox had to pull the string. The bait in the tray could be pulled out via a small gap at the bottom of the box.

Six adults came regularly to the garden to feed, but not all were interested in playing along with Gillian's game. First to try was female subadult Blondie. She grabbed and pulled the string but it happened so quickly that she startled herself. She jumped away, but returned cautiously to take the reward. Next up was Teardrop, a subadult male. He seemed much less concerned about the Perspex box, and quickly learned to pull the string, which had been placed on the right side of the box. He gained the reward, and he did it time and again, until, in his enthusiasm to get at the chicken, he nearly broke the apparatus.

Interestingly, no adult foxes investigated the box. They stayed clear. That a young male is more comfortable with such a strange device than a young female is understandable. Males disperse far and wide in the autumn, more so than young females. They tend to be more adventurous. It was time for a second experiment – the two-string test.

This time, there were two trays – one on the left and one on the right, each linked to the outside by a string, so the fox had to choose which one to pull to gain the reward. Gillian placed the chicken in the left-hand tray. Again, Teardrop stepped up to the mark. At first he pulled the right-hand string, from which he would have expected a reward, but there was none. He was clearly confused. However, after several hours, he pulled the correct string so, in subsequent tests, Gillian kept swapping the bait around, and eventually Teardrop was 100 per cent successful. It was looking as if he was learning.

It was then time for a third experiment in which the strings were crossed, so the fox had to pull the right string to get food in the left-hand tray, and vice versa. After several false tries he found the food, but was it a fluke? Given the same test, domestic dogs fail the cross-string test. Was Teardrop smarter than a dog and really learning? Apparently not. Out of 17 tests, he failed 12 times, and in the last 9 attempts he got it wrong 8 times. Teardrop was not as clever as was first thought.

But was he smarter than his rural cousins? Well, nobody knows. They wouldn't even approach the box!

 ## Arrivals and departures

The big birds have arrived. Flying in from their summer breeding grounds north of the Arctic Circle are the overwintering swans – whooper and Bewick swans. For some bird watchers, it marks the end of autumn and the real start of winter.

Some birds trickle in from October onwards, like the non-breeders that pitched up at Martin Mere on the 1st October, but the vast majority arrive later in the month or in November.

The whoopers are big birds, weighing up to 15 kg (the weight of a male wintering in Denmark) and maximum wingspan of 2.75 m. They can be recognised by the triangular patch of yellow. It forms a pointed V-shape on either side of their black bills, each bird with its own pattern. The birds migrate in family groups, covering the 1,000 miles from Iceland to south west Scotland in a single hop, a journey time of just 12 hours. They fly high, at altitudes around 8,000 metres, and at an average speed of 55 mph, depending on the wind. They announce their arrival with loud and deep honking 'whoop-whoop' calls, like vintage car horns.

Most of Iceland's breeding population of whooper swans over-winter in the British Isles, about 20,000 of them. About 60 per cent head for Ireland, with up to 1,500 dropping into Lough Neagh. *Autumnwatch*, together with swan enthusiast Darryl Grimason, filmed birds at nearby Lough Beg. At first, he pointed out, they are not the pure white birds we have come to know. They have 'rusty' heads and necks from the iron oxide in the wetland areas from where they have just come. It washes off after a few weeks.

The Bewick swans have an even longer journey, close to 4,000 kilometres. They breed on the Arctic tundra in Siberia, the more western breeders heading to our shores and to other overwintering sites in north-west Europe each autumn. The rest head the other way, to China, Japan and Korea. Journey time is dependent on the weather along the route. Generally, they take about ten weeks, with several stops along the way, sometimes with extended stopovers as long as a month. They fly above the clouds at about 2,800 metres (but have been spotted by aircrews at 3,650 metres) at speeds that sometimes reach 55 mph, and even 100 mph with a strong tailwind according to some reports.

They are smaller than the visiting whooper swans and resident mute swans, not much bigger than a Canada goose, making them the smallest species of swan in the British Isles. They have a maximum weight of about 7.8 kilograms and wingspan of about 1.9 metres. Their neck is shorter than a whooper's. They have yellow on the bill too, but they differ from the whoopers in having more rounded patches on either side of their black bills, and the pattern is highly variable so individuals can be told apart. Their calls have been described as being more like those of an excitable dog.

These birds are relatively rare so three overwintering sites in the UK are of international importance: Ouse Washes, Nene Washes and Severn Estuary, and three of national importance at Breydon Water/Berney Marshes, Dungeness to Pett Level, and Ranworth/ Cockshoot Broad.

Where to watch overwintering swans

- Welney WWT, Norfolk (also winter home to all Svalbard's breeding population of barnacle geese)
- Lough Foyle, Lough Neagh, and Lough Beg, Northern Ireland
- Caerlaverock WWT, Solway Firth
- Abbotsbury the Fleet
- Martin Mere, Lancashire
- Slimbridge, Gloucestershire

 ## What to look out for

- Listen out for the birds' distinctive calls.
- Scan fields adjacent to nature reserves as swan feed on stubble and sugar beet tops.
- In late afternoon, watch feeding swans. The heads of a few swans go up and down rapidly and shake from side to side, and wings are flapped, signs that they're about to take off. The signaller is usually the swan that leads the flight.
- Check out morning and evening swan-feeding sessions.

 ## Special departure

Twice each year, Montagu's harrier embarks on a long journey. It is a medium-sized, long-winged bird of prey, smaller than a buzzard, with more pointed wings than the hen harrier. The male is grey above, the female brown. It is an extremely rare breeding bird in the UK, and its nest sites – just five are known – are kept secret; but it's quite possible to see one on passage. In the autumn, the birds head south to sub-Saharan West Africa, and satellite tags have revealed just where they go.

Two individuals – Sally and Roger – became the unlikely stars of *Autumnwatch*, when Martin Hughes-Games was given the honour to release Sally, and see her on her way. Roger went to Senegal for the winter, travelling via Gibraltar, but Sally went on a mammoth trek. After her release on 14th August, she roosted in Kent before crossing the Channel. She then travelled across France and Spain, crossing the Mediterranean between Almeria and Morocco. She reached Mali a couple of weeks later on 8th September, but that was not the end of it. On 24th November she set off again, flying as far south as the Ivory Coast, and then on to Ghana. It was the farthest south that any UK breeding Montagu's harrier had ever flown.

Sunrise and sunset times for Britain's capital cities

30th November	☼ Sunrise	☼ Sunset
Belfast	08.21	16.03
London	07.43	15.55
Cardiff	07.55	16.07
Edinburgh	08.18	15.44

DECEMBER

Estuaries are choked full of waders and other waterfowl from all over Europe and beyond. Fungi are still pushing up fruiting bodies. Lapwings are feeding in fields. Robins are fighting to the death with their neighbours. Foxes are screaming blue murder. While much of our wildlife may *seem* to be dormant this month, there is clearly still sufficient to keep a dedicated British wildlife watcher busy, and, with the year's critical landmark having passed, increasingly longer days will trigger new growth and a renewed round of frantic and, for us, exciting activity.

Sunrise and sunset times for Britain's capital cities

1st December	☀ Sunrise	☀ Sunset
Belfast	08.23	16.02
London	07.44	15.54
Cardiff	07.56	16.07
Edinburgh	08.19	15.43

Burning the old year

Our tradition of bringing evergreen plants, such as fir trees, holly and mistletoe into the home over the Christmas period has its origins in pagan times when they were symbols of the continuity of life. Newly collected mistletoe was hung up when the clock struck twelve on New Year's Eve and the old mistletoe, which had been hanging there for a year, was burnt. Today, bonfires are a relic of the winter solstice celebrations that served to drive out last year's devils and bring a promise of fertility to crops and livestock for the coming year.

Most owls seem to hoot exactly in B flat according to several pitch-pipes used in tuning of harpsichords ...

Gilbert White, 4th December 1770

 Life's a hoot

Tawny owls and long-eared owls often establish their breeding territories in the winter, so December can be a very vocal time of the year. The familiar duet of tawny owls – the 'hoo' (pause) 'ha' (followed by) 'hu-hu-hu-hoo' of the male and the 'kewick' of the female – can be heard in woodlands throughout the country, their calls contrasting with the lower-pitched 'hooo-hooo-hooo' of the male long-eared owl, the female responding with a raspy buzz.

Established tawny owl pairs occupy their nesting territory all year round. The rest fight it out during October and November, so by December the males will have found an unoccupied territory to take over and the female a suitable nesting hole. During this transition from autumn into winter, male and female roost together more and more often, with courtship feeding taking place from now until the start of nesting in mid-March.

Tawny owls hunt at night. They wait on a perch, watching and listening, scanning the ground for any disturbance. When a target is located, the owl glides down silently or drops down vertically, pinning the prey to the ground in its powerful talons. Prey can be anything from as small as an earthworm to something as big as a rat; in fact, *Autumnwatch* thermal cameras revealed tawny owls to be feisty little birds.

In the woods at Sherborne, during the 2017 season, a tawny owl had a go at catching rats by the river. Water going over a weir made listening for prey movements impossible, so the bird must

Short-eared Owl

Long-eared Owl

Tawny Owl

have been using its amazing eyesight. Rats, however, are relatively large and very agile animals, and they are fierce fighters. Larger owls and kestrels tend to leave them well alone, but not the tawny owl. In previous programmes, the team also found tawny owls taking birds the size of magpies and wood pigeons, and one bird was seen hunting Daubenton's bats down by the Sherborne Brook.

Although long-eared owls roost in woodlands, they hunt at night over open land, taking mainly small mammals such as mice and voles, but they will catch birds, such as blackbirds. They fly low to the ground with the head slightly cocked to one side, listening for any movements. They pounce immediately, grabbing prey in their talons. Small items are swallowed whole, slightly larger ones are carried in the beak to a butchering site, and large items are carried in the talons. Like the tawny owl, nesting won't be until the weather improves in March.

A third owl to watch out for this month is the short-eared owl. While most owls hunt at night, this species hunts by day. It flies low, with slow flaps of its wings, quartering fields where mice and voles may be hiding. Open moorland and grassland around conifer plantations is a good place to see them. They also perch on fence posts, scanning the land for prey, but they are so well camouflaged that you probably won't see the owl until it moves.

 ## Flower of the Month

There's an old saying about gorse: 'when gorse is out of bloom, kissing is out of season', and, as kissing is clearly a year-round activity, so too can gorse be seen every month of the year. As very few other flowers are in bloom at this time, the bright golden-yellow gorse is a welcome sight for sore eyes, and, if the sun shines, a perfume of coconut and vanilla fills the nostrils.

It's a tough plant, a real survivor. It colonises waste ground, scrublands, forest margins, hedgerows and grasslands. To help it grow in nutrient-poor soils, its roots have nodules containing symbiotic bacteria that can fix nitrogen, so it produces its own fertiliser. The plant itself is covered with sharp spines, which deter animals from browsing, and its seeds are dispersed explosively (see also page 252); in fact, gorse is so successful that it's considered an invasive species, outcompeting most other plants. Its habit of retaining its dead and dry branches and leaves also makes it a fire hazard.

The flowers, however, have their uses. They make a strong yellow dye, and when added to white wine or cider they make gorse vinegar, a culinary delight for 'foraging' cooks. They can also make gorse tea, gorse blossom water can be used to colour icing on cakes and, apparently, a few drops of gorse water on the face is refreshing on a hot day.

Gorse's common name comes from the Old English *gors* or *gorst*, meaning 'rough or prickly'.

 ## Fungus foray

Frost and fungi generally do not mix, but there are still some hardy species producing their exquisite fruiting bodies. There are the jelly fungi, with no stems or caps; instead, they are folded blobs of gelatinous material. Tree tripe fungus looks like the lining of a cow's stomach, while the light brown-coloured Jew's ear looks and feels to all the world like a human ear. It was once known as 'Judas' ear', for it grows on common elder, the tree from which Judas Iscariot was supposed to have hanged himself. A 400-year-old legend tells that the fungus is the visible remains of Judas' tormented spirit.

For colour, the scarlet elf cup fungus is hard to beat. It shows as bright scarlet-red or orange cup shapes growing out of rotting wood. If the weather is dry, listen closely and you might hear the little puffs as the fungus disperses its spores into the air rather than down onto the ground like many other fungi.

For a surprise, nothing does it better than the little green wood-cup fungus. Growing on the outside of fallen oak logs, the fruiting body is a dark blue-green cup, but break open the log and inside the filaments of the fungi have coloured the wood the same colour. This 'green oak', as it is known, was once sought after in the making of Tunbridge ware, a form of inlaid woodwork, in the late 19th century.

 ## Killer fungi

Most fungi gain nutrients either by breaking down dead material or by parasitising living organisms, but there are few that are predators. Many of these are microscopic soil fungi. They have hyphae that form into loops that entrap any tiny eelworms that wander into them. The worm's wriggling stimulates special cells on the inside surface of the loop to inflate rapidly, effectively strangling the prey. Then, hyphae grow into the victim, digesting its soft tissues and absorbing the nutrients released.

The hyphae of oyster mushrooms behave in a similar way. The difference is that they have an adhesive coating so any round worm that brushes against them is stuck fast. The hyphae then secrete a narcotic that reduces the worm's wriggling so filaments can grow more easily into its body. Enzymes do the rest.

 ## Highest and lowest rainfall in millimetres recorded for December since 1910

	Highest		Lowest	
England	179.0	1914	21.5	1933
Wales	334.7	2015	34.0	1926
Scotland	328.2	2015	40.2	1933
Northern Ireland	224.1	1919	29.1	1963

The big sleep

By December, most animals due to hibernate for the winter are tucked away in some warm, safe place and are out for the count. Our main mammalian hibernators are bats, hedgehogs and dormice.

Having fattened up on hips, haws and hazelnuts, our native hazel dormouse should be snug in its hibernation nest, spaces usually under tree roots, hazel stools or log piles that it has lined with grass, leaves and moss, but could also be in an old bird nest box. A few weeks previously, when the temperature reached a critical 15°C, the dormouse rolled itself up, tucked its nose into its belly, legs under its chin and curled its tail around its body. Its heartbeat slowed, body temperature fell and its general metabolism wound down. It'll stay this way until April, when it can snack first on food it stored away last autumn. Curiously, shutting down its body temporarily might not end there. In spring and summer the dormouse sleeps during the day and is active at night, and, if there is a spell when food is scarce, it will remain in its summer nest in a state of 'torpor'. This way it can sometimes spend seven months of the year asleep!

Dormancy through winter

Insects and other invertebrates that opt out during winter are not true hibernators; instead, they have a behaviour known as diapause, a long-term state of suspension like a pause in their life. It's the insect equivalent of hibernation, when individuals seek a suitable place to shelter from the cold and become dormant. Some burrow underground, others hide in trees or under rocks. Falling temperatures in autumn are not the trigger. Shorter days are. And, when it's too cold to fly and there's not a lot to eat, many insects take a break.

Some insects cluster together for warmth. Worker honey bees, for example, gather around their queen, and, fuelled by their sugar-rich honey, vibrate their wing muscles to keep the colony significantly warmer than outside. Some clusters are in more exposed places.

Ladybirds cluster together in dry crevices in walls and tree trunks. They produce a scent that in summer is a predator-warning signal, but in winter it serves to gather ladybirds together in small aggregations at suitable hibernation sites. Cream-spotted ladybirds prefer the crevices in the bark of deciduous trees. You might find native 2-spot and invasive harlequin ladybirds in your house, hiding in cracks around windows, or in garden sheds. The common 7-spot gathers in groups of about a dozen in the leaf debris underneath low plants, and the beige-coloured 16-spot occurs in groups of up to 100 on low bramble leaves. The orange ladybird clings to sycamore tree trunks, while other species are packed tightly in the dead stems of verbascum and in the centre of marjoram plants. There can be up to 1,000 ladybirds clustered together in any one spot.

Teasels have good dormancy sites. The compartments vacated by its seeds are hiding places for many types of small insects, and the bristles of the seed head deter birds from probing around. Likewise, hollow plant stems are good for insects like earwigs. Overwintering hoverflies hide behind the ivy on garden walls, and blowflies and cluster flies find safe places in lofts and attics. Female drone flies like sheds, and they will have mated and stored sperm so that as soon as spring is sprung, they can lay fertilised eggs almost immediately.

Unheated outhouses are often the choice of peacock and small tortoiseshell butterflies, two of Britain's handful of butterfly species that enter a state of dormancy as adults in winter, rather than truly hibernate. They might even spend the winter inside houses. Brimstone and comma are two more, and they might overwinter like this for up to five months, which means they are among the longest living butterflies in the world.

Red admirals do not hibernate or go into long periods of dormancy like the other four. They are migrants from Africa, and, although they may roost here in mild winters, they tend to select exposed places, on tree trunks and under branches, so during a cold snap they perish. They were probably late in pupating, and conditions were too cold for flying south. Even so, individuals are sometimes seen flying on mid-winter days, probably because they developed from caterpillars and then pupae in particularly warm spots, and there is some evidence to suggest that these butterflies get on with their life cycle even during the harshest days of winter.

 ## Who hibernates as what?

Most butterflies spend the winter as eggs, larvae or pupae. The reason butterflies have radically different strategies for living through the winter is not about keeping warm, but timing. Each species of butterfly depends on a small range of plants as food for their caterpillar, and in some cases it is a single plant species. So the butterfly arranges its life cycle so that its caterpillar emerges when the plant is at its best or when there is least competition.

The chalkhill blue, for example, overwinters as an egg, whereas the closely related Adonis blue does so as a caterpillar. The reason is that they both share the same food plant – horseshoe vetch. In spring, the Adonis blue caterpillar has a head start, and has the vetch all to itself. Six weeks later, the chalkhill blue hatches out and starts to feed, by which time the Adonis blue is a chrysalis.

Here is a summary of 59 British butterflies and the stage in their life cycle at which they overwinter.

EGG (OVUM)

* Black hairstreak
* Brown hairstreak
* Chalkhill blue
* Essex skipper
* High brown fritillary
* Purple hairstreak
* Silver-spotted skipper
* Silver-studded blue
* White-letter hairstreak

LARVA (CATERPILLAR)

* Adonis blue larva
* Brown argus
* Chequered skipper
* Common blue
* Dark green fritillary
* Dingy skipper
* Gatekeeper
* Glanville fritillary
* Grayling
* Heath fritillary
* Large blue
* Large heath
* Large skipper
* Lulworth skipper
* Marbled white
* Marsh fritillary
* Meadow brown
* Mountain ringlet
* Northern brown argus
* Pearl-bordered fritillary
* Purple emperor
* Ringlet
* Scotch argus
* Silver-washed fritillary
* Small blue
* Small copper
* Small heath
* Small pearl-bordered fritillary
* Small skipper
* Speckled wood (or pupa)
* Wall
* White admiral

PUPA (CHRYSALIS)

- Cryptic wood white
- Duke of Burgundy
- Green hairstreak
- Green-veined white
- Grizzled skipper
- Holly blue
- Large white
- Orange-tip
- Small white
- Speckled wood (or larva)
- Swallowtail
- Wood white

ADULT (IMAGO)

- Brimstone
- Comma
- Peacock
- Small tortoiseshell

MIGRANT

- Clouded yellow
- Painted lady
- Red admiral (mainly)

 ## Have house, will hibernate

Garden snails shut down for the winter too. They slither into sheltered places, under flowerpots, the holes in house bricks, and under ledges, rocks and the folds of plastic compost bags. They secrete a mucilage seal, which dries into a tough membrane that not only glues them tightly to their chosen hibernation site, but also excludes predators and reduces water loss to a minimum. The interesting thing for gardeners is to locate these hibernation clusters and remove the snails that damaged your vegetables last summer. If you release them on some waste ground some distance away, they'll settle back down and ride out the winter in their new home.

Winter flying moths

Surprisingly, several species of moths are still flying during the winter. Moth of the month is the December moth, a plump, furry moth with a wavy cream pattern across its charcoal grey-brown wings. It doesn't feed, which is just as well as there is not much nectar around at this time of year. It gets all its energy from the food eaten as a caterpillar. It will be attracted to the light from windows until the middle of the month, by which time it will have laid its eggs and died.

Less easy to recognise is the winter moth. It has pale brown wings with darker cross bands. The male is attracted to light, but the female isn't: she can't fly. She spends most of the day at the base of a tree, climbing higher at dusk to attract a mate and lay eggs. In spring, blue tits arrange their breeding season to coincide with the emergence of winter moth caterpillars. A single brood can eat 10,000 of them before fledging.

 # Little robin redbreast

The robin is one of the few birds that sing the whole year round, bar a short period in late summer when it is moulting. Both sexes sing. During the early part of December, however, they appear to be singing in a half-hearted way, defending winter territories, but come the winter solstice, the males will have already started their spring song. They have a rich repertoire of several hundred short phrases, which they rarely repeat in a single song bout, and the more sudden pitch changes they can slip in, the more impressed the females will be. Streetlights can cause them to sing way into the night, and if they're disturbed they'll even sing in the dark!

Little gentlemen in black velvet

Moles don't hibernate. They're active throughout the winter, but heavy rain can be a problem for them. Their tunnels become natural drains, and they collapse, so you are likely to see many more molehills after wet weather as the incumbents battle to keep their underground empires sound. The British Mole Catchers' Register estimates there are 35–40 million moles in the UK, so their tunnels must underpin a good few fields and cricket pitches.

Moles are well adapted to live in their claustrophobic tunnels. Here they work shifts – four hours digging and four hours resting, but not on the 31st December – St Sylvester's Day. It was said that if you picked up a molehill on that day, the moles would not make a mound in your field again.

Moles feature frequently in old superstitions, including weather sores. If a mole enters a meadow, it's a sign of good weather. If it tunnels down deep, expect a severely cold winter. In Wales it was said that if a mole tunnels under the dairy or washhouse, the mistress of the house would die within a year, and if molehills appeared in the cabbage patch, the master of the house would be dead before the year is out. In Wiltshire, farm labourers would carry a pouch hanging from their neck containing the two forelegs and one hind leg of a mole to prevent toothache!

Folklore aside, the mole has frequently been misrepresented. There is the common belief that moles are blind, but that's not true. It has small eyes, although they are hard to see amongst his fur, but it led William Shakespeare to write in *The Tempest*:

Pray you, tread softly, that the blind mole may not
Hear a footfall; we are now near his cell.

Well, clearly Shakespeare was no naturalist.

Highest and lowest average temperatures (°C) recorded for December since 1910

	Highest		Lowest	
England	12.1	2015	-3.5	2010
Wales	11.5	2015	-3.8	2010
Scotland	8.5	2016	-5.1	2010
Northern Ireland	10.0	2015	-4.2	2010

Nature's landscape engineers

Wild boar are ecological engineers. By grubbing in the woodland floor, they increase the diversity of the plants that can grow there. They dig up bracken rhizomes, allowing tree seedlings to rise through what would otherwise be an impenetrable mat. Their wallows are a useful habitat for water-loving plants, insects and amphibians.

Wild boar are in our countryside because they escaped from farms, when storms brought down trees that broke down the fences of their enclosures. Now they are at large in several parts of the countryside, but they are threatened by the government's policy of allowing landowners to decide whether or not they should be allowed to survive.

Wild boar have stocky, powerful bodies with grey-brown fur. Mature males have tusks that protrude from the mouth. Piglets are a lighter ginger-brown in colour, with stripes on their coat for camouflage. Large animals, wild boar can stand up to 80 cm at the shoulder and typically weigh between 60–100 kg, although males in excess of 200 kg have been reported in some parts of the world.

WHERE AND WHEN TO SPOT

The history of wild boar in the UK is complicated. A native species, they were hunted to extinction at some point in the Middle Ages. In the 1980s, boar farming became prevalent and many animals are believed to have escaped – or been illegally released – into the wild. There are established breeding populations of boar in south east and south west England, with the highest numbers in the Weald and Forest of Dean. Smaller populations have also been reported across the UK, including south Wales and the Scottish Highlands (boar have been sighted at Loch Arkaig).

A woodland species, wild boar are shy and primarily nocturnal, meaning your chances of coming across one are slim. In the majority of cases, boar will flee upon detecting people, but can become aggressive if they feel threatened, especially females with young. Dogs should be kept on leads in woods where boar are known to be present and, if you encounter one, the best advice is to move away slowly in the opposite direction.

FEEDING

Boar are not fussy eaters and will consume a wide variety of food. Much of their diet is made up of plants, roots, seeds and fruit, but they will eat carrion and even small mammals, birds' eggs and chicks if the opportunity arises.

BEHAVIOUR AND BREEDING

Most boar live in groups, known as sounders, that are comprised of females and their young. Adult males tend to live alone, only coming together with females to mate. Typically, four to six piglets will be born in spring. A boar's maximum lifespan in the wild is thought to be around 14 years, although the majority of animals will not survive this long.

THREATS

The presence of wild boar in our woods is controversial. It has been suggested the species can have both a positive and negative impact on woodland biodiversity, but the exact impact is currently unclear. While some welcome the return of a once-extinct native species, others are concerned about agricultural damage and collisions with traffic. Boar have no natural predators in the UK, meaning culls are being carried out in some areas in a bid to control population growth.

DID YOU KNOW?

- The wild boar is the ancestor of the domestic pig. It is thought to have been first domesticated around 15,000 years ago.
- Wild boar occur naturally across Eurasia from the UK in the west to Japan in the east; they have also been introduced to North and South America and Australia.
- Boar have poor eyesight but an extremely strong sense of smell, relying on their nose to find food and detect danger.

 Year of the Fox

Apart from the routine matter of finding food, foxes' thoughts are turning to mating. Already dominant males and females have apparently teamed up, in what seems to be a statement of intent. Together they will drive other foxes away from the stretch of land they call home. Noise levels are on the rise. The screams of early starters followed by the commonly heard triple bark convince some householders that the neighbourhood foxes are killing their cats. Sometimes people suspect a more heinous crime is being committed. But one sniff of the night air should be enough to reassure those with concerns about what's going on nearby under cover of darkness. The musty musk that's issued by dog foxes as they pursue a mate lingers long after the animal has disappeared.

Highest and lowest hours of sunshine recorded for December since 1929

☼	Highest		Lowest	
England	75.7	2001	20.0	1956
Wales	73.5	2001	22.3	1988
Scotland	43.7	2001	15.6	1934
Northern Ireland	61.5	2010	18.1	1931

 ## Changing coats

Just as we change from summer to winter clothes, so do some animals. Deer, for example, grow thicker coats to help keep them warm throughout the winter months. Some animals, though, even change colour. Mountain hares (see page 30) are not the only mammals to sport a white coat when the snow falls. A reduction in day length, a drop in air temperature, increased snow cover and the resulting production of hormones causes the stoat to moult into its white ermine winter coat. You're more likely to see ermine in the north of the country, where the winter is harder. They can be pure white aside from their button eyes and the black tip to their tail, and female stoats are more likely to be white than males. Further south, stoats tend to be skewbald, with only patches of white.

The only British bird to turn white is the ptarmigan. It lives in the Scottish Highlands, where it is well insulated against the cold weather. Its dense feathers keep the body warm, and they extend to the nostrils and the legs. Both sexes are white with black tails, but you can tell the male apart for he has a black line running from the black bill across the eye. The male also has a red comb above the eye that reflects ultraviolet light: the brighter the reflection, the healthier the bird. In severe weather the birds dig down into hollows to shelter, and effectively disappear from view. If the going gets too tough, they leave the high tops and head for the forest edge.

Winter solstice

The winter solstice generally occurs on the 21st or 22nd December, but it is not just a day, but a specific time on that day. In 2018 it is at 22:22 Greenwich Mean Time precisely, in 2019 it will be 04:19 on the 22nd December, and in 2020 it will be 10:02 on 21st December. The day can vary between the 20th and 23rd December, although 20th and 23rd solstices are rare. The last 23rd solstice was in 1903, and the next will be in 2303. The point is that the winter solstice is at a very precise moment in our annual calendar, when the Sun is exactly over the Tropic of Capricorn in the Southern Hemisphere and the North Pole is tilted farthest from the Sun. Here in the British Isles, it is our shortest day and our longest night.

'Solstice' means literally 'when the sun stands still', because on this day it appears to reach its most southerly point in the sky, pauses momentarily, and then reverses its direction. For astronomers, it's the first day of winter, rather than midwinter, which ends on the March or spring equinox, whereas meteorologists consider winter started three weeks ago on 1st December, and biologists still opt for 1st November as the start of winter … and it often feels like it!

Sunrise and sunset times for Britain's capital cities

21st December	Sunrise	Sunset
Belfast	08.44	15.59
London	08.03	15.53
Cardiff	08.15	16.06
Edinburgh	08.42	15.40

Pleased to meet you … again

If you head to the Cairngorms in December, you might find a surprising sight: free-ranging reindeer. Conservationists have tried many times to re-introduce them to the wilder parts of Britain, but early attempts failed. In the 1790s, the Duke of Atholl brought over animals from Russia, but these were used to living on the Arctic tundra, and the Scottish Highlands were not a suitable substitute. It was not until 1952 that the penny dropped.

Swedish reindeer herder Mikel Utsi and his wife Dr Ethel Lindgren were on their honeymoon in Aviemore when they realised that the ground, rock and tree lichens were similar to those growing in open woodland settings in Swedish Lapland. Driven more by the promise of valuable meat, hides and horn than by any thoughts of 're-wilding', the husband and wife team introduced a small herd to the Rothiemurchus Forest. They bred successfully and, in 1954, the

Forestry Commission granted the couple permission to turn out the reindeer onto the northern slopes of the Cairngorms, and they have been living on the high ground ever since. Today, the herd consists of about 150 animals that are still managed, and which is split between the Cairngorms and the Cromdale Hills, near Glenlivet. The Cairngorm animals are free ranging, but are fed daily, and you can go and visit them.

At one time reindeer were probably the most numerous large mammals in the British Isles. Remains have been found in caves in Somerset dated 12,500 to 13,000 years old, and in Cattedown Caves, near Plymouth, dated 14,500 years old. The youngest remains from Scotland are dated to about 8,300 years before the present. They were hunted in more recent times. An Orcadian saga known as the *Orkneyinga*, tells how the Earls of Orkney hunted red deer and reindeer in Caithness about eight centuries ago but, shortly after, by the end of the 13th century, the species was extinct in Britain. The cause of its demise is unknown – climate change and hunting pressure are two possibilities.

 ## Red list, yellow list

Since 1996 Britain's birds have been monitored on three colour-coded lists that indicate whether or not they are thriving. The latest red list contains the names of 67 species, more than 27 per cent of the British bird population, including those once considered ubiquitous in this country.

- White-fronted goose
- Ringed plover
- Golden oriole
- Nightingale
- Pochard
- Dotterel
- Red-backed shrike
- Pied flycatcher
- Scaup
- Whimbrel
- Willow tit
- Black redstart
- Long-tailed duck
- Curlew
- Marsh tit
- Whinchat
- Common scoter
- Black-tailed godwit
- Skylark
- House sparrow
- Velvet scoter
- Ruff wood warbler
- Tree sparrow
- Black grouse
- Red-necked phalarope
- Grasshopper warbler
- Yellow wagtail
- Capercaillie
- Woodcock
- Savi's warbler
- Grey wagtail
- Grey partridge
- Arctic skua
- Aquatic warbler
- Tree pipit
- Balearic shearwater
- Puffin
- Marsh warbler

❄ Hawfinch

❄ Shag

❄ Roseate tern

❄ Starling

❄ Linnet

❄ Red-necked grebe

❄ Kittiwake

❄ Ring ouzel

❄ Twite

❄ Slavonian grebe

❄ Herring gull

❄ Fieldfare

❄ Lesser redpoll

❄ White-tailed eagle

❄ Turtle dove

❄ Song thrush

❄ Yellowhammer

❄ Hen harrier

❄ Cuckoo

❄ Redwing

❄ Cirl bunting

❄ Corncrake

❄ Lesser spotted
woodpecker

❄ Mistle thrush

❄ Corn bunting

❄ Lapwing

❄ Merlin

❄ Spotted flycatcher

The red list has increased from 52 birds in 2009. Some birds that were elevated from the amber list to the red list this time include the shag, curlew, kittiwake, nightingale, puffin, merlin and grey wagtail.

Troublingly, the white-fronted goose and the long-tailed duck went straight from the green list to the red this time, without pausing at amber.

Among the 96 on the amber list are the gannet, oystercatcher, common tern, house martin and bullfinch.

Yet there are some success stories in the 81 species that make up the green list. Most remarkable of all is the red kite, once endangered but now a familiar sight across middle England. Other birds on the green list include the tufted duck, little egret, barn owl, green woodpecker and firecrest.

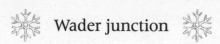

Wader junction

Britain's estuaries are buzzing this month. Over 3 000,000 migrating waders flock to feed on the food-rich muds and sands, all 2,600 square kilometres of it at low tide. Some birds will have already continued south, following the East Atlantic Flyway to warmer climes; others stay with us all winter.

Many waders are 'little grey jobs', and notoriously difficult to tell apart, even with a good field guide, but there are a few things to look out for. Firstly, they're not actually grey but various combinations of black, white and buff, and to tell them apart, you need to look at their bills. The long slightly down-curved bill of the dunlin contrasts with the shorter straight bill of the knot (see also pages 291–2). The grey plover has a short bill and big eyes, and calls with a 'pee-oo-ee', like a wolf whistle. Godwits have upturned bills, and curlews have very long down-turned bills, although their melancholy calls are a dead giveaway.

Many of these birds use their bills like tweezers, lifting out mainly worms, crustaceans and molluscs. Before the rising tide erases them, you can see the numerous pockmarks in the mud caused by the hundreds of probing bills. Many of the birds simply push their bills into the mud randomly, like a row of sewing machines, hoping they make contact with potential food. Lugworms are accessible to birds with long bills, like the curlew, while those with medium-length bills catch shallow-living invertebrates, such as red or green-coloured ragworms. This probing, however, only works for birds with relatively long bills. Plovers rely on their eyesight. They watch for almost imperceptible movements on the surface of the mud, then dart in and peck.

Oystercatchers have bold black-and-white plumage and stout red bills, and they too have a distinctive call as they fly in small flocks along the tideline. They chisel away at molluscs. Sanderlings have dark shoulder patches, and they race back and forth in small groups at the water's edge on sandy beaches. They rely on the waves disturbing the sand and whatever is buried beneath it.

Then, of course, there are the stunningly beautiful avocets. Over 7,000 of them overwinter in the UK. White with black wingtips and head, this leggy wader has a long and slender upturned bill. It gathers in large numbers in estuaries and coastal lagoons along the south and east coast of England, and the best way to see them is by boat. Excursions regularly go to see flocks on the Exe Estuary, Poole Harbour and along the River Ore to Havergate Island in Suffolk.

 ## Where to see waders

Almost any estuary with mud or sand at low tide will have waders present, but notable hotspots include:

- RSPB Marshside on the Ribble estuary claims to have more birds than any other estuary in the country
- Dee estuary, between North Wales and Cheshire, is still one of the best locations with over 100,000 waders
- The Wash, Norfolk, has huge areas of sand and mud
- Pagham Harbour, West Sussex, but you'll need scopes and bins
- Poole Harbour, Dorset, is the second biggest shallow natural inlet in the world, after Sydney Harbour, Australia
- Exe Estuary, Devon, especially for avocets
- Blackpill, Swansea Bay, is an easy to reach location
- The Swale, Kent, for its waders and their predators
- Elmley, Isle of Sheppey, Kent, has a long walk to the hides; go either side of high tide, or the birds will be too distant and spread out.

In fact, for the most exciting spectacles at all these sites, it's best to visit about an hour or two either side of high tide, when the birds are pushed into tight flocks by the tide.

 ## Arrivals and departures

Saw-billed ducks use their serrated bill to catch fish, and three species – merganser, goosander and smew – are on the move to find winter fishing sites.

Red-breasted mergansers, which breed in more northerly parts, can be seen overwintering in flocks a hundred strong around the coast, their numbers swelled by birds from Scandinavia and Russia. The male has a green-black head in winter, with a wispy punk-like crest that reflects a 'bad-hair day'. Its bill is red, long and slim and turns upwards slightly. It's a fast flyer. A top speed of about 100 mph has been claimed, which means it's a contender for the 'fastest bird in level flight' award.

Goosanders and smew head for freshwater lakes and reservoirs.

Male goosanders, recognised by their dark green heads, white body and red bill with a hooked tip, embark on an unusual annual journey. Some breed in this country, mostly near lakes and rivers in the north, but shortly afterwards they suddenly disappear. It was a mystery for many years until it was discovered that all the goosanders head for Tanafjord in Norway, where they moult their flight feathers. They stay there for about three months, returning to the UK from October onwards, the bulk of them arriving in December.

The male smew is a beautiful white bird with a black mask and back. The female is grey with a reddish-brown head and white cheeks. Smew appear most often when Arctic weather systems, like the 'beast from the east', bring especially cold weather to north west Europe. Birds arrive at the last minute from their normal overwintering sites in Holland and Denmark, such as IJsselmeer, a large closed-off bay in Holland where 10,000 smew settle for the winter.

Good places to see smew and goosanders in this country include: Abberton Reservoir, near Colchester, Essex, where there are also wigeon and tufted ducks; Staines Reservoir, Surrey, with goldeneyes and pochard; Grafham Water, Cambridgeshire; Chew Valley Lake, near Bristol, with large rafts of goosander, mixed in with goldeneye, wigeon, pochard and teal; Fairburn Ings, West Yorkshire, which is the most northerly place for smew; and The Mere, Ellesmere, Shropshire.

 ## Christmas crackers

Christmas wouldn't be complete without holly and mistletoe, and wildlife in the British Isles is dependent on them too. The berries are a valuable food source for songbirds, such as resident mistle thrushes, as well as visiting redwings and fieldfares, particularly at this rather barren time of the year. The thrushes guard their trees against all-comers, although blackcaps seem to have a knack of stealing the waxy white berries of mistletoe from right under the thrush's nose; in fact, the birds help disperse the mistletoe's seeds. When they wipe their beaks they leave the seeds behind, and when they defecate they deposit seeds covered in a sticky substance called viscin. The viscin survives passage through the birds' gut so the seeds attach firmly to the trunk of a tree and then germinate, because mistletoe is a parasite. It obtains most of the water and nutrients it needs from its host tree via filaments, known as haustoria, which infiltrate the tree's tissues.

At one time, mistletoe went hand in hand with apple orchards, but the countrywide loss of old apple trees has meant wild mistletoe is not as common as it once was. It is mainly found these days in limestone regions in the southern half of the country, where it grows on oak, lime, hawthorn, blackthorn, rowan, poplar and willow trees. Even so, cider counties, such as Gloucestershire, Herefordshire and Worcestershire, are still strongly associated with mistletoe.

The tangled ball of mistletoe, with its leathery green leaves, can be up to a metre across. With the host tree devoid of leaves, the mistletoe looks like a large bird's nest. The leaf-mining caterpillar of the mistletoe moth probably causes any brown patches you might find on its leaves.

Mistletoe has featured prominently in folklore since the third century BCE. In Greek mythology passage to the underworld was smoothed with mistletoe and, in Roman times, mistletoe was used as a decoration for celebrating Saturnalia, the festival of Saturn in December, the predecessor of Christmas. The tradition of kissing underneath the mistletoe is recorded first in the 16th century, and the custom is to remove a berry for every kiss that's claimed.

In days gone by, holly was not merely a decoration. Sheep and cattle browsed on it as an emergency food supply in hard winters. You can see how important this once was by visiting the 200 ancient holly trees or 'Hollins' on the north-east ridge of the Stiperstones in Shropshire or in the Olchon Valley in Herefordshire. These holly trees were not grown for berries, but for livestock feeding. The cows and sheep were kept on smallholdings by lead miners, their mines once the most productive in Europe. Today, these trees are hundreds of years old and tucked under the frost-shattered tors and crags of heather moorland. Alongside, there are the remains of flues, shafts and spoil heaps, and even the old grinding machines that were used to tenderise the holly before it was given to livestock.

Holly's prickliness varies from tree to tree. Foliage that is regularly browsed, say, by deer, becomes very prickly, whereas that left alone, above a height of about two metres, tends to be prickle-free, the soft-edged leaves known as 'silke' in Shropshire. Birds take the berries. Mistle thrushes covet holly bushes and trees in the same way they protect their balls of mistletoe, and overwintering field-fares and redwings muscle in on the bounty. The caterpillars of the holly blue butterfly and the privet hawk-moth count holly as a key food plant.

Both holly and mistletoe are dioecious – they have male and female flowers on different plants. Only female holly plants will have red berries. The fruit is the stone in the middle, but birds are attracted to holly berries for the scarlet exocarp and the orange flesh of the mesocarp. Like mistletoe berries, the seeds travel through the bird's gut unharmed and are carried some distance from the parent tree and deposited with a convenient dollop of fertiliser … and there another holly tree grows.

 ## Sunrise and sunset times for Britain's capital cities

31st December	Sunrise	Sunset
Belfast	08.45	16.08
London	08.06	16.01
Cardiff	08.18	16.13
Edinburgh	08.43	15.48

WEBSITES

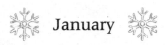

January

Big Garden Birdwatch

https://www.rspb.org.uk/get-involved/activities/birdwatch/
everything-you-need-to-know-about-big-garden-birdwatch/

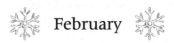

February

Snowdrops

https://www.nationaltrust.org.uk/lists/top-spots-for-snowdrops
https://www.ngs.org.uk/whats-new/news/category/snowdrop-festival/
https://www.greatbritishgardens.co.uk/seasonal/snowdrops.html

National Nest Box Week

https://www.bto.org/about-birds/nnbw

March

World Frog Day

https://www.froglife.org/

World Sparrow Day

https://www.worldsparrowday.org/

International Day of Forests

http://www.un.org/en/events/forestsday/index.shtml

World Meteorological Day

https://public.wmo.int/en/resources/world-meteorological-day

World Osprey Week

http://www.ospreys.org.uk/world-osprey-week/

Hare Preservation Trust

http://hare-preservation-trust.com/helping-hares/sightings/

Toad patrols

https://www.froglife.org/what-we-do/toads-on-roads/tormap/

Mapping earthworms

https://www.earthwormsoc.org.uk/ners

Nature's Calendar

https://naturescalendar.woodlandtrust.org.uk/

 May

Surveying bats

http://www.bats.org.uk/pages/nbmp.html

Recording migrant butterflies

https://butterfly-conservation.org/110/recording-and-monitoring.html

Get a licence to record wildlife

https://www.gov.uk/get-a-wildlife-licence

International Dawn Chorus Day

http://www.idcd.info/

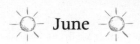 June

National Insect Week
http://www.nationalinsectweek.co.uk/

Stag beetle sightings
https://ptes.org/get-involved/surveys/garden/great-stag-hunt/
stag-hunt-survey/

Random acts of wildness
http://action.wildlifetrusts.org/page/20877/petition/1

Environment Agency
https://www.gov.uk/guidance/prevent-the-spread-of-harmful-
invasive-and-non-native-plants

Surveying water voles
https://ptes.org/get-involved/surveys/countryside-2/national-
water-vole-monitoring-programme/

Bee survey
https://friendsoftheearth.uk/bee-count

 July

British sharks
https://www.sharktrust.org

Woodlands and wildlife
https://www.woodlandtrust.org.uk

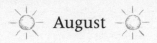 August

Wild flowers
https://www.plantlife.org.uk

Whales and dolphins
http://www.seawatchfoundation.org.uk/recentsightings
https://www.mcsuk.org

 September

Swans and migration
http://www.swan-trust.org

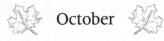 October

Insects
https://www.buglife.org.uk

Galls and other plant topics
https://www.rhs.org.uk

British deer
https://www.bds.org.uk

Grey seals and knots
https://www.norfolkwildlifetrust.org.uk

Red squirrels
https://www.nationaltrust.org.uk/lists/top-places-to-spot-red-squirrels

British dragonflies
https://british-dragonflies.org.uk

 November

The Mammal Society
http://www.mammal.org.uk

Swan migration
https://www.wwt.org.uk

 December

Winter moths
https://butterfly-conservation.org/moths/december-moth

Goosander and other water birds
https://scottishwildlifetrust.org.uk

INDEX

Page numbers in *italics* refer to illustrations.